Approaches to
Teaching Boccaccio's
Decameron

Approaches to Teaching
World Literature
Joseph Gibaldi, series editor

For a complete listing of titles,
see the last pages of this book.

Approaches to Teaching Boccaccio's

Decameron

Edited by

James H. McGregor

The Modern Language Association of America
New York   2000

© 2000 by the Modern Language Association of America
All rights reserved. Printed in the United States of America

For information about obtaining permission to reprint material from
MLA book publications, send your request by mail (see address below)
or by e-mail (permissions @mla.org).

Library of Congress Cataloging-in-Publication Data

Approaches to teaching Boccaccio's Decameron / edited by James H. McGregor.
p. cm. — (Approaches to teaching world literature ; 69)
Includes bibliographical references and index.
ISBN 0-87352-761-5 (cloth) — ISBN 0-87352-762-3 (pbk.)
1. Boccaccio, Giovanni, 1313–1375. Decamerone.
2. Boccaccio, Giovanni, 1313–1375.—Study and teaching.
I. McGregor, James H. (James Harvey), 1946– II. Series.
PQ4287.A77 2000
853'.1—dc21   00-057860
ISSN 1059-1133

Cover illustration of the paperback edition: Illustration from
ms. Douce 213 (late 15th cent.), fol. i recto, The Bodleian Library,
University of Oxford

Published by The Modern Language Association of America
26 Broadway, New York, New York 10004-1789
www.mla.org

CONTENTS

PREFACE TO THE SERIES

In *The Art of Teaching* Gilbert Highet wrote, "Bad teaching wastes a great deal of effort, and spoils many lives which might have been full of energy and happiness." All too many teachers have failed in their work, Highet argued, simply "because they have not thought about it." We hope that the Approaches to Teaching World Literature series, sponsored by the Modern Language Association's Publications Committee, will not only improve the craft—as well as the art—of teaching but also encourage serious and continuing discussion of the aims and methods of teaching literature.

The principal objective of the series is to collect within each volume different points of view on teaching a specific literary work, a literary tradition, or a writer widely taught at the undergraduate level. The preparation of each volume begins with a wide-ranging survey of instructors, thus enabling us to include in the volume the philosophies and approaches, thoughts and methods of scores of experienced teachers. The result is a sourcebook of material, information, and ideas on teaching the subject of the volume to undergraduates.

The series is intended to serve nonspecialists as well as specialists, inexperienced as well as experienced teachers, graduate students who wish to learn effective ways of teaching as well as senior professors who wish to compare their own approaches with the approaches of colleagues in other schools. Of course, no volume in the series can ever substitute for erudition, intelligence, creativity, and sensitivity in teaching. We hope merely that each book will point readers in useful directions; at most each will offer only a first step in the long journey to successful teaching.

Joseph Gibaldi
Series Editor

PREFACE TO THE VOLUME

Not so many years ago Giovanni Boccaccio's *Decameron* ranked as a famously scandalous text, which circulated in privately printed editions; today it is widely read in undergraduate courses, though more often in excerpts than in toto. Indeed the full text of the *Decameron* is almost as imposing as that of *War and Peace*; the standard edition in Italian runs to more than 950 pages of text, while G. H. McWilliam's English translation is well over 800 pages. The scandal of the *Decameron* is neither its torrid past nor its unseemly bulk. What separates the *Decameron* from most of the canon is that it is fun to read. Though its narrators sometimes weep, they laugh much more often. Such laughter plays a serious and important part in the rehabilitative role that was assigned to recreational texts in the Middle Ages, but it is laughter that is unselfconsciously echoed by contemporary readers.

Boccaccio's admirers have been at work for over six hundred years, commenting on and explicating the *Decameron* and, in the last century and a half, writing numerous dissertations, articles, and monographs about it. The work plays an important part in contemporary narrative theory and gender studies, and many readers emphasize its role as a conduit of oral folk traditions and of tale-telling traditions that have their origin in the East. During its long lifetime, the *Decameron* has also inspired hundreds of imitations. It is not the first collection of novelle in Italian: the *Novellino*, known in English as the *Hundred Old Tales*, precedes it by more than a generation. It is, however, the acknowledged inspiration of the more than two hundred collections of framed tales in Italian written before the seventeenth century. In the Renaissance these tale collections were imitated in or translated into every European language; they influenced the development of the Renaissance dialogue, Renaissance drama, the picaresque, and ultimately the modern novel and short story.

Even today Boccaccio finds imitators as well as commentators. Many films have been based directly or indirectly on the *Decameron*. The best known of these is Pier Paolo Pasolini's celebrated version, but there are many others. Writers like Italo Calvino and the Russian novelist Julia Voznesenskaya have produced modern, or, perhaps more accurately, postmodern versions of it. Calvino responds to the formal conventions of the novella collection in such works as *Invisible Cities* and *The Castle of Crossed Destinies*. Voznesenskaya's *Women's* Decameron consists of a hundred stories told by ten women over a ten-day period of confinement in a Saint Petersburg maternity hospital. Playing Boccaccio to the Dante of Aleksandr Solzhenitsyn's *First Circle*, Voznesenskaya makes the women's storytelling and their growing friendship a positive statement of productive collaboration across class and party lines.

Of course, like every great author, Boccaccio has had his share of detractors.

He himself begins the tradition of disparagement of his work through fictionalized authorial statements within the *Decameron* and later warnings in letters to friends about who should and should not read it. The text was bowdlerized and censored in the sixteenth century, at the very moment that Boccaccio's language was enshrined in the first Italian dictionaries as the highest standard of correct usage. The religious scruples that led to its suppression by the Counter-Reformation and its polemical adoption by the more daring among Protestant writers find their echo in modern debates about the canon and the multiple and sometimes contradictory roles that literature is asked to play in today's world.

Given the magnitude of Boccaccio's work, the extent of its literary heritage, and the enormous critical history it has accumulated, presenting it to students whose experience and interest vary widely is no easy task. Courses in which the *Decameron* is read in whole or in part are legion. They are far from uniform, however; they range from seminars in Italian medieval literature taught in Italian for language majors to courses in the humanities or women's studies. Italian literature courses, surveys of medieval and Renaissance literature, courses on the background of the novel and short story, even surveys of non-Western literature routinely include excerpts from it. Both the *Norton Anthology of World Masterpieces* and Macmillan's *Literature of the Western World* include portions. The HarperCollins *World Reader* includes it among selections that range beyond the confines of the European tradition. It has also found a place in St. Martin's *Western Literature in a World Context,* an equally wide-ranging anthology.

In approaching this vast field of creative reflection and critical study, this volume benefits from the experience of many of the most highly skilled readers and teachers of Boccaccio's masterpiece. Many of the contributors are among the acknowledged experts in the world of Boccaccio studies. All are teachers in American colleges and universities, and their essays reflect their own proven approaches to the text in a variety of undergraduate courses. The volume begins with a series of discursive bibliographical sorties compiled by the volume editor on the basis of a survey of Boccaccio instructors. The second section of the volume, which is focused on classroom approaches, consists of seventeen essays by participants in that survey and one by the volume editor.

Part One

MATERIALS

Editions and Translations

The standard edition of the *Decameron* is the fourth volume in the series *Tutte le opere di Giovanni Boccaccio*, published by Mondadori. Both the series and the *Decameron* volume were edited by Vittore Branca. Branca's edition is based primarily on a fourteenth-century manuscript now in Berlin that is known as Codex Hamilton 90. Working independently, Branca and Charles Singleton proved that this manuscript was written and corrected by Boccaccio in his own hand. They agree that Hamilton 90 is a revised copy of the complete *Decameron* that Boccaccio made for himself in 1370 or 1371, very near the end of his life. Despite the superiority of the Branca edition, which is also available in reasonably priced paperback editions from both Mondadori (1985) and Einaudi (1980) for classroom use, many instructors substitute the Mursia edition, edited by Cesare Segre. The primary virtue of this text, which is not based on the Codex Hamilton and which as one instructor notes "suffers from a paucity of footnotes," is that it is more affordable than the others.

In English there are two translations of the *Decameron* that instructors appear to rank about equally. The G. H. McWilliam translation (Penguin), now in its second edition, was revised in 1995 and the introduction and notes updated and expanded. The translation by Mark Musa and Peter Bondanella is also available in an inexpensive paperback format. This translation is used in a number of anthologies as well. Selections in the *Norton Anthology of World Masterpieces* (both the regular and expanded versions) are taken from this translation, as are the selections included in *The Italian Renaissance Reader*, edited by Julia Conaway Bondanella and Mark Musa. The Norton Critical Edition of twenty-one novelle also uses the Musa-Bondanella translation. There it is combined with introductory materials that describe the structure and contents of the *Decameron* and an anthology of responses to the text by Boccaccio's contemporaries. The final section of the volume includes excerpts from significant critical assessments of the text by leading figures such as Ugo Foscolo, Francesco De Sanctis, Tzvetan Todorov, Erich Auerbach, and others. A translation by Guido Waldman was published in 1993 in the United Kingdom for the Oxford World's Classics series. The Victorian translation by John Payne, republished in 1982, is reckoned by many to be the most accurate representation of the *Decameron* in English, but its archaisms of syntax and diction make it very challenging for undergraduate students.

Required and Recommended Reading for Undergraduates

Many instructors responding to the survey indicated that because of the length of the *Decameron*, few outside readings were required of their students. The texts most frequently mentioned by instructors requiring or recommending outside readings are the following: Vittore Branca's *Boccaccio medievale e nuovi studi sul* Decameron and, in English, *Boccaccio: The Man and His Works*; Francesco Bruni's *Boccaccio: L'invenzione della letteratura mezzana*; Giuseppe Mazzotta's *The World at Play in Boccaccio's* Decameron; Millicent Marcus's *An Allegory of Form*; Guido Almansi's *The Writer as Liar*; David Wallace's *Giovanni Boccaccio:* Decameron; Joy Potter's *Five Frames for the* Decameron; Aldo Scaglione's *Nature and Love in the Late Middle Ages*; James V. Mirollo's "Renaissance Short Fiction"; Teodolinda Barolini's "Giovanni Boccaccio (1313–1375)." Some instructors assign a sampling of the critical and background essays included in Musa and Bondanella's Norton Critical Edition of the *Decameron*; and in Robert S. Dombroski's *Critical Perspectives on the* Decameron. Others include historical introductions such as Anthony Molho's *Social and Economic Foundations of the Italian Renaissance* and treatments of the Black Death such as Charles L. Mee, Jr.'s "How a Mysterious Disease Laid Low Europe's Masses."

The Instructor's Library

Reference Works

The bibliography on Boccaccio is enormous and growing. Up-to-date bibliographic surveys have recently been completed. The most important of these is Joseph P. Consoli's *Giovanni Boccaccio: An Annotated Bibliography*. This invaluable work covers most of the books, articles, and dissertations on Boccaccio in the period from 1939 to 1986. The book is divided into eleven subsections, and there are ample indexes since each entry is included in only one subsection. The languages of original publication surveyed include English, Italian, French, Spanish, Portuguese, and German. Editions as well as criticism for the period 1939–74 are covered in Enzo Esposito's *Boccacciana*. Although Esposito's arrangement is chronological and his work is not limited to the *Decameron*, a number of indexes make topical searches possible. Both Consoli and Esposito refer their readers to Branca's *Linee di una storia della critica al* Decameron, which is the definitive bibliography of Boccaccio research before 1939. A few survey respondents included Guido Traversari's *Bibliografia boccaccesca* among their suggested bibliographical resources. *Boccaccio in English*, by F. S. Stych, covers the whole of Boccaccio's oeuvre and the entire span of English language editions, selections, and adaptations as well as criticism. Six indexes, which include references to individual *Decameron* novelle, facilitate detailed searches.

Serial bibliographies of Boccaccio studies are widely available. *Studi sul Boccaccio*, which is the only international journal devoted exclusively to Boccaccio studies, is an essential resource in every area of contemporary *Decameron* research. It began its bibliographical review in 1963. In Branca and Giorgio Padoan's "Integrazioni alle bibliografie di studi boccacciani pubblicati dal Traversari e dal Branca" in 1963 and in subsequent years, it covered items that had been overlooked in the earlier bibliographies. Selected Boccaccio bibliography is annotated in *Year's Work in Modern Language Studies*. The *MLA International Bibliography*, which is available in both print and online versions, gives access to the bulk of this material as well.

Only one concordance to the *Decameron* has been published: Alfredo Barbina's *Concordanze del* Decameron.

There is no dictionary devoted exclusively to Boccaccio. The multivolume *Grande dizionario della lingua italiana* provides nearly complete information on Boccaccio's vocabulary. A more compact dictionary, edited by Giacomo Devoto and Gian Carlo Oli, is *Dizionario della lingua italiana*. In English the *Cambridge Italian Dictionary*, edited by Barbara Reynolds, is the best available. The *Enciclopedia dantesca* provides guidance in areas of language and historical reference that Boccaccio shares with Dante. The most valuable philological resource, however, is the notes to Branca's Mondadori edition. Many of Boccaccio's sources are recorded in Alfred C. Lee's The Decameron: *Its Sources and Analogues*. Renzo Bragantini and Pier Forni's *Lessico critico decameroniano* includes useful articles on important topics in Boccaccio studies.

Biographies and Background Works

The standard biography of Boccaccio is Branca's *Giovanni Boccaccio: Profilo biografico*. In English much of the same material can be found in Branca's *Boccaccio: The Man and His Works*. Many participants in the survey referred to Carlo Muscetta's *Giovanni Boccaccio*, Thomas Bergin's *Boccaccio*, as well as Judith Serafini-Sauli's *Giovanni Boccaccio*. Portraits of Boccaccio are cataloged in Victoria Kirkham's "A Preliminary List of Boccaccio Portraits from the Fourteenth to the Mid-Sixteenth Centuries."

Fourteenth-Century Italian Background   Two books by John Larner present useful overviews of the social, political, and cultural landscape of trecento Italy: *Culture and Society in Italy, 1290–1420* and *Italy in the Age of Dante and Petrarch, 1216–1380*. *Medieval Italy: Constraints and Creativity*, by Marvin B.

Becker, is an economic and cultural history of the early modern period with an emphasis on the relation between faith in the religious realm and credit in the mercantile sphere. The pioneering work of Roberto S. Lopez in the field of mercantilism and international banking culminated in such works as his *Commerical Revolution of the Middle Ages, 950–1350* and Lopez and I. Raymond's *Medieval Trade in the Mediterranean World.*

Florentine Background: Primary Sources   Florentines began to examine their own history in the time of Dante, and many chronicles describe Florence in the time of Boccaccio. Outstanding among these is Giovanni Villani's *Nuova cronica*, which comes to an end in the plague year of 1348 when the author became a victim of the disease. The chronicle was continued by Giovanni's brother Matteo and his son Filippo. To date there has been only one English translation of selections from these chronicles, edited by Rose E. Selfe and Philip H. Wicksteed; a second may soon be published. Louis Green's *Chronicle into History* examines the changing approaches and presuppositions of the chroniclers before and after the black death.

Florentine Background: Secondary Sources   Perhaps the single most informative book on the history of Florence in the fourteenth century is Gene A. Brucker's *Renaissance Florence.* Marvin B. Becker's *Florence in Transition* is an intellectual and political history of the same period. Among the many books of Richard C. Trexler on Florentine civic ritual and social life, *Public Life in Renaissance Florence* deserves special notice. Paul F. Gehl's *A Moral Art: Grammar, Society, and Culture in Trecento Florence* gives a view of the literary and intellectual life of the period. Florentine art is described in Frederick Antal's *Florentine Painting and Its Social Background.* Patterns of daily life in the period are described in the excellent essay by Charles de la Roncière, "Tuscan Notables on the Eve of the Renaissance."

Black Death   Contemporary descriptions of the bubonic plague that echo and extend Boccaccio's can be found in Matteo Villani's *Cronica* (vol. 1, chs. 1–2); and in the *Cronaca fiorentina*, by Marchionne di Coppo Stefani. On the etiology of bubonic plague, the classic study by Hans Zinsser, *Rats, Lice, and History*, is illuminating and engrossing. Two instructors mentioned the article "How a Mysterious Disease Laid Low Europe's Masses," by Charles L. Mee, Jr. Scholarly accounts of the plague and its social effects include Samuel Kline Cohn's *The Cult of Remembrance and the Black Death*, Ann G. Carmichael's *Plague and the Poor in Renaissance Florence*, and Brucker's "Florence and the Black Death." Other popular books on the subject include Philip Ziegler's *The Black Death* and William McNeill's *Plagues and Peoples.* On the broader issue of the relation between illness and literature, Susan Sontag's *Illness as Metaphor* and her more recent *AIDS and Its Metaphors* are especially important.

Literary Background   For the general literary history of the fourteenth century, the classic study remains *Il Trecento* (1987 ed.), edited by Natalino Sapegno. For the history of prose narrative, the best source is Achille Tartaro's "La prosa narrativa antica." The background, sources, techniques, and development of Boccaccio's prose are best described in Branca's *Boccaccio medievale e nuovi studi sul* Decameron (chs. 1–6, collectively titled "Tradizione letteraria e genio narrativo del *Decameron*," and chs. 11–13, collectively titled "Tre nuovi studi sui procedimenti narrativi"). These chapters are included in the English translation of Branca's *Boccaccio: The Man and His Works* (197–332). Branca argues for the author of the *Decameron* as a "medieval Boccaccio," one who, despite his vast knowledge of classical texts, "seems to avoid them deliberately" in his masterpiece (203). Others have been at pains to show that such classical texts as those of Petronius, Apuleius, and Ovid offer interesting structural parallels to the framed narrative Boccaccio is, in the novella tradition, the first to adopt. On the classical background of the *Decameron* and its links to framed tales, see James V. Mirollo's excellent "Renaissance Short Fiction." One example of the numerous articles citing Boccaccio's indebtedness to individual classical authors is Douglas Radcliff-Umstead's "Boccaccio's Adaptation of Some Latin Sources for the *Decameron*."

The Novella Tradition   Only the anonymous *Novellino* antedates the *Decameron*. It is a collection of one hundred unframed stories, most of them brief and anecdotal, often with an appended commentary that points out a moral or gives advice on social behavior. Boccaccio's transformation of this humble genre paved the way in the following centuries for a flood of generally framed tale collections, first and most frequently in Italian, but quickly expanding to all European languages. While these collections are often popular in origin and nonliterary in approach, the weight of Boccaccio's authority lends literary respectability to the genre. Aldo Scaglione's "Storytelling, the *Novella* and the *Decameron*" surveys the narratological theorists who have attempted to define the novella as a genre. These include Viktor B. Shklovsky's *Theory of Prose* and Tzvetan Todorov's *Grammaire du* Decameron. Citing the relative failure of the narratological tradition to open the discussion toward the historical engagement of the novella, Scaglione ("Storytelling,") proposes an alternative definition based on the convergence of sociological and hermeneutic approaches. Mirollo's "Renaissance Short Fiction" offers a rapid guide through this maze of texts and the surprising paucity of relevant criticism. On the novella tradition in general see *Formation, codification et rayonnement d'un genre médiéval: La nouvelle*, edited by Michelangelo Picone, Giuseppe Di Stefano, and Pamela D. Stewart. Older studies include Walter Pabst's *Novellentheorie und Novellendichtung*; Salvatore Battaglia's *Contributi alla storia della novellistica*; Aldo Borlenghi's *La struttura e il carattere della novella italiana dei primi secoli*; Leonie Graedel's *La cornice nelle raccolte novellistiche del*

Rinascimento e i rapporti con la cornice del Decameron; Pamela D. Stewart's "Boccaccio e la tradizione retorica: La definizione della novella come genere letterario"; and Marga Cottino-Jones's "Observations on the Structure of the *Decameron* Novella." Very little has been published in English on this topic. Of exceptional value is *The Anatomy of the Novella* by Robert J. Clements and Joseph Gibaldi. See also Yvonne Rodax's *The Real and the Ideal in the Novella of Italy, France, and England* and John Addington Symonds's "The Novellieri."

The Decameron *and English Literature*   Since the influence of the *Decameron* and the novella tradition has been extensive in English and American literature, the details of that tradition are likely to be well-known by the readers of this volume. In addition to specific studies on Shakespeare, Dryden, and others, general introductions to the influence of Boccaccio in England can be found in *Il Boccaccio nella cultura inglese e anglo-americana*, edited by Giuseppe Galigani; Herbert G. Wright's *Boccaccio in England, from Chaucer to Tennyson*; Wallace's *Giovanni Boccaccio:* Decameron; and Ernest Hatch Wilkins's *A History of Italian Literature*.

Critical Studies

Despite its age, the cornerstone of contemporary Boccaccio studies remains Francesco De Sanctis's *Storia della letteratura italiana*. Perhaps the most influential modern study of Boccaccio is Branca's *Boccaccio medievale*, currently in its fifth edition. Branca's approach is philological on the one hand—he is a founder of Italy's post-Fascist critical movement called *la nuova filologia* 'the new philology'—and biographical on the other. No one can compare with Branca in his reading of the intertextual *Decameron*, especially when the texts invoked are popular and devotional. His comedic reading of the *Decameron* has had widespread influence in Italy and particularly in America. Branca's *Boccaccio: The Man and His Works* includes substantial portions of *Boccaccio medievale* in translation. Giorgio Padoan's *Il Boccaccio, le muse, il Parnaso e l'Arno* is a magisterial study of Boccaccio's work and its background in the culture of Florence. Among the innumerable critical works in Italian on the *Decameron*, the following were most often cited by respondents: Umberto Bosco's Il 'Decameron': *Saggio*; Giuseppe Billanovich's *Restauri boccacceschi*; Giovanni Getto's *Vita di forme e forme di vita nel* Decameron; Giorgio Barberi Squarotti's *Il potere della parola* and *Prospettive sul* Decameron; Mario Baratto's *Realtà e stile nel* Decameron; Franco Fido's *Il regime delle simmetrie imperfette*; Francesco Bruni's *Boccaccio: L'invenzione della letteratura mezzana*; Giuseppe Velli's *Petrarca e Boccaccio: Tradizione-memoria-scrittura*; Giuseppe Petronio's *I miei* Decameron; Laura Sanguineti White's *La scena conviviale e la sua funzione nel mondo del Boccaccio*.

A number of excellent studies of the *Decameron* have appeared in English. Among those most often singled out are Potter's *Five Frames for the* Decameron; Scaglione's *Nature and Love in the Late Middle Ages*; Wallace's *Giovanni Boccaccio:* Decameron; Marcus's *An Allegory of Form*; Janet Smarr's *Boccaccio and Fiammetta*; Mazzotta's *The World at Play in Boccaccio's* Decameron; Almansi's *The Writer as Liar*; Cottino-Jones's *Order from Chaos*; Lucia Marino's *The* Decameron *Cornice: Allusion, Allegory, and Iconology*; Kirkham's *The Sign of Reason in Boccaccio's Fiction*; Robert Hastings's *Nature and Reason in the* Decameron; Cormac O Cuilleanain's *Religion and the Clergy in Boccaccio's* Decameron.

Collections of Essays

Inspired by celebrations of the sixth centenary of Boccaccio's death in 1974, scholars assembled essay collections focusing on Boccaccio and his international influence. The most significant collections are Carlo Ballerini's *Atti del Convegno di Nimega sul Boccaccio*; Carlo Pellegrini's *Il Boccaccio nella cultura francese*; Cottino-Jones and Edward F. Tuttle's *Boccaccio: Secoli di vita*; Branca and Padoan's *Boccaccio, Venezia e il Veneto*; Galigani's *Il Boccaccio nella cultura inglese e anglo-americana*; Francesco Mazzoni's *Il Boccaccio nelle culture e letterature nazionali*; and Gilbert Tournoy's *Boccaccio in Europe*. Other important collections include the multivolume Festschrift for Branca, which includes a volume entitled *Boccaccio e dintorni*, and Aldo S. Bernardo and Anthony L. Pellegrini's *Dante, Petrarch, Boccaccio: Studies in the Italian Trecento in Honor of Charles S. Singleton*. Essay collections in English include Dombroski's *Critical Perspectives on the* Decameron. A number of useful critical essays are reprinted in Musa and Bondanella's Decameron: *A Norton Critical Edition*.

Articles

Among the hundreds of essays on the *Decameron*, the following are often cited: Carlo Delcorno's "Metamorfosi boccacciane dell'exemplum"; Raffaello Ramat's "L'introduzione alla 'quarta giornata'"; Michel David's "Boccaccio pornoscopo?"; Robert M. Durling's "Boccaccio on Interpretation: Guido's Escape"; Charles Singleton, "On Meaning in the *Decameron*"; Thomas Green's "Forms of Accommodation in the *Decameron*"; Franco Fido's "Dante personaggio mancato del *Decameron*"; Ferdinando Neri's "Il disegno ideale del *Decameron*"; Joan Ferrante's "The Frame Characters of the *Decameron*: A Progression of Virtues"; Michael Sherberg's "The Patriarch's Pleasure and the Frametale Crisis: *Decameron* IV-V"; Michelangelo Picone's "Dal lai alla novella: Il caso di Ghismonda (*Dec.* IV.1)"; Paul Watson's "The Cement of Fiction: Giovanni Boccaccio and the Painters of Florence."

Audiovisual and Electronic Resources

Boccaccio's influence has by no means been limited to writers. As Kevin J. Harty points out in his essay in this volume, "The *Decameron* on Film," more than thirty motion pictures based in some way on the *Decameron* have been produced. Three of these—Hugo Fregonese's Decameron *Nights* (1952), Pier Paolo Pasolini's *Decameron* (1971), and Mino Guerrini's Decameron *N.º 2: Le altre novelle del Boccaccio* (1972)—are available on videotape for classroom use. Long before the era of film, however, Boccaccio had an enormous influence on the visual arts. In a series of articles Victoria Kirkham, Branca, and Paul Watson have chronicled the multitude of late medieval and Renaissance paintings based on *Decameron* novelle. The most significant of these articles are Kirkham, Susy Marcon, Watson, and Branca's "Boccaccio visualizzato, II" and Paul Watson's "A Preliminary List of Subjects from Boccaccio in Italian Painting, 1400–1550." The essay by Kirkham in this volume, "Early Portraits of Boccaccio," with its extensive iconography, pinpoints the location of many of these images. Instructors who have access to the resources of an art historical slide library can make extensive and effective use of the paintings identified in these works.

Among composers inspired by Boccaccio are Franz von Suppé, Giuseppe Verdi, and Maurice Ravel. Suppé's operetta *Boccaccio* (1879) is a fictional depiction of Boccaccio's life and times that draws on tales from the *Decameron*. There is a famous recording of *Boccaccio* (EMI, 1975) with Hermann Prey as Boccaccio, Anneliese Rothenberger as his beloved Fiammetta, and the Bavarian Symphony Orchestra and Bavarian State Opera Chorus, conducted by Willi Boskovsky. In Verdi's *Falstaff* (1893) the magical, recurrent phrase sung by the lovers Nannetta and Fenton—"Bocca baciata non perde ventura, / Anzi rinnova come fa la luna" ("A kissed mouth does not lose freshness, rather it is renewed like the moon")—is a musical setting of the last line of novella 2.7 (e.g., Verdi 99; 1.2). Ravel's ribald, *Decameron*-like *L'heure espagnole* (1911) concerns a clockmaker, his restless wife, her two ineffectual would-be lovers, and an indefatigable muleteer. The one-act opera, with a libretto by Franc-Nohain (the pen name of Maurice-Etienne Legrand), concludes with an ensemble that contains a direct allusion to the Italian author:

> C'est la morale de Boccacce:
> Entre tous les amants, seul amant efficace.
> Il arrive un moment dans les déduits d'amour
> Où le muletier a son tour.   (Ravel 191–200; sc. 21)

> It is the moral of Boccaccio: Among lovers, only the efficacious lover succeeds. There arrives a moment in pursuit of love when the muleteer has his day.

In addition, the music making and dancing of the *brigata* in the frame narrative permits exploration of music from the late Middle Ages and early Renaissance. The recording *Chominciamento di gioia: Virtuoso Dance-Music from the Time of Boccaccio's* Decamerone (Naxos, 1994), performed by Ensemble Unicorn, contains instrumental pieces derived from a fourteenth-century Italian manuscript found in the British Library (ms. 29987). Among the dance forms featured are the *trotto*, saltarello, and *istanpitta*. In an album entitled *A Song for Francesca: Music in Italy, 1330–1430* (Hyperion, 1988), the Gothic Voices offers songs from a Vatican manuscript (Rossi ms. 215) dating from around 1340 that, as the program notes state, "may represent the kind of music which the well-born young men and women of Boccaccio's *Decameron* sang and played in their Tuscan villas during the time of the plague in 1348." The recording also includes music written by the fourteenth-century Florentine composers Andreas de Florentia, Johannes de Florentia, and the celebrated Francesco Landini.

The *Decameron* Web at Brown University, created under the direction of Massimo Riva (described in detail in his essay in this volume, "The *Decameron* Web: Teaching a Classic as Hypertext") offers a multitude of resources for Boccaccio students. The Web site includes a chronology of the life and writings of Boccaccio; the text of the *Decameron*, both in Italian and English translation; a list of the storytellers with links to the tales they tell; maps illustrating the world of the *Decameron*; an extensive bibliography; and a number of short essays under such rubrics as literature, the plague, the arts, society, religion, and history. Each essay is divided into subtopics. The URL of the *Decameron* Web is http://www.brown.edu/Research/Decameron.

NOTE

Except where stated otherwise, Italian-language quotations from the *Decameron* in this volume are taken from volume 4 of *Tutte le opere di Giovanni Boccaccio*, edited by Vittore Branca, and English-language quotations are taken from the Mark Musa and Peter Bondanella translation in the New American Library edition.

Part Two

APPROACHES

Introduction: The *Decameron* in the Classroom

Courses Taught

The range of courses in which the *Decameron* is read in Italian is broad. Their organization tends to be historical rather than thematic. Students of Italian are likely to encounter Boccaccio for the first time in a survey course on the literature of the Middle Ages and Renaissance. Depending on how such a course is structured, students may read as few as seven novelle from the *Decameron* or as many as twenty. Usually in such courses no critical works are assigned. For more advanced students in Italian, there are courses in which extensive portions of the *Decameron* are combined with a few other texts. Typical upper-level courses combine Dante, Petrarch, and Boccaccio or just Petrarch and Boccaccio and cover anywhere from seventeen to forty *Decameron* novelle.

Aldo Scaglione teaches a course in the Italian Renaissance in which portions of the *Decameron* are combined with readings from Baldassare Castiglione, Giorgio Vasari, and Benvenuto Cellini. Michael Sherberg teaches the course Boccaccio and the Novella, in which the entire *Decameron* is studied along with "selections from the *novellieri* of the fifteenth and sixteenth centuries [. . . and] a few source tales from the *Novellino* and the Provençal tradition."[1] Only a handful of undergraduate courses devoted exclusively to Boccaccio are offered. Many of these combine undergraduate and graduate instruction. Typical is a course taught at Cornell by Marilyn Migiel, described as a "combined undergraduate and graduate seminar, in which the average class size is about six to eight students, about three of whom are likely to be undergraduates." The entire *Decameron* is taught in Italian, "though students have the option of reading the work in English translation." Steven Grossvogel, at the University of Georgia, describes a similar course. While graduate students are expected to read the entire text, undergraduates are required to read slightly fewer than half the novelle.

Many Italian departments and programs offer courses in translation. Under such titles as Masterpieces of Italian Literature in Translation, Italian Civilization in Translation, and Italian Literature of the Medieval Period and Renaissance, these courses, which introduce a wide range of students to the *Decameron*, are similar to those taught to Italian majors.

Some instructors have introduced the *Decameron* into freshman seminars. Cornell offers The Craft of Storytelling, taught in multiple sections each year and limited to seventeen students, who read the entire *Decameron*. Robert Hollander, at Princeton, has taught a freshman seminar on Boccaccio's *Decameron* three times in the last eight years to a group of eleven to fifteen. The course includes readings from Ovid's *Art of Love*, Dante's *Inferno*, and Boccaccio's *Amorosa visione*. On a more advanced level, Janet Smarr teaches the course The Renaissance Novella in translation. Giuseppe Faustini teaches a course on Italian cinema in translation in which students read the *Decameron* novelle alluded to in Pasolini's film plus a handful of others. David Wallace and Janet Smarr teach courses on Chaucer and Boccaccio.

The greatest variety of settings for the *Decameron* is likely to be found in courses taught outside the Italian department. Movement away from the context of Italian literature often means a shedding of historical moorings for the *Decameron*. Courses based on themes replace courses organized historically. Frank G. Hoffman of the English department at Susquehanna University has taught a number of literature and composition seminars focusing on the *Decameron*. These include Medieval Stories and Storyteller, in which the text is combined with the *Canterbury Tales* and Calvino's *Castle of Crossed Destinies*. In From Italy and Russia with Love, students compare the *Decameron* with Voznesenskaya's *Women's* Decameron. In an honors course on constructions of sexuality in the Western tradition, Hoffman has paired *Decameron* 6.7 with the Supreme Court case *Bowers v. Hardwick*. Bonnie D. Irwin, at Eastern Illinois University, teaches the *Decameron* in English courses at all levels. In upper-level courses she teaches it along with *Thousand and One Nights* and Chaucer's *Canterbury Tales* "in a unit on framed narratives."

Novelle Taught

Because of the detailed syllabi supplied by respondents to the survey, it is possible to rank the *Decameron* novelle on the basis of how frequently they are taught. Every instructor responding teaches 1.1 (Day 1, novella 1), the story of Cepparello; 4.1, the story of Ghismonda; and 5.9, Federigo degli Alberighi. Day 1, story 3, "the three rings," and 6.10, the novella of Frate Cipolla, are only slightly less popular. Three-fourths of the respondents teach Day 4, story 2, Frate Alberto, and story 5, the "pot of basil"; as well as 5.8, the story of Nastagio degli Onesti; and 10.10, the Griselda story. Two-thirds of the respondents add the "Introduction to Day 1"; 1.2, the story of Abraham (Abraam) the Jew; 2.5, Andreuccio; 2.7, Alatiel; 3.1, Masetto; 3.2, Agilulf; the "Author's Preface" to Day 4; 5.1, Cimone; and 8.3, the first of the Bruno, Buffalmacco, and Calandrino stories. Stories taught by a majority of the respondents include 1.4, 4.9, 5.3, 6.4, 6.9, 10.3, and 10.9.

It is also possible to determine the most popular Days within the *Decameron*. Days 1 and 4 are the most widely taught, and Day 5 is a close third. Days 6 and 10 are in the second rank. Days 2, 3, and 7 rank next in popularity. The Days that are least often taught and from which stories are least likely to be assigned are Days 8 and 9. The most neglected area of the *Decameron*, whether students study the text in Italian or English, are the final sections of each day, in which dispositions for the following day are discussed and a *canzone* is sung.

Approaches and Difficulties

The variety of approaches to the *Decameron* reported by respondents to the survey is large, but some themes appear more often than others. Setting the text in its historical and cultural context tops the list, and issues of gender are a close second. Tommasina Gabriele listed many of the most common approaches in her summation of the themes she points out to her students. These include the *Decameron's* "view of women (elsewhere contradicted in Boccaccio's work), its critique of religious intolerance and religious institutions, its view of sex (as explicated in part by Scaglione), its popularity, the importance Boccaccio places on human nature, its reflection of bourgeois (in a positive sense) values as contrasted to the waning ideals of courtly love and courtly values."

Both Hollander and Smarr emphasize ethical aspects of the work. Hollander sees it as a "satire with roots in Ovid's minor works and Dante" and advocates a "post-Robertsonian" approach to the text. Smarr, following Boccaccio's lead in the proem, reads the work as "a collection of examples of behavior to admire and imitate or to laugh at and avoid." Marilyn Migiel and Pier Massimo Forni emphasize rhetorical approaches to the text. Forni places particular emphasis on the "intersection of rhetoric and narrative."

In addition to such thematic considerations, most instructors pay attention to the style of the work. Boccaccio's style is difficult even for native speakers of Italian, but the difficulties vary. The introduction of any novella is always the most challenging part. As the narrator frames his story, he or she speaks at levels of abstraction and of stylistic complexity that are abandoned as the story itself unfolds. Boccaccio's notion of rhetorical decorum demands these complexities, and so they are present among all his fictional narrators. These distinct levels of style are often washed out in translation, but the most distinctive features of Boccaccio's style—his snide comedy and vivid description of events, his sense of character and comic dialogue, his occasional absurdity verging on the surreal, and his mock solemnity—all come through.

Study of the form and structure of the work usually focuses on the elements that have traditionally defined the *cornice*, or frame, of the *Decameron*. These include the title, subtitle, proem, introduction to Day 1, introduction to Day 4, and author's conclusion. Attention to the *cornice* might be supplemented by consideration of the text's audiences. Irwin has her students "look at layers of audiences: the internal audiences, the contemporary audience, the modern audience, and the audience of authors who borrow from the *Decameron*." Structural readings can also shade into ethical readings of the text. Michael Sherberg draws attention to "order as the *brigata* creates it and as a reflection of [the *brigata's*] need to re-establish order in the wake of the plague." Many respondents give some attention to the comedic reading of the *Decameron* most closely associated with Branca and amplified by Cottino-Jones in her book

Order from Chaos. This tradition argues for the aesthetic ordering of the *Decameron* as a model for social reformation in Boccaccio's society.

Whatever approach participants in the study take, the length of the *Decameron* is the primary difficulty they must overcome in presenting the work to students. The solution almost always appears to be some form of excerpting. As the section in this volume "Novelle Taught" illustrates, however, there are many approaches to excerpting the text. But all of them must come to terms with the complex and often subtle structures interconnecting words and ideas within the *Decameron*. Understanding these structures enables students to appreciate the way Boccaccio turns a collection of one hundred short stories into something more unified.

A Note on the Essays

While the general focus of the volume is pedagogical, some of the essays are more direct in their discussion of classroom experience than others are. Every essay, though, can deepen an instructor's understanding of the text as well as guide his or her classroom approach. Bonnie Irwin and Janet Smarr lead off the first group of essays, "Teaching the *Decameron* in Its Traditions," by addressing Boccaccio's engagement with the world beyond Europe and religions other than Christianity. Irwin's subject is the frame tale as a genre, while Smarr's essay examines the text's thematic excursions into the territory, both physical and ideal, of Arabs and Jews. Unlike many of his contemporaries, Boccaccio shuns anti-Semitic stereotypes, and in the *Decameron's* third novella he seems to be arguing that within the limits of human knowledge the claims to spiritual authority of Christians, Muslims, and Jews are indistinguishable.

Robert Hollander addresses the debt Boccaccio owes to his great predecessor and sometime foil Dante and the *Divine Comedy.* Hollander's essay explores the burden that Boccaccio's dependence on Dantean words and phrases imposes on the instructor. A central aspect of the relationship between Boccaccio and Dante, but one that is not limited to the influence of an individual author, is discussed by Julia Reinhard Lupton in her essay on secular designs in the *Decameron.* Lupton argues that Boccaccio's creation of secular literature is not a creation ex nihilo but a transformation of sacred literature into something new and unprecedented.

In the essay that follows, Michael Papio discusses a variety of structures that readers have observed in the *Decameron* ranging from the geometric and numerological patterns beloved of medieval readers and writers to those discerned by structuralists and historical critics. Steven Grossvogel describes the historical situation of the *Decameron* and some of the issues raised by Boccaccio's intertwining of history and fiction. After a discussion of Boccaccio's presentation of this subject in his *Genealogie deorum,* the essay focuses on Vittore Branca, the most influential of contemporary Boccaccio scholars and a critic who has often foregrounded the interplay of history and fiction in his extensive work on the *Decameron*. The next essay describes major currents in Boccaccio criticism in the last hundred years. Giuseppe Mazzotta, the author of the influential *The World at Play in Boccaccio's* Decameron, looks at the text's "deep entanglement" with critics, violence, and love. In the long scholary history of the text, Mazzotta argues, critics have far too often oversimplified the *Decameron* and reduced a polyvocal text to one or another systematic univocality.

In the section of essays entitled "Gender and Sexuality in the *Decameron*," F. Regina Psaki discusses the multiple and complex roles that women play in the *Decameron* and the role of gender-related approaches to the text in the classroom. The essay examines the voices given to women as characters; the ironic representation of genres within the *Decameron* and the way female characters are refracted by this process; and, finally, the way the *Decameron* looks—often voyeuristically—at the female body. Marga Cottino-Jones turns from the real world Boccaccio compellingly describes to a consideration of the magic and supernatural worlds that the *Decameron* frequently evokes. While this essay might be read as a complement to Smarr's essay on Arabs and Jews in the *Decameron*, Cottino-Jones focuses on how gender is highlighted and critiqued through the contrast of real and fantastic worlds. In the final essay in this section, Raymond-Jean Frontain uses the concept of sexual festivity to describe Boccaccio's frequent references to sexual encounters in the *Decameron*. He argues that the text exemplifies an attitude toward life that he finds echoed in many contemporary responses to the AIDS epidemic.

In the next section, "The Influence of the *Decameron*," topics range from essays on the literature of Europe in the Middle Ages and Renaissance to Boccaccio's appearances on film and in the modern world of hypertext. Robert W. Hanning compares the *Decameron* with Chaucer's *Canterbury Tales*. He looks in the *Tales* for internal evidence of Chaucer's knowledge of the *Decameron* and addresses the common cultural work being carried out by the two texts. He then describes the different textual worlds that each author has created and the way their agendas diverge.

Next James McGregor looks at the novella tradition in Italy after Boccaccio. Drawing on an observation by Erich Auerbach, the essay describes the role of the novella—a popular, nonliterary form for the most part, despite its distinguished ancestry—as a chronicle of new ways of life and thought in the period. Aldo Scaglione, whose pioneering approach to the *Decameron* is discussed in Mazzotta's essay, looks at the influence of the novella tradition on the *Heptaméron* of Marguerite de Navarre. Robert Bayliss focuses on Boccaccio's influence on the novella in Spain and, more specifically, on Cervantes's *Novelas ejemplares* and on novelle of María de Zayas. Angelo Mazzocco and Elizabeth H. D. Mazzocco examine one of the many transformations of the Boccaccian novella in the Renaissance. While story collections like the *Decameron* proliferate from the fourteenth century on, in the Renaissance the novella begins to have a significant influence on the new dramatic forms that are springing to life.

The theme of Boccaccio's influence as it spreads beyond the confines of the literary tradition is addressed at length in the last section of the volume, "Boccaccio and the Visual Arts." Victoria Kirkham surveys the enormous field of Boccaccio illustrations begun by the poet himself, then burgeoning in manuscript and print. She argues for the use of one subgroup of this avalanche of visual materials, Boccaccio portraits, to link the elusive writer with the interpretations of his work. Her essay includes an iconographic bibliography pinpointing the location of the most important illustrations. Kevin J. Harty brings the story of Boccaccio illustration down to the present day. He discusses two films—both readily available on videotape for classroom use—the 1952 film Decameron *Nights*, directed by Hugo Fregonese, and Pasolini's 1970 film, *Il Decameron*. His essay includes a complete filmography. The final essay in this section, by Massimo Riva, is not, strictly speaking, about Boccaccio's influence. Instead it focuses on the way computers equipped with hypertext can be used to open the text for simultaneous and complex investigation by a diverse group of students. Not only is it an exciting introduction to the newest form of literary research and pedagogy, but it is also a fine summation of the theme of the entire collection. Hypertext readings emphasize the very features in the text that the essays as a group demonstrate: the plurality of voices in Boccaccio's text, its complex interweaving of themes, and its multiple perspectives.

NOTE

[1]All unattributed quotations in this section were taken from responses to the MLA survey of Boccaccio instructors.

Narrative in the *Decameron* and the *Thousand and One Nights*

Bonnie D. Irwin

Teaching the *Decameron* in conjunction with the *Thousand and One Nights* offers students the opportunity to examine many different aspects of medieval narrative: the influence of oral tradition; shifting roles of authors, narrators, and readers; Eastern influence on Western texts, and the vitality of the tale genre in medieval literary traditions. The two tale collections are quite different. The *Thousand and One Nights* dates back to the ninth century, is of anonymous authorship, and although the tales it contains are timeless, is steeped in Muslim and Arabic traditions.[1] The *Decameron* has a named author whose biography we know a little about, can be dated in the mid-fourteenth century (c. 1349–53), and although many of its stories are also timeless, the frame is well situated in a particular time and place. Narrative differences are obvious as well: one versus ten narrators, an infinitely expandable frame versus one with a set limit of stories. Despite these differences, however, the fact that both works depict storytelling in all its complexity and deal with the moral and social issues of their separate cultures allows us to develop fruitful comparisons as well as contrasts that illuminate our understanding of both texts.

Decameron, Thousand and One Nights, and the Oral Tradition of the Frame Tale

Although generally categorized as a collection of novelle, the *Decameron* falls within the genre of the frame tale since it consists of a story that contains other stories. As such, it joins the company of the *Thousand and One Nights*, Buddhist jataka tales, numerous versions of the *Seven Sages*, and such European works as Petrus Alfonsi's *Disciplina clericalis* and Chaucer's *Canterbury Tales*, among many others. The frame tale may be defined as a fictional narrative in either prose or poetry that is composed primarily for the purpose of presenting other narratives. It depicts a series of oral storytelling events (in the *Decameron,* a total of one hundred) in which the characters in the framing story become the narrators of the interpolated tales. The framing tale derives its meaning primarily from what it encloses and thus generally cannot stand alone, although Boccaccio's *cornice,* or frame, is among the more complex. The frame of the *Thousand and One Nights* is more typical, in that it outlines a narrative situation without fully developing the characters and in some versions even lacks a conclusion. Its framing story tells of Shahrayar, whose unfaithful first wife has caused him to murder each subsequent wife on their wedding night. Shahrazad, the daughter of his vizier, elects to marry Shahrayar and change his ways, which she does through telling stories night after night, ending each on a note of suspense, thus guaranteeing her survival one more night. By the time she finally runs out of tales, she has also given birth to three sons, and Shahrayar spares her life both for their sake and because of her virtuous character. Boccaccio and Chaucer represent a much later stage in the evolution of the frame tale, a stage at which the narrative, while retaining traditional elements, also becomes more self-conscious. Their many narrators, while each less productive than Shahrazad, have distinct personalities and comment on their tales and those of others.

Among all the other themes that will be discussed in this volume regarding the *Decameron*, one that cannot be overlooked is the theme of traditional storytelling and its depiction in the Middle Ages. The frame tale is unique among medieval genres in the extent to which it both derives from oral traditions and depicts them. We cannot determine exactly how oral performance took place just from reading these collections, but by analyzing two works at opposite ends of the developmental spectrum of such tales, we can better see not only the range of frame tale dynamics but also ways in which they may have been orally performed. The *Decameron* and the *Thousand and One Nights* exhibit what John Foley has termed the "rhetorical persistence of traditional forms" (60), meaning that we can see traces of oral language and style in the written text.

In the *Thousand and One Nights*, this means language with hallmarks of oral dialect, which in Arabic is quite distinct from written language, reiterative structures, and simple characterizations. Of course, in most classes one will have to limit the discussion to the last two aspects, as few undergraduate students have mastered Arabic and Italian. Even through translations, however, students can recognize that Boccaccio, consciously constructing a literary text rather than transcribing an oral one, is aware of the oral-literate differences. His structure is also very regularized and reiterative; even though he changes the events of each day, the similar patterns of the days recall oral storytelling sessions. He demonstrates an awareness of the differences between the two modes of communication in the second paragraph of the author's conclusion:

> [D]ico che più non si dee a me esser disdetto d'averle scritte, che generalmente si disdica agli uomini e alle donne di dir tutto dí *foro* e *caviglia* e *mortaio* e *pestello* e *salsiccia* e *mortadello*, e tutto pien di simiglianti cose.   (960)

> [L]et me say that it is no more improper for me to have written these words than for men and women at large to fill their everyday speech with such words as "hole," "peg," "mortar," "pestle," "wiener," and "fat sausage," and other similar expressions.   (685)

Statements such as this, compounded by Boccaccio's decision to break with tradition and write his work in Italian prose rather than in Latin poetry, reflect his knowledge of and control over the narrative choices he makes. He also recognizes and explains differences among the various kinds of oral speech. Place, time, and company dictate the nature of any oral performance:

> Appresso, assai ben si può cognoscere queste cose non nella chiesa, [. . .] ma ne' giardini, in luogo di sollazo, tra persone giovani.   (960)

> What is more, one can see quite clearly that these tales were not told in a church [. . .]. But they were told in gardens, in a place suited for pleasure, in the presence of young people [. . .].   (686)

These two excerpts serve other functions—Boccaccio inserts them primarily to distance himself, albeit ironically, from the more risqué tales—but they do reveal that he recognizes the comparative freedom of oral tradition as well as its potential complexity. With that knowledge, he freely uses those forms adopted from oral tradition in his written text.

In teaching the two works side by side, an instructor may point out the variety of ways a written text may open windows onto oral performance and the extent to which authors are dependent on traditional narrative forms over and above the mere borrowing of tales from oral sources. We can be relatively certain that, during the fourteenth century, both collections were usually read or recited aloud. Both texts can be described at one level as transitional, taking material from oral as well as written sources, but students can also recognize some subtle differences in the way the oral tradition influences these tales. The *Thousand and One Nights*, apparently closer to its oral roots, contains traditional language and forms primarily because it is oral-derived. Muhsin Mahdi has pointed to many literate aspects of this work, but the fact remains that much of the literacy in the different versions seems to be at a scribal level, where various redactors have tried to make the text more literary and less traditional. Boccaccio, however, may very well be using certain forms consciously and intentionally just as he makes careful use of Latin rhetorical structures. The conclusion to the *Decameron* shows that he is aware of the differences among the various traditions from which he draws, and his use of oral narrative devices points to his decision to make his text resemble the performance situation.

One place this contrast becomes most obvious is in the portrayal of narrator-audience dynamics within the works. Scholars of folklore and oral tradition show us that, among other distractions, there are often interruptions in performances when the audience disagrees with the content or style of a storyteller's narrative. Oddly enough, the *Thousand and One Nights* contains little of this; the only thing that consistently interrupts Shahrazad is the coming of dawn. Her audience, that is, her husband and sister, make comments that are almost identical from one night to the next and never until a story telling session is completed. In the *Decameron*, however, we see more interference incorporated in the text itself. When the servants run in on Day 6, for example, we see the impact of this disturbance on the oral performance itself, as it helps Dioneo to choose the theme for Day 7:

> Valorose donne, in diverse maniere ci s'è della umana industria e de' casi vari ragionato, tanto che, se donna Licisca non fosse poco avanti qui venuta, la quale con le sue parole m'ha trovata materia a' futuri ragionamenti di domane, io dubito che io non avessi gran pezza penato a trovar tema da ragionare. (575)

> Worthy ladies, we have discussed so often and in a variety of ways the subject of human endeavor as well as its different kinds of adventures that if Mistress Licisca had not arrived on the scene a short time ago and said something which gave me material for a new topic tommorow, I am afraid I would have found it very difficult to turn up a theme for us to talk about. (410)

As a frame tale becomes more literate, authors such as Chaucer and Boccaccio seem to find it necessary to include more of the keys of oral performance: interruptions, a variety of audience responses, and a variety of narrative styles matched to individual narrators. It appears, however, that redactors of older texts, like the *Thousand and One Nights*, assume the oral performance of the text will include these textures of performance whether or not they appear in the manuscript. Approaching an issue like this in regard to the *Decameron* can only be accomplished by offering students another frame tale with which to compare it.

Narrators and Audiences, Authors and Readers

In addition to providing a basis for studying the orality-literacy continuum of the Middle Ages, comparing the structure of the *Decameron* with that of the

Thousand and One Nights allows students to delve into many issues of medieval narrative that the story-within-a-story format may present. Frame tales come in a variety of shapes and sizes. The *Decameron* represents what John Jaunzems terms a "tight" frame (45), although it is not nearly so tight as those employed in sermons and by medieval authors of "Mirrors for Princes," advice books in which each tale illustrates a moral or practical lesson. In the *Decameron*, however, there is a theme for each day except the first and the ninth, and the narrators, with the exception of Dioneo, succeed in holding to these restrictions. This tight framing structure unifies and delimits the text in a way that the loose frame of the *Thousand and One Nights* does not. The tales enclosed within the *Thousand and One Nights* do not have to conform to any particular theme, length, or style. The only restriction is that they be sufficiently entertaining. Thus the redactors of the several versions of the *Thousand and One Nights* have considerably more freedom to include whatever tales they choose, and while the tales often share themes, the collection is far less unified than the *Decameron*.

Frame tales also provide great occasion for irony. The multiple layers of narrators and audiences filter the stories through several different perspectives before they reach a reader. In the *Decameron*, the overall narrator is clearly an ironic persona, even though he has much in common with Boccaccio himself. The author can manipulate the multiple voices to absolve himself of responsibility for his text while, at the same time, clearly claiming credit for its wit. By having several internal narrators, Boccaccio can play one off another. For example, the unhappy Filostrato can request sad tales while the playful Emilia allows her storytellers free reign; both are included within the *Decameron* without Boccaccio's seeming inconsistent. He brings a vitality to his narrators lacking in those of earlier frame tales. This development of character gives him even more possibilities to exploit. The complexity of the *Thousand and One Nights*, however, is achieved more through multiple layers than through highly developed narrators. This layering is five levels deep in certain sections: "The Hunchback Tale" and "The Porter and the Three Ladies of Baghdad" both show Shahrazad telling stories of people telling stories of people telling stories, and so forth. These layers present to audiences a series of lenses through which to view a story. Some are colored by gender, others by religion or social class. Asking students to penetrate the multiple layers and discuss the motivations of the various narrators leads them to realize how complex these collections are. Secondary sources, such as Joy Potter (*Five Frames*) and Sandra Naddaff are helpful here. Moreover, comparing the two texts deepens the analysis. How does the nature of irony change if we know the individual author responsible for the text? What difference does it make if the primary narrator is juggling one or more voices in the interpolated tales?

The multiple layering allows the *Decameron* and the *Thousand and One Nights* to call attention to the process of narration as it is simultaneously depicted and commented on. The reader moves in and out of the frame depending on the length and depth of any interpolated tale. If the story being narrated by a character is long and involved, one may temporarily forget that the framing tale even exists and that someone is telling the story of a merry *brigata* fleeing the plague or of a queen narrating to save her life. Other times, when a particular narration is brief or frivolous or particularly apt to the situation being portrayed in the framing story, readers will be more aware of the puppetmaster behind the scenes pulling the strings of both narrators and reader alike. In the *Thousand and One Nights*, much of this awareness is dependent on the watchfulness of the reader. Boccaccio, clearly cognizant of the potential of the form that he has chosen for the *Decameron*, manipulates it in a variety of ways to highlight the narrative craft as well as his talent as an author.

On the fourth day of the *Decameron* alone, many of these manipulations can be observed. First of all, Boccaccio's introduction to the day is longer than usual. In his discourse he takes up the issue of his responsibility, or lack thereof, for the stories of his narrators. While reading this passage, one comprehends the author's attempts to guide his readers. When the storytelling commences, however, the king for the day, Filostrato, reacts at length to the first two stories, complaining that they are not sad enough. During these speeches, it is easier to forget or at least ignore the author's presence behind the scenes. To carry the process further, one can imagine that during the second story of the day, which depicts a friar pretending to be the angel Gabriel in order to make his way into a widow's bed, a reader might get immersed in a complex and amusing story and lose track of Filostrato's request for a sad story. This phenomenon is precisely what Boccaccio describes in his introduction to the day. How can we blame him for its content if we can forget his presence while we read the story?

The framing stories of both the *Decameron* and the *Thousand and One Nights* reveal an obsession with time. Both narrative situations arise out of the need to fill time in a pleasant and absorbing way: in the *Thousand and One Nights*, Shahrazad must fill an entire night with stories while causing her husband to forget his promise to kill his bride in the morning, and in the *Decameron*, the tales are meant to separate the company mentally from the effects of the plague just as they have chosen to separate themselves physically from Florence. At the same time, however, the narration time does not always agree with the narrative time. We are given to understand that the storytelling takes much more time than it would in reality. Because both frames use the threat of death as a backdrop, the narration is well served by this stretching of time. Outside the storytelling events lies death; not only must the narrators continue relating their tales in order to thwart it, but they also must use as much time as possible. Moreover, the time frame of each narrated story is different from the temporal movement of the framing story. This creates a kind of pushing and pulling movement as each interpolated tale stops time and forwards it simultaneously. As readers, we will not reach the end of the framing story without passing through the interpolated ones, but each interpolated tale effectively stops time for the reader while it is being narrated, although it fills time for the audience within the text. Depending on the intellectual level of a class, these temporal aspects of narrative can be explored either as merely an interesting phenomenon of the frame tale or as a challenging issue of narrative dynamics that is compounded with each additional layer of framing.

East and West

The *Decameron* and the *Thousand and One Nights* indeed have many similarities and differences that can be explored fruitfully, and although they may represent a single genre, they emerge from two very different traditions. Many instructors will find it useful to compare the two works in the area of East-West literary relations. No one suggests that Boccaccio ever read a version of the *Thousand and One Nights* or any other Arabic frame tale popular in the Middle Ages, but the *Decameron* and the *Nights* certainly share stories or analogues of stories. What difference does context make in the interpretation of a tale? How does the significance of a story change when it appears within a different frame? The frame tale facilitated the transmission of tales across linguistic and cultural boundaries since both oral and literary versions of the tales were translated and transmitted from one language to another. Hearing or reading these collections then provided other redactors and authors with the raw materials for their own works. Thus Boccaccio could have been indirectly exposed to much of the material from Eastern collections through such intermediaries as versions of the *Seven Sages* (Runte, Wikeley, and Farrell) in Italian and Latin and the *Disciplina clericalis* (Petrus Alfonsi), a Latin collection heavily dependent on Eastern sources. The fourth story on Day 7 of the *Decameron*, for example, is nearly identical to the fourteenth tale in the *Disciplina clericalis*, "The Well." In it, an adulterous wife, who has been locked out of her home by her husband, feigns her death by appearing to drown in a well in order to lure him out of the house and subsequently lock him out. Comparisons such as these show students that Boccaccio was writing within a worldwide tradition of storytelling.

The best source for analogues, despite its age, remains Alfred Lee's The *Decameron: Its Sources and Analogues*, which conveniently lists analogous stories in the order in which they appear in the *Decameron*. This work, in combination with folklore resources such as Antti Aarne's *The Types of the Folktale*, enables one to find which tales in the *Thousand and One Nights* and the *Decameron* have the most in common. A good example is the tale told by Fiammetta on Day 1 (fifth story) in which, by symbols and clever words, the marchioness of Monferrato protects her honor from the desires of the king of France. In many ways, this tale resembles that of the "Lion's Track," which appears in the Eastern *Seven Sages* versions and also in later manuscripts of the *Thousand and One Nights*, such as the one translated by Richard F. Burton. Juxtaposing the two versions can inspire class discussion of possible source material for the *Decameron* and, perhaps more important, of how the interpretation of a tale changes in different contexts. In the context of the *Seven Sages* the tale is used to show the devious nature of women, although one can assume that the placement of the entire *Seven Sages* frame tale within the *Thousand and One Nights* allows Shahrazad to use the same story to praise the woman's fidelity. Boccaccio's Fiammetta, by contrast, uses the story to demonstrate the woman's skill with language. This approach to teaching these collections is valuable because it can be accomplished through reading excerpts. In the traditional undergraduate class, most instructors would be hard-pressed to read both of these rather lengthy works in their entirety. Comparing individual tales in context offers many options: individual students could choose different stories and present their findings to the class, an entire class could read the *Decameron* and then selections from the *Thousand and One Nights*, or an instructor could assign selections from each text.

Aside from comparisons involving individual tales and their analogues, many thematic comparisons can be made between these two works, both of which contain many tales of love and adultery, deception and gullibility. Analyzing how the common themes work in each collection (for instance, how culture and religion affect the depiction of marriage and adultery) can lead students to discover medieval attitudes toward such issues as gender and sexuality. One difference that may immediately be noticed is that the clergy plays a much larger role in Boccaccio's work than in its Eastern counterparts. Boccaccio feels free to ridicule the apparent hypocrisy of the clergy in many tales (e.g., 3.8, 4.2, 7.5), but religious leaders are hardly included at all in the *Nights*. One reason for this difference lies in the differences between the religions themselves. Catholicism has a firmly established clerical hierarchy, whereas Islam reveres religious scholars but not as intermediaries between lay people and God.

Similarities in the tone and nature of adultery tales far outweigh the differences. Boccaccio devotes two entire days (seven and eight) to women's guile in deceiving their husbands, while this theme is the catalyst of most of the action of the narrative frame of the *Thousand and One Nights*. Clearly, in both Arab and Italian medieval storytelling traditions, women's infidelity and men's gullibility are favorite topics. If one chooses to use an edition based on a later version of the *Thousand and One Nights*, such as the Burton translation, still more specific parallels may be drawn. A popular story in these later versions of the *Nights* is the "Woman with Five Lovers." In this tale, a woman manages to have five different lovers and hide them all in a chest with five compartments, built specifically for that purpose. This tale clearly brings to mind several stories in the *Decameron* where women shut men in tight spaces in order to hide them from a jealous husband (8.8, 7.6). The absence of "The Woman with Five Lovers" from earlier manuscripts of the *Thousand and One Nights* allows for discussion of whether or not influence and analogues could have traveled West to East as well as East to West. In any case, for centuries both the *Decameron* and the *Thousand and One Nights* have raised the ire of conservative audiences while delighting those in search of entertaining tales. Reading them in conjunction with one another shows students how Boccaccio fits into an international tradition of storytelling that is didactic and diverting at the same time.

Another aspect of East-West cultural relations that can be covered through teaching these two works together is the medieval perception of the other. While Boccaccio is rightly concerned about how his audience will receive the more licentious and sacrilegious of his tales, he harbors no such qualms about his depiction of Eastern characters. Jews and Muslims are the source of much amusement in the tales. Panfilo's tale on Day 2 (seventh story) revolves around Western perceptions of Arab sexuality, depicting a young woman who is married off as a virgin after she had "lain with eight men perhaps ten thousand times" (126). Boccaccio's depiction of Arab characters can be compared with medieval Arabic portrayals in the *Thousand and One Nights*. Even in the Arabic text, some of the Arabs are foolhardy, prejudiced, and deceitful. The investigation can also be made in the opposite direction, juxtaposing, for example, Arab views of Christians as drunkards and Jews as greedy in "The Hunchback Tale" and Boccaccio's satiric portraits of his own people as foolish, selfish, and lustful.

Even historical characters cannot escape revision in these frame tales. Often noted by scholars of the *Decameron*, Boccaccio's portrait of Saladin (10.9) is largely positive. He repays the kindness of a Christian with generosity and understanding. The opening of the tale where Saladin disguises himself as a merchant to see what the Christian crusaders are preparing for his army recalls the many tales in the *Thousand and One Nights*, such as "The Porter and the Three Ladies of Baghdad," in which Harun al-Rashid, an Arab caliph (ruled 786–809), dons the disguise of a merchant to see how his subjects are faring. Both rulers are spirited and beneficent, these portrayals relying more on legend than on history. Both Boccaccio's portrait of Saladin and the Harun al-Rashid of the *Thousand and One Nights* were developed approximately 100–150 years after their actual deaths. Comparing these tales can add a historical component to the multicultural studies that continue to be an important part of many literature courses. In addition, these tales may be used to study the relation among history, legend, and tale.

Myriad similarities and differences between the *Decameron* and the *Thousand and One Nights* greet the reader, creating endless possibilities for classroom discussions and assignments, only a few of which have been covered here. What must not be forgotten, however, is the diversion that the stories provide for medieval audience and modern student alike. Boccaccio, as well as the many storytellers and redactors of the *Thousand and One Nights*, obviously revels in his task of presenting tales in their traditional context to the reading public, and both collections celebrate the tale and the storytelling tradition. Amusing and enlightening stories have a remarkable effect on an audience when they are well told, and by exposing our students to the spirit of medieval storytelling we allow them, too, to become a part of one of the traditions of the *Decameron*.

NOTE

[1]Husain Haddawy's translation (*The Arabian Nights*), the only English one to be based on a medieval version of the *Nights*, is by far the most accurate and student-friendly English edition. More familiar translations by Richard F. Burton and Edward Lane are based on nineteenth-century Arabic versions and include many more tales, but both translators have taken considerable liberties with the Arabic texts.

Non-Christian People and Spaces in the *Decameron*

Janet Levarie Smarr

Although most of the *Decameron*'s adventures take place in Europe and among Christians, some of the tales occur in Asia or Africa or concern people of other races and religions. How are non-Christian people and places represented in this work? How do they relate to the people and places of Europe that are, of course, predominant? And what are the functions served by introducing these "other" spaces? Other peoples interact with Europeans in three types of cases: that of non-Christians in Europe, that of non-Christians in Africa or Asia, and that of Christians traveling to the non-Christian world.

Students can be asked to think about the representations in each of these cases as a part of their mapping of the *Decameron*'s world, the values it offers, and the strategies by which it engages these values. In courses where the *Decameron* is taught along with Dante's *Commedia*, as in our Masterpieces of Western Literature survey, the differences between the two works' representations of non-Christians and of the possibilities for relationships across cultures can also be fruitfully explored, and students can be asked to speculate on what might make for divergences even among Florentines of the same half-century. They can also be asked to suggest what other categories, such as genre, might be relevant to this analysis and to consider the connection with questions of gender.

There are, of course, important differences between Jews and Muslims: for one thing, the Jews lacked a geographical area of their own and were not political military foes as were the Muslims; for another, because Boccaccio had deep connections with the business world, he was more likely to have actually known Jews in Italy than to have met real Muslims. The first difference means that the Muslim world offered not only a separate race and faith but also a separate space that appears in Boccaccio's narratives. The second difference is reflected in the fact that while Boccaccio can tell a story about a Jewish merchant living in France, his Muslim characters are either women in clearly fantastic tales or else the legendary Saladin, but not ordinary Muslim businessmen. Notwithstanding these important differences, Jews and Muslims were frequently linked in late medieval thought as simply non-Christians, especially in law (Daniel, *Islam* 116; Camille 164), and were often dehumanized in popular texts. Thus it makes some sense to treat Jew and Muslim together under the rubric of the cultural other.

Non-Christians in Europe

As early as the second tale the *Decameron* introduces a Jew who lives in Paris on friendly terms with a French businessman. Abraam is described initially as "diritto e leale" (48) ("honest and upright" [33]), the almost identical terms that in the same sentence describe Giannotto: "lealissimo e diritto." Giannotto sees Abraam as "valente e savio e buono" (49) ("valiant, wise, and good" [33]) and as marred solely by his lack of Christian faith. Although Abraam is content with his religion, Giannotto never ceases to press the issue.

In contrast to the character of this Jew is that of the papal court, the very center of Catholicism, which has supposedly the right faith but is marred by every imaginable sin. The virtues of Christianity reside more often among honest merchants—even Jewish ones—than among the leaders of the church. Nonetheless, the very wickedness of the curia persuades Abraam that God must be favoring the Christian religion since it grows despite its priests.

Ultimately, Abraam is baptized with a version of his friend's name, "Giovanni." The two friends have become totally indistinguishable. Thus we are reminded that the two men were always almost entirely the same, except for their religion. The period of their observance of different faiths does not seem to create any meaningful differences in their ways of life, nor does the conversion lead to any other specified changes in Abraam. He is the same good man he was, and the same friend, but now a Christian. That difference, however, is important in itself.

Perhaps as a structural mirror to the second tale, the penultimate (10.9) also offers a non-Christian in Europe and a friendship that traverses faiths. As the setting involves Saladin's coming to spy on European preparations for a religious war in the Middle East, the context is one of hostile relations. Nonetheless, the tale presents an exchange of loving generosities. The sultan and his companions "apertamente conobber messer Torello niuna parte di cortesia voler lasciare a far loro" (927) ("they clearly saw that Messer Torello meant to omit no aspect of courtesy in their regard [660]). Messer Torello's behavior is closer to the aristocratic emphasis on liberality (the very word *cortesia* names its social context) than to the merchant ethic of calculation and profit. Yet Messer Torello senses that his guests are nobler than they appear, and his courtesy wins the sultan's love.

Part 2 of the tale takes place in Alexandria where Messer Torello has been taken as a prisoner of war. Just as Abraam was called "the Jew" in Christian Europe, so Torello in Muslim Alexandria is called "the Christian" until the sultan happens to recognize him. Saladin's opportunity to return the extravagant courtesies he had received enables the two men to become equal; the sultan even expresses his improbable invitation that they rule together "equally lords": "Sarebbemi stato carissimo [. . .] che quel tempo, che voi e io viver dobbiamo, nel governo del regno che io tengo parimente signori vivuti fossimo insieme" (934) ("I should have liked nothing more than for the two of us to spend the rest of our lives here together, ruling as equals over the kingdom I possess" [666]). Thus class distinctions have been overcome along with distinctions of race and religion. The two men continue to correspond and remain fast friends, this time without any anxiety about the Muslim's salvation. Given Saladin's popular reputation for extreme wealth and generosity, the tale seeks to show how a gentleman of Pavia can equal him in spirit if not in material wealth. The Muslim, his religion seemingly forgotten, has become a model worthy of emulation.

In both these tales, two cultural worlds are compared. In one, the Christian world is found to be clearly inferior in its behavior to the other but nonetheless truer in its belief. In the tale of Messer Torello, religious issues are left aside. The other world far surpasses in wealth and power, even magical power, the world of Italy; yet the Italian is seen as nonetheless equal in personal qualities. In both tales, a strong bond of affection connects good men across the divisions of religion and race.

The case is different in two tales in which the Muslim visitor is female. One is the story of Alatiel (2.7), a Saracen with an Arabic-sounding name. The men through whose hands she passes in a series of misadventures are all foreign to her and do not speak her language; they are Christians. The first, knowing the Muslim is unaccustomed to wine, intentionally gets her drunk to satisfy his lust; most of the subsequent lovers are quickly willing to commit murder to obtain her, "lasciando ogni ragione e ogni giustizia dall'una delle parti" (169) ("put[ting] aside all reason and justice" [116]). Not the bonds of brothers or of host and guest or of friends can restrain these acts of violence and betrayal. The foreign woman is an object, but a desirable object. Men do not perceive the danger she brings, for it is not the danger of an external enemy but the peril of their own inner sinfulness, aroused by her exotic beauty.

At last she comes into the hands of men who can speak her language, one, in the service of the king of the Turks, who takes her to Rhodes and later his friend who takes her to Cyprus. There she encounters the old merchant who can return her to her father's court. Once she is among people speaking her language, men not only treat her more kindly but also treat each other more considerately. The acts of violence end, and the men even ask her what she wishes to do. At her return home she will have a proper wedding, a rite none of the men in the West cared to honor. Civilized behavior lies in the land of the other, while Christians are full of treachery, murder, lust, and disregard for the institutions of the church. Yet the narrator's warning seems to be addressed not to the men but to the woman: one should not wish for beauty because it is a cause of harm. Although this tale does not explicitly contrast Muslim and Christian behavior, it does take the measure of Western mores (somewhat like the stories of Abraam and Saladin) by stringing together from the two cultures a continuous series of men who take possession of Alatiel.

Very similar is the case in tale 3.10, in which Alibech, a woman who has an Arabic-sounding name, comes from Tunis into the desert to learn how to serve God. Like Abraam, she has heard the Christian faith frequently recommended by its adherents; as in the tale of Abraam, Christian behavior does not live up to its tenets. The Christian hermit Rustico who takes her in first sins with pride, thinking he can use her to test his willpower, then sins with lust, and is finally ridiculed by his inability either to maintain his vows or to fulfill her desires. He is revealed to be lacking in both spiritual and physical potency. Dioneo's tale is more humorous and less grim in its depiction of Christian failings than the story of Alatiel, but again the allure of the Arab woman unleashes the worst in the Christian male. Rustico's metaphor about the devil raising its head is only too true. Alibech and Alatiel may represent the perceived sexual laxity of Islamic law, which was accused of seducing Christians and others who encountered it (Daniel, *Islam* 98–102, 137–50, esp. 137, and *Arabs* 42–43, 235; Southern 68–69; Polo 58). The Eastern female comes as an unexpected test, and the Christian man fails it miserably. The men who desired these two women are left either dead or, at best, exhausted and humiliated. Whereas the visiting male, Jew or sultan, openly criticizes or praises the West, the female does not comment on the behavior of the men she encounters. Either ignorant or helpless, or simply unable to communicate, she accepts whatever men do. It is we who are left to comment and judge.

Non-Christians in Africa or Asia

If Christians at home are not always on their best behavior, a remarkably positive presentation is given to non-Christians on their own turf. We have noted already the dazzling splendor and generosity of Saladin in tale 10.9 and his willingness to befriend a foreigner—even an enemy—whose personal qualities are worthy. On the same day, on which the topic is magnanimity, tale 10.3 gives another example of a foreigner's supreme generosity. It is worthy of note that this last day, which explicitly offers positive examples to "correct" the follies and vices of the previous nine, presents two exemplary figures from beyond the Christian West. Positive examples on that day also come from ancient Greece (10.8), from a female of the lowest class (10.10), and from both Guelph and Ghibelline parties (10.6 and 10.7). There seems to be an intent here to demonstrate that admirable behavior can be found anywhere. The implication, of course, is that virtue is universal and not culturally bound in any way by history, gender, class, or faith.

The shift to a non-Western site follows a tale in which it is proclaimed almost a "miracle" that a clergyman would demonstrate gratitude, compassion, and generosity. The third tale on Day 10, though actually originating from Persian and Arabic sources (it appears in Saadi's *Bustan* about the ruler of Yemen and an Arab chieftan), is set, unusually, in China. This tale claims to follow the reports of Genovese merchants to that distant land, though it continues to use names belonging more to the Middle East than to the Far East.[1] Being on a trade route and eager to make himself known in some good way, the Chinese ruler Natan builds a magnificent palace in which he plays splendid host to all who come. His neighbor Mitridanes, equally wealthy, envies his reputation and tries to imitate his behavior. So far the Chinese rulers appear similar to the sultans as possessors of fabulous wealth and an abundance of beautiful goods. Travel accounts such as Marco Polo's or the romances of Alexander and the widely circulating letter supposedly from Prester John all described the East as a place of fabulous wealth and splendor. Mitridanes's increasingly envious desire to get rid of Natan only allows Natan the opportunity to demonstrate the ultimate generosity in his willingness to give away his life. Shamed, Mitridanes becomes his friend and the tale ends with their exchange of courteous sentiments.

Within their final conversation lies the critical comparison to unspecified other emperors and kings who seek to augment their fame not by acting generously but by killing innumerable people, burning villages, and destroying cities. This behavior is clearly associated with the "perverse desire" (614) of which Mitridanes totally repents. Moreover, the story's audience within the *Decameron* comments that Natan's liberality with his own blood surpasses the day's previous examples of Spanish king and French clergyman. Once more, the foreigner serves as a vantage point from which to assess and criticize behavior in the West.

There is no attempt at a realistic presentation of either Saladin's or Natan's court; each is an extreme or ideal against which the West is to be measured. Fabulous wealth is required to sustain the initial liberality; the ultimate gift of one's own life, however, lies within anyone's reach. Nonetheless, only in faraway places can such total generosity be imagined to exist until the very last tale of the *Decameron*, when an Italian peasant girl caps all other examples.

A more puzzling tale, different from any discussed so far, is the famous story of the three rings (1.3). The Saladin of this tale, in need of money for his wars, looks for an excuse to confiscate the wealth of a Jew in Alexandria. This story follows the tale about the Jewish and Christian merchants whose friendship leads to the Jew's conversion; and it seems to comment on this conversion, but the implications of the comment are far from clear. Like Abraam and Giannotto, Saladin and Melchisedech are two of a kind, not in justice and reliability but in avarice and shrewdness. Their fast friendship, across religious lines, results from their recognition of this similarity; there is no suggestion of a change of faith but rather a shared complicity in the refusal to acknowledge Christianity's truth.

The issue of faith is raised by the snare Saladin sets, by asking the Jew which of the three religions, Islam, Judaism, or Christianity, is best. He anticipates one of two possible answers: Islam, to flatter the sultan, or Judaism, in loyalty to the Jew's own faith; Christianity is never a serious option here. The Jew's response makes all three religions equal in both sincerity and uncertainty: each thinks his own faith is true, but no one knows which is right. Indeed, the father in the Jew's story makes two more rings because he indeed loves all three sons and wants to "satisfy" them all. It would be easy to take this tale as a cautious exhortation of tolerance.

However, another message may equally be implied. In the tale of three rings which Melchisedech tells as an analogy, the father who had two copies made of the ring "appena conosceva qual si fosse il vero" (56) ("could hardly tell which was the real one" [38]); his sons "qual fosse il vero non si sapeva conoscere" (56) ("could not recognize the true one" [38]). Thus the three religions are not in fact indistinguishable. Filomena might expect her totally Christian audience to enjoy a sense of superiority in being able to know how to recognize that their own faith is the true one. She might expect them to find amusing the mutual assurances of two infidels that no one can know the real truth. Perhaps Abraam's disinterested acknowledgment in tale 2 of the superiority of the Christian faith prepares the ground for the Jew's self-serving disclaimer in tale 3. In the latter case, the first tale to be set in non-Christian lands specifically emphasizes the Muslim and Jew's religious difference and the ignorance or self-interest that prevents their recognition of the true faith. Any smugness of a Christian reader, however, quickly comes up against the criticisms of Christian behavior discussed above.

Christians in the Non-Christian World

Two tales, 2.9 and 5.2, present the travels of a Christian into the lands of the East. The European protagonists, one male and two females, are driven eastward by troubles at home that their sojourn abroad allows them to resolve. The Orient becomes that generic "other" space—like the pastoral realm or the forest—where a healthy inversion of the home situation makes possible its ultimate amelioration. As in the stories of generosity, it is an idealizing fantasy rather than a realistic representation.

Tale 2.9 is actually a double border crossing: Zinevra becomes a man as well as an Arab. The racial other and sexual other are equated; and both transformations work with perfect ease. Bernabò had praised his wife's abilities to ride, hawk, read, write, and keep accounts as well as any man. All she needs to do, when her husband sends orders to have her killed, is to don male clothes, and no one can tell that she is female. Having left the dangers of Italy for Alexandria and mastered the Arabic language, she becomes the sultan's captain of the guard, in charge of a market where both Christians and Muslims do business together. As her abilities have made sexual difference irrelevant, so commerce has apparently rendered racial or religious differences negligible. It is through this market and its circulation of goods from all over the world that Zinevra is able to find the clues and explanation for what had caused her husband's mysterious fury. Moreover, if in Italy she was at the mercy of men (her husband, Ambrogiuolo, and the pitying servant ordered to kill her), in Alexandria she is in a position of official power that can summon both Ambrogiuolo and her husband to justice before the sultan. The East provides a justice denied in the West.

The wealth of the East reappears in the gold, silver, and jewels that the sultan showers on her; however, the real value to Zinevra of the East lies in its escape from the structures of home. Just as the merchants and goods of the world circulate here out of their original contexts, so her own position in life is free to change—from female to male, from servant to captain, from victim to winner, from tricked to tricker ("l'ingannatore rimane a' piè dello'ngannato" [204, 218] is the repeated proverb that frames the tale: "the deceiver lay at the mercy of the deceived" [141, 152]). Interestingly, amid this total flux, it is her *constanzia* ("constancy") that is especially praised. But it is the swirl of goods and people that enables her to find once again her lost goods, her deceiver, and her husband and to recover her original social position.

As Zinevra was praised for constancy, so the woman of tale 5.2 is even named Gostanza, a name she deserves for her constancy in love. Her beloved Martuccio, rejected as too poor a suitor by her upper-class father, goes off to make his fortune. His own excessive greed leads to his capture by Saracen pirates, who leave him in a prison in Tunisia. Thinking him dead, Gostanza commits herself to sea in a small boat, only to end up also in North Africa. There Gostanza, like Zinevra, learns Arabic and takes up a new life in a Muslim household.

War not commerce provides the opportunity in this tale for Martuccio, who, by giving a bit of clever advice, brings himself to the attention and favor of the king. Now the roles have been reversed, for he is wealthy and of high status while Gostanza has become a modest artisan working in silk and leather. This reversal is underscored when, seeking to meet him again, she has herself announced (albeit with double meanings) as his servant from their old country. Enriched by the usual splendid gifts of the Tunisian king, they are able to go home and marry, that is, to obtain the situation they had sought in the first place.

Just as in tale 2.9, the Muslim world is, on the one hand, similar enough to their own culture to allow them to adapt and flourish; on the other hand, it is an other space in which their previous differences in status and wealth can be completely reversed. Thus their temporary displacement into the Muslim world enables them to overcome their own world's social obstacles to their marriage.

Boccaccio had access to a wide range of attitudes toward Jews and Muslims through the ecclesiastical writings, chronicles, romances, and tales that he might have encountered. Excerpts from some of these texts may be introduced to students in a seminar. He shares many of these attitudes, and if he seems to be situated in a fairly tolerant end of the spectrum, it is not through any noticeably deeper knowledge of the other culture. When considering Islamic religion in his scholarly writings, such as the *De Casibus* and *Esposizioni*, Boccaccio joined the clerical tradition in dismissing Islam with contempt. So, too, he clearly considers it a good ending that the Jew of tale 1.2 becomes Christian. But when considering the secular side of Muslim society in his novelle, he presents it not only as an outside place from which Europe can be criticized or its hierarchies reversed but also as a place of justice, liberality, and honor, readily open to friendships that cross the cultural divide.

NOTE

[1]This tale is also translated in Hitti 155–56 and in Crane 199–201.

Boccaccio's Hidden Debt to Dante

Robert Hollander

Boccaccio's knowledge and use of the works of Dante, as reflected in his *Decameron*, constitute a challenging topic, one that has only recently begun to receive the attention it deserves. It had simply been an unexamined common-place among his commentators that the young Boccaccio either did not know well or did not understand sufficiently the texts of Dante (even though the young Boccaccio is construed as including the thirty-eight-year-old author of the *Decameron*). In a magisterial essay published in 1979, Carlo Delcorno demonstrated, once and for all, that Boccaccio's *Elegia di madonna Fiammetta* (c. 1344) is filled with obvious borrowings from Dante, particularly the *Commedia*. If this is true (and no one has come forward with reasons that would cast it into doubt), then those of us who believe that we frequently find citations of Dante in the *Decameron* are relieved of one burden of proof, the argument that it was possible for Boccaccio to be closely familiar with Dante's texts by 1350. That may now be taken as a given.

By acknowledging this fact, those obliged to teach the *Decameron* are put under a second burden, that of confronting, in a carefully thought-out way, the relation of Boccaccio to his great precursor or, more particularly, the dependence of Boccaccian formulations, both large and small, on Dantean originals. And there are several layers to this problem. Is the teacher well versed in Dante? If he or she is, what of the students? There is not much that is less amusing in the classroom than discussion of a preceding literary text that students have not read. Those who are teaching the work in Italian will almost certainly be able to count on students' knowing at least anthologized portions of Dante's *Divine Comedy*. Those who are teaching it from an English translation (I use the one by Mark Musa and Peter Bondanella), in a course in which Boccaccio is covered for only a week or two, may be able to count on few students' having any familiarity with Dante's poem. It seems clear that magisterial desires and discipular abilities may only rarely match. As a result, I have tried to set down here something for all.

I have been able to offer a freshman seminar on the *Decameron* several times at Princeton. I think that a description of that experience may be helpful not only to those who will have that much time at their disposal but to others as well. My approach to Boccaccio presents him as indebted primarily to Ovid and to Dante. Of the fifteen or so students who take this seminar, I can count on perhaps one to have read some of the amatory works of Ovid and perhaps two or three to have read at least a bit of Dante in translation. I must therefore either steal some time from Boccaccio or forget about Ovid and Dante. The choice that I have made seems to work. The Ovidian texts are difficult (I distribute a full outline of both *Ars* and *Remedia* to help the students follow the development of Ovid's argument) but worth the effort for three reasons at least:

(1) If, as I insist, Boccaccio is an ironic writer, Ovid is excellent preparation for him; (2) Boccaccio's other vernacular fictions, of which we read one, are filled with references to these texts (the *Decameron* less so), and thus we are reading works that were extremely well known to him; (3) Ovid is simply not known to many of our entering students and therefore, in a small way, we are making up a bit of their cultural deficiency.

Dante's *Inferno* is, in its strange and wonderful way, the ancient text that one can most surely count on to rouse untutored minds to excitement. My students never seem to have any difficulty in letting Dante seize their attention. Our only problem arises from having to say good-bye so quickly; nonetheless, our two weeks with Dante help to set up the *Decameron*. Students with investments in Ovid and Dante are also aware that they are now acquainted with the authors that meant most to Boccaccio. This is not a small thing.

Our fourth week puts both the amatory Ovid and Dante to excellent use. The *Amorosa visione*, a text beloved by few, is filled with Boccaccian learning, and certainly with references to Ovid and to Dante. That is not the principal reason that we read it. Rather, it stands as perhaps the most egregious example that we possess of Boccaccio the maker of mythographic fiction. (In our opening meeting I give a descriptive overview of all Boccaccio's works that precede the *Decameron*.) The students find the *Amorosa visione* the least agreeable work that we read (and in such company, who will not forgive them that reaction?), but they agree that it also sets up the *Decameron* by helping them see its radical newness, even with respect to Boccaccio's own previous career in letters. We read it as a text in itself, trying to determine how serious it is (or how ironic). The last group with whom I studied the poem actually claimed to have enjoyed the experience of reading and discussing it. It remains my belief that even an unhappy meeting with an erudite dream vision about an (apparently traditional literary) enamorment is excellent preparation for a first encounter with what is now accounted Boccaccio's sole masterwork and one of the landmarks of European literature.

As for the *Decameron* itself, I assign each member of the seminar a particular identity (from among the ten frame characters and the narrator; when there are more than eleven students one poor soul may be asked to make sense of the songs that conclude each day while still others may double up on a hard character [e.g., Dioneo]). This tactic puts a spine through their first reading of Boccaccio. What impresses me most about our mutual experience as readers is how much the *Decameron* changes as one moves from day to day. By the end of Day 3 Boccaccio seems nothing so much as the Italian Ovid, satirizing the lustful and other cupidinous habits of humankind. By the end of Day 5 things seem to have brightened and to have become more serious. Then the next four days in succession make life among the inhabitants of the cento novelle seem even more self-centered. Day 10 is supposed to change all that. The success or failure of the entire semester hinges on our reading of the work's conclusion. Is the *Decameron* a post-Dantean comedy, as many maintain? Or is it, rather, a satire, along the lines of Ovid's texts about the amorous Romans (see Hollander and Cahill)? It is up to the students to decipher Day 10. I have been astounded and pleased by how well this final class has gone each time the seminar has been offered, with almost all the talking done by the students.

I hope that the foregoing has been of interest to my fellow teachers. It should give some idea of what, at least by my lights, comes close to being an ideal arrangement for serious dealing with Boccaccio on the part of young students who neither speak his language nor arrive with more than a little of the necessary literary background. My only complaint is that we have twice to deal with two of his days in one of ours. That is the price for spending four of our twelve weeks away from the *Decameron*; I consider that price worth paying in the light of what we gain thereby.

As one may sense from the above, the concerted effort of each three-hour seminar is to make sense of the texts under scrutiny that week. Nonetheless, the Dante that we read in the second and third weeks is never totally away from our attention as we move through Boccaccio. In what follows I delineate three ways in which I think the text of the *Commedia* may help illuminate that of the *Decameron*. I put these remarks into three categories of the relation between the two works: general likeness and difference; strategic difference (from Boccaccio's point of view); details of Boccaccio's borrowing from Dante.

General Likeness and Difference   The overall similarities and differences between the *Decameron* and its major vernacular precursor are too obvious to have gone undetected. They are commonplaces, requiring little in the way of supporting evidence or ingenious demonstration. The hundred cantos of Dante's "divine" *Comedy* are echoed in the hundred novelle of Boccaccio's all-too-human comedy. Both works seem to celebrate their Italianness, that is, their use of the vernacular in work that is obviously meant to be considered significant. (Neither Dante nor Boccaccio would have, I think, been amazed to know that guides to their works would be written for denizens of an as-yet-unknown continent some six centuries later.) But Dante's language is seen as noble, lofty, even austere (this is not my own unswerving view, I wish to make it known), while Boccaccio's is streetwise, low mimetic, and playful. Each of the similarities is intrinsically conjoined with a distancing difference. In such a view Boccaccio is conceived to have had Dante very much in mind, but only as a general idea or as a rather distant model. His purpose is held to be so far from Dante's that no one seems prepared to argue that he was not only Dante's greatest champion (see *Filocolo* 674; *Amorosa visione* 5.70–6.24) but was also deeply involved in thinking about Dante's magnum opus as he created his own. Boccaccio may emulate Dante in general terms, but he is not thinking of the *Comedy* as a challenge to his own extended effort in prose. In this view the *Comedy* is for Boccaccio a monument, an idea of a potential model, but not a pressing literary presence.

Strategic Difference   While in no way denying that the two works are greatly different in nearly every respect, this writer would like there to be no confusion about the strength of his disagreement with the earlier view of the issue. Boccaccio is heavy with reminiscences of the text that he believed the greatest modern work and the only one that had achieved a status similar to that reserved for the greatest writers of antiquity. He could hardly make a move without thinking of how Dante had moved before him. The *Decameron*, we now realize, is peppered with not dozens but hundreds of citations of the *Comedy*. (See Bettinzoli's two important studies of Dantean borrowings.) The only surprising thing is that it has taken us so long to acknowledge so obvious a phenomenon, especially given the plethora of Dantean personages from the *Comedy* who find their way to Boccaccio's attention: for example, Gallehault (title), Charles of Valois (1.1), Cangrande della Scala (1.7), Guglielmo Borsiere (1.8), Corrado Malaspina and Manfred (2.6; the latter also in 10.6), Giotto (6.5), Guido Cavalcanti (6.9), Michele Scotto (8.9), Ciacco, Corso Donati, and Filippo Argenti (9.8), Pope Boniface VIII (10.2). There is an obvious reason for readers' traditional difficulty in perceiving what everyone must now cede as being true. Since, in the traditional view of Boccaccio's relationship to Dante, Boccaccio was not writing a text that had anything much in common with Dante's *Comedy*, there was no reason to believe he was frequently thinking of that text. A countering view claims that Boccaccio was so totally involved in thinking of Dante's poem that, no matter how different his purposes might have been, he could not fail to cite Dante's text, which for him contained a sort of lingua franca, words that came to him on the slightest pretext. For him to write in the Italian vernacular was, in good part, to rewrite Dante. It is fair to say that such a view is currently (and finally?) the dominant one. Nothing written by Boccaccio, from his very early work (*Caccia di Diana*) through the *Decameron*, reflects the textual presence of any author so much as it does Dante. This is no less and no more than a fact. What follows is speculation. If the *Decameron* is filled with *dantismi*, why has their presence been imperceptible to many students of the work? The answer, one might argue, is simple. The tone of the *Decameron* is "wrong." That is, when Boccaccio cites Dante concerning the validity of visions of the afterworld or the actual moral behavior of humankind, Dante will always come out the loser in Boccaccio's view of such matters. "That is beautiful, Dante," Boccaccio seems to be saying, "but you cannot expect us to believe it, can you?" Thus, at the strategic level, Boccaccio's references to Dante are gently, but firmly, derisory and frequently generic (a bourgeois gentleman who thinks he is in Purgatory [3.8], a lady in the pine forest outside Ravenna who behaves like a denizen of *Inferno* 13 [5.8], a friar who claims he has visited other worlds [6.10]).

It is, perhaps, these two issues that trouble Boccaccio most: Dante's granting himself visionary knowledge of the world to come and his unyielding belief that humankind can learn how to live with justice in political and moral community. Boccaccio, man of the world, loves Dante for his optimism but knows in his all-too-human heart that these are impossible dreams. And so his fictive world is filled with the ornaments of Dante's, but these lovely bits and pieces tend to be deracinated from their contextual habitat. In the *Decameron* we hear nothing true of the world to come, only lies about it (mainly purveyed by friars); and we see little positive about the human family, which spends, if not all, most of its time seeking its own pleasures (sex, money, getting the best of another human being) or the avoidance of pain or blame. There is not much room for anything Dantean but his words.

Boccaccio's Borrowing from Dante   This essay is not the occasion for a study of the numerous and arresting Boccaccian citations of Dante. We might begin at the beginning, the *Decameron*'s subtitle, "Prencipe Galeotto," an obvious reference to the verse "Galeotto fu 'l libro e chi lo scrisse" (*Inferno* 5.137), in which Francesca da Rimini blames a book for kindling passion in her and in her brother-in-law. No one insists that this is not a reference to that text. Some insist on some fairly incredible things about the reference, for instance, that it has no negative sexual resonance or that, if it does, it was only added by Boccaccio late in his life (thus placing credence in the notion that the old fellow had to make his way around northern Italy, sneaking into people's houses to add the subtitle to the many circulated copies of the work). While there are many, many instances of Boccaccio's appropriating a phrase from Dante (as I would from Louis Armstrong if I played jazz trumpet) without really being aware of what he is doing, there are some remarkable moments in which we can see him playfully and meaningfully pillaging his poet for a passage that enters his work with its full Dantean context. Readers may consult some recent works that concern specific textual confrontations.[1] It is enough to conclude by saying that our work on this aspect of Boccaccio's keen awareness of Dante's text has only begun. Few aspects of the *Decameron* are as exciting and as understudied. It is a good thing that, after all these centuries, there are major tasks that still confront us. I once encountered a colleague in the hard sciences who, when I told him that I worked on Dante, asked, "Hasn't that all been worked over?" I told him we were in fact just beginning to get down to serious, mature effort. The subject of this brief discussion is, after six centuries and more, still in its infancy.

NOTE

[1] For example, Franco Fido's "Dante personaggio mancato del *Decameron*"; Giuseppe Mazzotta's "Games of Laughter in the *Decameron*"; Robert Durling's "Boccaccio on Interpretation: Guido's Escape (*Decameron* VI.9)"; Victoria Kirkham's "Painters at Play on the Judgment Day (*Decameron* VIII 9)"; and Robert Hollander's "Boccaccio's Dante: Imitative Distance," "The Sun Rises in Dante," "Boccaccio's Dante," and "The Proem of the *Decameron*: Boccaccio between Ovid and Dante." The Hollander studies are now available in *Boccaccio's Dante: The Shaping Force of Satire*.

The *Decameron*'s Secular Designs

Julia Reinhard Lupton

A few years ago, a serious young man in my course The Western Literary Tradition: Homer to the Renaissance approached me just before Thanksgiving break. So far in the course, he had painfully worked his way through the *Odyssey*, the *Aeneid*, the *Metamorphoses*, the *Confessions*, and the *Inferno*, along with a few Greek tragedies and related material. The penultimate assignment was substantial selections from the *Decameron*, and he informed me solemnly that he had been "reading ahead" in this work. Distracted and a bit impatient, I nodded my approval of his diligence and prepared to move on. "Professor Lupton," he persisted, "I'm worried. This book was fun to read. Am I missing something?"

I instantly understood his concern. Throughout the course I had emphasized the mechanics of tradition: the myriad ways in which texts locate themselves in a canon through the contracts of genre and the signatures of allusion. For eight weeks this student had slowly learned to follow the paths of the epic simile, the invocation to the Muses, and the descent to the underworld in these conventions' itineraries through the *selva oscura* created by Homer, Vergil, and Dante. Now, entering into the prosaic clarity and easy wit of the *Decameron*, he found himself lost in a text that was suddenly too familiar, too much like home. Could the same labyrinthine patterns of poetic recollection possibly apply to this simpler, sharper world?

The answer, of course, is yes. My goal in teaching the *Decameron* is precisely to demonstrate how the special lucidity of Boccaccio's cityscapes is itself the product of a set of concerted literary operations. Among these procedures I place special weight on the process of literary secularization that unfolds in relation to the monumental example of Dante as well as to the widely disseminated conventions of Catholic liturgy, literature, and art. If, as critics have long liked to comment, Boccaccio's great work is a human comedy in relation to Dante's *Divine Comedy*, I insist that this shift in perspective could only occur through a series of systematic negations executed on the inherited motifs and exegetical habits of the medieval Christian imagination. I argue that it is in large part through this allusive dynamic, established in the classroom through a number of foundational instances, that the *Decameron* fashions itself as a major voice in the Western literary tradition.

Naming the Secular

Both the title and subtitle of Boccaccio's collection announce the sacred-secular dialectic that determines the character of the work as a whole. Boccaccio's decision to call his work a *galeotto* locates the *Decameron* in the romance library that brought together Paolo and Francesca, the sinful lovers familiar to my students from canto 5 of the *Inferno*, where the lovers first kiss when reading the story of Lancelot and Guinevere, the book serving as a *galeotto*, or panderer, between them. I try to get the class to produce different interpretations of this famous subtitle: Does it defend art, or demonize it? Does Boccaccio present his text as an actual go-between designed to facilitate sexual relationships, or is it rather a *galeotto* of the imagination, reinforcing social mores by transgressing them through fantasy? (This problem becomes the basis for the course's final writing assignment.)

Less immediately accessible to the students is the import of the work's main title: the word *decameron*, meaning ten days, alludes to the medieval genre of hexameral literature, comprising sermons and commentaries on the six days of creation.[1] By naming his work the *Decameron*, Boccaccio identifies the creative faculties of the poet with those of God himself, an analogy made explicit in the little homily that opens the first story of Day 1:

> Convenevole cosa è, carissime donne, che ciascheduna cosa la quale l'uomo fa, dallo ammirabile e santo nome di Colui, il quale di tutte fu fac-itore, le dea principio. Per che, dovendo io al vostro novellare, sí come primo, dare cominciamento, intendo da una delle sue maravigliose cose incominciare [. . .].   (32)

> Dearest ladies, it is fitting that everything done by man should begin with the marvelous and holy name of Him who was the Creator of all things; therefore, since I am to be the first to begin our storytelling, I intend to start with one of His marvelous deeds [. . .].   (21)

Although at first glance the passage appears to be a straightforward praise of the Creator, it also boldly casts the storyteller as a figure parallel to God, since Panfilo also must make a beginning by setting the narrative sequence of the *Decameron* into motion. In the comic story of the false saint Ser Cepparello that follows, divine creation gives way to poetic re-creation, and God's sublime making of the world out of speech comes to mirror the verbal fabrications of a consummate sinner. Expanding God's six days into ten, the poet-maker of the *Decameron* creates his world not ex nihilo (out of nothing), but rather through negation, that is, through the selective appropriation and rewriting of sacred categories and imagery.

I schematize this process for my students as a movement from a vertical axis linking humanity to God, to a horizontal axis that connects neighbor to neighbor. Developing this allusive structure allows me to begin establishing some of the thematics peculiar to secularization as the literary process of modernity par excellence (ideas of authorship, creativity, and canon as they devolve from sacred models). It also permits me to restate a central argument of the course: unlike God, poets must work with what's there, with the existing tradition, which provides both the limits and the resources for future innovation.

Afterlives of the Saints

Ser Cepparello's deliciously diabolical countercreation is also the story of a "canonization": the making of a saint through the acts of false confession and postmortem memorialization (de' Negri; Lupton 85–89). I point out to my students that the word *canon* originally referred to the books that make up the Bible, and *canonization* to the legal process of registering saints in the official calendar of the church. The stories of the *Decameron* are *legends* in a special sense: associated in modern diction with fiction and folklore, the word comes from the Latin *legendum*, meaning "that which must be read" and designating the day's reading in the church's lectionary, or calendar. It soon came to indicate any saint's life or collection of saints' lives, as in Jacobus de Voragine's *Golden Legend*. Boccaccio's *Decameron*, borrowing and negating the conventions of hagiography, begins to peel the modern sense of legend as story or fiction from the medieval sense of legend as saint's life. In the process, Boccaccio canonizes the modern prose novella as a secular form derived from sacred types. Moreover, Boccaccio installs the modern poet as the new saint by parodying the canonizations performed by the church as a human institution. In story 1.1, the hero's title Ser, indicating his profession as a notary, signals the devious affiliation between the secular writer and the false saint, the clerk and the cleric, the hagiographic legend and the secular novella.

The hagiographic parody that inaugurates the novelle of the *Decameron* is in turn answered by the very different story that ends the collection (10.10), the tale of the patient Griselda. It is also a kind of secular saint's life, but now conducted in the mode of moral exemplarity rather than parodic negation. Here Boccaccio manages to distill secular domestic virtues from the vitae of the saints, discovering Job-like patience in the trials of married life. By counterpointing negative and positive modes of secular hagiography at either end of the *Decameron*, Boccaccio maps his collection as "the afterlives of the saints," fashioning the prose novella as a genre that derives both its sacred satires and its protohumanist exempla from the legendaries of the church.

This framing of the *Decameron* as an exercise in hagiographic rewriting in turn opens up analyses of stories contained in the work. For example, the story of Alibech and Rustico (3.10) is modeled on the lives of the desert hermits, making the trials of such figures as Saint Anthony (familiar to my students from the *Confessions*) and Mary Magdalene in the desert into the material for sexual innuendo and literary play.[2] In Day 4, Ghismonda's confinement by her jealous father, Tancredi (4.1), resembles Saint Barbara's imprisonment in a tower by her pagan parent, and the various dismemberments incurred by Boccaccio's martyrs for love recall the fragmentation of saintly bodies in medieval martyrology, now resituated in the framework of secular romance.

Rather than assign actual saints' lives from *The Golden Legend* or similar works, I use slides to teach the iconography of the saints. Giotto's *Saint Martin Dividing His Cloak* presents the kind of moral exemplum reworked to such different effects in the stories of Ser Cepparello and Griselda. Hieronymus Bosch's *Saint Anthony* paintings and Donatello's statue of the hermit Magdalene are useful supplements to the Alibech and Rustico story. Lucas Cranach's *Decapitation of Saint Barbara* illuminates the relics of martyrology scattered throughout Day 4. Although most of these paintings postdate the *Decameron*, these vivid and accessible images help reconstruct the larger iconographic universe of the late Middle Ages and early Renaissance for students unfamiliar with visual art and religious motifs.

Enunciating the Annunciation

Visual art also elucidates 4.2, the story of Friar Alberto and Madonna Lisetta, one of the two comic tales that break the tragic mood of Day 4. Using images of the Annunciation by painters such as Giotto, Botticelli, Leonardo da Vinci, and Jan van Eyck, I establish the basic features of the Annunciation theme in visual art. Such paintings are above all visualizations of a speech act, the angel Gabriel's announcement, or annunciation, of Christ's birth to Mary; sometimes, as in van Eyck's *Annunciation*, the message is actually written out in golden letters between the Virgin and the angel (from the Greek *angelos*, messenger). Alternatively, especially in the Italian Renaissance, artists such as Leonardo separate the two figures by a large space to charge the field between them with the invisible weight and energy of the message. The medieval doctrine of *conceptio per aurem* (conception through the ear) is sometimes pictured as a dove flying toward Mary's head; although the idea sounds strange to students at first, I remind them that the word *conception* still applies to both the act of becoming pregnant and to the realm of ideas, or concepts. If Christ is "the Word made flesh," how better for him to be conceived than through the porches of the ear?[3]

This visual background is activated in the story of Friar Alberto (4.2), who, to seduce the pretty but vain Madonna Lisetta, convinces her that the angel Gabriel is in love with her. Catholic iconography underwrites the seduction's conceit:

> Madonna baderla allora disse che molto le piaceva se l'agnolo Gabriello l'amava, per ciò che ella amava ben lui, né era mai che una candela d'un mattapan non gli accendesse davanti dove dipinto il vedeva; e che, qualora egli volesse a lei venire, egli fosse il ben venuto, ché egli la troverebbe tutta sola nella sua camera: ma con questo patto, che egli non

dovesse lasciar lei per la Vergine Maria, ché l'era detto che egli le voleva molto bene, e anche si pareva, ché in ogni luogo che ella il vedeva le stava ginocchione innanzi.   (371)

Lady Silly then said that it pleased her very much that the Angel Gabriel was in love with her, for she loved him as well and never failed to light a cheap candle in his honor whenever she found a painting of him in church; and whenever he wished to come to her, he would be most welcome, and he would find her all alone in her room, and he could come on the condition that he would not leave her for the Virgin Mary, whom, it was said, he loved very much, and it was obviously true, because everywhere she saw him, he was always on his knees before her [. . .].   (262–63)

Students quickly see that Madonna Lisetta is a literal-minded interpreter who mistakes the divine birth announcement for a mundane scene of courtship. At the same time, insofar as the Annunciation is indeed a scene of physical conception, Madonna Lisetta's misreading contains a kernel of truth, a not so hidden erotic possibility that Friar Alberto (and with him Boccaccio) elaborates into an extended sexual encounter. By tracing the scenes of communication, interpretation, and eroticism embedded in religious iconography, students encounter the poetic complexities of religious motifs in the full flower of their secular revision.

Cannibalism, Sacred and Profane

In story 4.1, Ghismonda, presented by her rageful father with the heart of her lover in a chalice, mixes poison with her tears in the same cup and then drinks the fatal mixture. In 4.9, the wife of Guiglielmo Rossiglione, realizing that her husband has just served her the heart of her murdered lover, leaps from a window rather than ever taste any other food. My students immediately recognize the motif of cannibalism from our earlier study of classical literature. Yet the resonances of the act have changed significantly from one historical moment to the other. Rather than recoil in horror from the act (like Tereus in Ovid's story of Procne and Philomela), Boccaccio's heroines actively choose or willingly embrace the cannibalistic meal. And instead of taking place as part of the travesty of a scene of hospitality (like Odysseus in the cave of Polyphemos) or as the gravest possible sign of generational disruption (the Tereus story), these love stories concern not the guest or the child but rather the lover whose flesh is consumed, and consumed with a certain macabre joy.

How do we explain the movement from the scandal of classical cannibalism to Boccaccio's cuisine of love? In the *Decameron*, eucharistic imagery—the sacrificial love of Christ reenacted by the Mass—transfigures the women's acts of cannibalism. The cup cradling the lover's heart in 4.1 resembles the chalice used in Communion, while in 4.9, it is the body not the blood of the beloved that nourishes Mme Rossiglione in death. Boccaccio inherits this eucharistic strand of redemptive love from Dante and the larger liturgical culture of Catholic Italy. Throughout his poetry, Dante had used courtly love—the set of formalized romantic rituals governing aristocratic courtship in medieval Europe—as a pathway to divine love through the mediating figure of Beatrice, both earthly beloved and saintly intercessor. Boccaccio takes up the same equation but reverses the direction, serving up a new version of the Christian image of the Sacred Heart to sweeten illicit sexual relations for a new epoch of secular romance.

A final brief comparison of Day 4's romantic tragedies with Dante's tragedy of conflicted attitudes toward Paolo and Francesca in the *Inferno*, canto 5, rounds out our sense of the debts and differences that join and separate Dante and Boccaccio and prepares the students to write their final essays on the *Decameron* as a *galeotto* that goes between the sacred and the secular. In the process, the class has learned that Boccaccio's world, for all its tactility and humor, is just as crafted a place as the literary underworlds of Homer, Vergil, and Dante.

APPENDIX

Story Selection

Proem and introduction (frame of Day 1, *Dec.*, trans. Musa and Bondanella 5–20).
Stories 1.1, 3.10, Day 4 (complete), 10.10.
This selection can be covered in one to two lectures as part of a sophomore survey of the Western literary tradition.

Slide List

Giotto, *Saint Martin Dividing His Cloak* (1.1), Basilica Superiore di San Francesco, Assisi.
Hieronymus Bosch, *Temptation of Saint Anthony* (3.10), Museo Nacional de Arte Antiga, Lisbon.
Donatello, *Desert Magdalene* (3.10), Bargello, Florence.
Lucas Cranach, *Decapitation of Saint Barbara* (Day 4), Metropolitan Museum of Art, New York.
Giotto, *Annunciation* (4.2), Arena Chapel, Padua.
Botticelli, *Annunciation* (4.2), Uffizi, Florence.
Leonardo da Vinci, *Annunciation* (4.2), Louvre, Paris.
Jan van Eyck, *Annunciation* (4.2), National Gallery, Washington, DC.

NOTES

[1]This tradition, whose medieval exemplars include the *Hexameron* of Saint Ambrose, would be most fully realized, of course, in book 7 of *Paradise Lost*. David Wallace notes the allusion (*Giovanni Boccaccio* 13).

[2]For the stories of these saints, see Jacobus de Voragine's *The Golden Legend*. The Magdalene's desert adventures are easily substituted for those of Mary of Egypt, a female anchorite on the model of Saint Anthony; on the desert careers of these two Mary's, see Benedicta Ward's *Harlots of the Desert* (10–56).

[3]For a fine history and analysis of Annunciation imagery, see Gertrud Schiller, *Iconography of Christian Art*.

Patterns of Meaning in the *Decameron*

Michael Papio

One of my students not long ago stumbled on an interesting narrative pattern in the *Decameron* and, scratching his temple, asked, "Does this mean something?" Although at first glance such a reaction may seem to reveal ingenuous reading strategies, I believe that the opposite is true. Whereas most scholars are intimately acquainted with the famous structure-oriented readings of the *Decameron* (not only Tzvetan Todorov, Viktor Shklovsky, and Cesare Segre but also Vittore Branca, Teodolinda Barolini, and others), students often overlook or undervalue the meaning inherent in the arrangement of novelle as each relates to another and in the work as a whole. In fact, Ernst Robert Curtius reminds us that Wisdom of Solomon 11.21 ("But thou hast arranged all things by measure and number and weight" [504, 1990 ed.]) was one of the most common biblical references in all medieval Latin texts. To communicate the importance of the *Decameron*'s structure in the classroom, we must move beyond the simple observation that the novelle are grouped in ten sets of ten. We must strive to recuperate, at least in part, a medieval attention to patterns of composition while simultaneously invoking a timeless, universal sensibility to aesthetically pleasing symmetry and perfection of form. This approach does not mean, however, that we all have to become formalists or fill the blackboards with sigmas and superscripts. Indeed, we should not choose between form and content but should instead teach each in its precise and complex relation to the other. Luckily, several intelligent proposals have been suggested to help us in this endeavor (for an overview of these proposals, see appendix).

In the late 1930s, Ferdinando Neri published a brief but influential essay in which he posed a rhetorical question that has served as a touchstone of criticism for decades. Having noticed that Day 1 seems to have a consistently satirical tone that runs counter to the lofty qualities celebrated in the tenth, he asks, "Non vi è qualche segreta intenzione perchè la prima giornata sia aggressiva, e l'ultima «esemplare»? Dalla negazione ch'è in principio all'ideale che risplende come termine, si giunge per una via che l'autore abbia segnata e si possa riconoscere ancora?" (74). ("Is there not some secret reason why the first Day is aggressive and the last 'exemplary'? why we start out in negation and at the end reach a resplendent ideal by way of a path that the author predetermined and that we may still recognize?")[1] Neri is among the first to intuit the presence of a secret level of meaning in the organization of the novelle, a pattern purposefully created in the *Decameron*'s composition. In his opinion, the *Decameron* is an intensely coherent work that depends not on the frame fiction for unity but on a planned transition from a negative pole (an aggressive day) to a positive one (an exemplary day). Between these extremes Boccaccio develops additional themes dear to him, beginning in Day 2 with Fortune's unpredictable, almost whimsical intervention into the lives of the protagonists. These are the adventure stories among which we meet characters such as Andreuccio da Perugia, the castaway Landolfo Rufolo, and Alatiel. The following set of ten novelle again takes up the theme of Fortune but with a twist; here Neri (77) places great emphasis on the term *industria* (*Dec.* 229), which we might translate into English as industriousness. The characters of Day 3, like Masetto the "deaf-mute" gardener (3.1) or King Agilulf's groom (3.2), shrewdly turn to their own advantage the hand that Fortune has dealt them.

Similarly, the fourth and fifth days function together as a thematic diptych in much the same way as the second and third do. Filostrato's reign is, in Neri's opinion, not so much a study of the emotions of its ill-starred characters as it is a study of tragic destinies. We are invited to consider the sad fates of Ghismonda (4.1), Lisabetta (4.5), and the others as the intervention of misfortune into the lives of lovers. In this way, some of the themes present already in Day 2, such as humankind's powerlessness in the face of forces larger than life, resurface in conjunction with another of the typically Boccaccian themes, love. Day 5, also greatly dependent on the caprices of Fortune, serves as a correction of Day 4, not through the active use of *industria* but, as in the inspiring example of Federigo degli Alberighi (5.9), through virtuous resignation and an enduring adherence to the codes of courtly love.

Neri makes a neat division between the first half of the *Decameron* and the second at the close of Day 5, the text's geographic midpoint. All the novelle that come before this turning point, he explains, are widely classifiable as "errori del caso" ("whims of chance") and those that come after as "una scherma d'ingegno" (79) ("an intellectual skirmish"). Day 6, devoted to "be' motti e [. . .] risposte pronte" (*Dec.* 527) ("clever remarks" and "ready replies"), prepares the reader for the next two, which deal with *beffe*, tricks played either by wives as in Day 7 or in general as in Day 8. Day 9 in this scheme is a miscellaneous collection of tales that did not fit in elsewhere ("la nona giornata ha radunato le novelle sparse" [81] ["the ninth Day brought together the extra tales"]), and Day 10, of course, contains the artistic high point of the *Decameron*'s structure, the exemplary virtues that in the satire of the first day are represented as uncorrected. Neri's principal contribution to the thematic analysis of the *Decameron* lies to a great degree in his bipartite partitioning of the text. The line he draws between two extremely important leitmotifs, fortune and intelligence, at once underscores the symmetrical perfection of the work and defines the moral character of Boccaccio's text in its anticipation of the Renaissance. "Sono le linee maestre di quella morale semplice e pratica," Neri writes, "che possiamo seguire fino al Machiavelli, il quale oppone, più reciso e più serio, Fortuna e Virtù; fino all'Ariosto, il quale sorride bonario: «Vincasi o per fortuna o per ingegno[. . .]»" (81) ("These are the artful lines of that simple and practical morality that we can follow all the way to Machiavelli, who juxtaposes Fortune and Virtue more resolutely, more seriously; all the way to Ariosto, who smiles good-naturedly: 'whether victory comes through fortune or shrewdness[. . .]' ").

In the fundamental study, *Boccaccio medievale*, Branca described Neri's basic notion of the *Decameron*'s artistic integrity as "elegant" (12) but expanded the two thematic categories to three, promoting love to the level of fortune and intelligence. The whole of life is now represented in what he calls "la commedia dell'uomo" (12) ("the comedy of man"). The *Decameron* displays the ideal medieval "comedic" structure inasmuch as, like Dante's *Divine Comedy*, it opens during a time of strife or troubles and concludes on a decidedly more positive note. Unlike Dante's epic poem, however, the *Decameron* is an exaltation of human being qua human being; Boccaccio unabashedly holds up for the reader's inspection numerous authentic specimens of lived reality—from Ciappelletto to Griselda—and each of them is in his or her own way testimony to "le grandi verità umane" (80) ("the great human truths"). Far from a discordant array of personages, the collection is, as Branca explains, a remarkably congruous masterpiece:

> Il *Decameron* si presenta come un'opera unitaria, retta saldamente da un disegno ideale, inquadrata in un'architettura morale precisa. [. . .] Dalla prima all'ultima giornata [. . .] le novelle si svolgono secondo un chiaro ordine prestabilito ubbidendo ai canoni delle più autorevoli poetiche medievali. Illustrano cioè un ideale itinerario morale, che dalla riprensione aspra e amara dei vizi dei grandi nella prima giornata, attraverso la raffigurazione delle prove che gli uomini danno nella lotta quotidiana fra loro stessi e con le più grandi forze dominatrici del mondo, la Fortuna e l'Amore e l'Ingegno, ha il suo epilogo nell'elogio della magnanimità e della virtù nella decima giornata.   (105)

> The *Decameron* appears as a unitary work, solidly built from an ideal design and framed within a precise moral architecture. [. . .] From the first day to the last, the tales play themselves out in accordance with a clear, prearranged order that conforms to the most authoritative poetic standards of the Middle Ages. In other words, the stories illustrate an ideal moral journey that begins in the first day with a rough and bitter condemnation of the vices of the powerful, passes through depictions of men put to the test in their daily struggles amongst themselves and against the principal controlling forces of life (Fortune, Love, and Intelligence), and comes to a close in the tenth day with a celebration of magnanimity and virtue.

The wide-stroke depiction of these three forces (fortune, love, and intelligence) may initially strike the student as overstated or artificial. Nonetheless, such a breakdown provides a surprisingly effective approach to a contextually sensitive reading of the text. Two of the great literary traditions of the Middle Ages, the exemplum and the anecdote, are artfully united by Boccaccio in his sophisticated incorporation of the episodic into the thematically cogent. These motifs, in other words, consolidate two previously autonomous art forms.

To appreciate this concept fully, we must look at the text. Like Neri, Branca classifies the first day as a satiric commentary on vice and folly, the second as a portrait of the vicissitudes of Fortune, and the third as the defeat of Fortune through the operation of *industria* (*Boccaccio medievale* 12, 81–82). What is not immediately discernible in this shared delineation is, as Branca points out, that the novelle in each *giornata* have more than a general topic in common. Within the decade dedicated to the fickleness of Fortune, for example, it is noteworthy that all but the eighth (the tale of the count of Antwerp [2.8]) bears the unmistakable stamp of the merchant class. Similarly, in Day 3, there is a preponderance of highborn wives and nouveaux riches husbands, "quasi che il Boccaccio voglia qui illuminare," Branca says, "il contrasto fra l'ingegno umano e la Fortuna di una luce allusiva alla contrapposizione—a lui cara—fra la nobiltà fortuita e quella conquistata nelle continue lotte di un'esistenza sempre aperta ai rischi più súbiti e gravi, sempre tesa in un impegno deciso e totale" (82) ("as if Boccaccio wanted to illuminate here the contrast between human intelligence and Fortune by a light that alludes to a theme dear to him: the opposition between nobility gained fortuitously and that attained through the incessant struggles of an existence always subject to the most sudden and serious dangers, always in the throes of a decisive and absolute endeavor"). The singularity of each tale (no less than its capacity to entertain) remains intact at the individual level while its position in a larger, organized whole sheds light on the underlying message.

The following diptych, composed of Days 4 and 5, is set apart by the half-tale of Filippo Balducci and treats the subject of love. Here, too, almost all the novelle contain characters of the merchant class and here, too, there is a secondary meaning. When thinking back on Ghismonda's moving discourse on natural versus inherited nobility (4.1), it should perhaps not be unlikely that we may remember as well some of the other tragic—yet not noble—figures such as Lisabetta, who pined away over her pot of basil (4.5); Simona, who gave her life in a reenactment of her lover's death (4.7); and Gostanza, who cast herself into a rudderless skiff (5.2). When placed against a backdrop of mercantile pragmatism, greed, and self-serving aggression, even these common women assume a seductively enchanting heroism that rivals that of the more glamorous "gentildonne feudali" ("feudal noblewomen"). These are the *giornate* of love, set into a minicomedic form that echoes that of the larger collection, yet the love celebrated here is an earthly one, a type neglected by both the Dolce Stil Nuovo and Petrarch.

Days 6, 7, and 8 form the tragicomic triptych of *ingegno* ("intelligence"). The main characters, as elsewhere in this great mercantile epic, tend to be merchants or members of the lower social classes. The first of these decades features vignettes in which men struggle to assert themselves in competitions that are resolved in quick thinking or the bon mot. Whereas the successes of Cisti the baker (6.2) or Chichibio (6.4) may suggest an authorial bias in favor of the underling, Branca notes, however, a progression away from this position in the seventh and eighth days in which "la preferenza è data alle figure, agli ambienti, ai temi della nuova classe dirigente" (*Boccaccio medievale* 83) ("preference is given to the figures, ambiance, and themes that are associated with the new ruling class"). This preference, unmistakable in the invective of 7.8 against the "mercatantuzzi" ("yokels from the country"), fairly categorizes the transition, after the pause of the ninth, to the tenth day wherein is revealed the "pantheon delle virtù umane, naturalmente destinato ai ritratti ingemmati e encomiastici dei grandi del passato" (*Boccaccio medievale* 84) ("pantheon of human virtues, naturally dedicated to the flattering, jewel-studded portraits of great figures of the past"). The perfection reached in the close of Boccaccio's "ideal moral journey," in the graceful thematic arches that support the narrative architecture of the *Decameron*, comes to a splendid crescendo in the last day: Fortune reappears in tales 1, 2, and 3; love in 4, 5, 6, and 7; and intelligence in 8 and 9. The final tale of the collection, the exemplary story of Griselda's patient endurance, combines all three of the principal themes individuated by Branca: "la fortuna che fa di una povera pastorella una splendida castellana, l'amore che trasforma Gualtieri e fa eroica Griselda, l'ingegno che Gualtieri usa per provare la sposa" (14) ("Fortune that changes a poor little shepherdess into the splendid wife of a lord, Love that transforms Gualtieri and makes Griselda heroic, and Intelligence that Gualtieri employs in the test of his wife"). The upward journey comes to a close in a triumphant celebration of the virtuous purity of Griselda, a figure absolutely antithetical to Ciappelletto, who, at the level of exemplum, is her exact counterpart.

While Branca's comprehensive, yet not unreasonable, thematic theories have gained currency with many critics over the years, the complexity of the *Decameron*'s structure has enticed others to examine additional patterns and relations between the days. Pamela Stewart (in "La novella di Madonna Oretta"), seizing on a nearly exact repetition in the introductions of tales 1.10 and 6.1, observed a two-part structure in the *Decameron*, whose division is located, as in Neri's model, between the fifth and sixth days. According to this perspective, the tale of Madonna Oretta comes to be the inaugural novella of the text's second half as well as of a *giornata* that in several respects mirrors the first. Though Stewart is quick to point out the parallelisms between the tales of Madonna Oretta (6.1) and of Maestro Alberto (1.10) and the natural connection, both thematically and numerically, between the stories of Ciappelletto (1.1) and Frate Cipolla (6.10), she warns against the temptation to appreciate in these what amounts to a simple formalistic reading (cf. Almansi 63–107). Instead, she argues, we should understand the structural relation in its innate capacity to direct our attention to the content of these four tales and, by extension, to the two halves of the *Decameron* (31–32).

In a reading of the text's structure, Stewart (perhaps unduly) breaks down Neri's observations into a binary equation: Days 1–5 deal with Fortune and

Days 6–10 with virtue (rather than intelligence). Naturally, simplification leads to unsatisfying exegesis and, to remedy the discrepancy, she proposes a complex new system:

> La prima parte tratta, nelle giornate II, III e V, di imprese o avventure (d'amore o d'altro) a lieto fine, e nella IV di amori infelici. La seconda parte tratta, nelle giornate VII e VIII, di beffe e, nella Giornata X, del contrario, e cioè della generosità nei «fatti d'amore o d'altra cosa». Ciascuna delle due parti ha così un tema dominante e in ciascuna di esse una giornata è dedicata al rovesciamento di esso. Inoltre, la Terza Giornata [. . .] riprende e continua il tema della Seconda, ma restringendolo. [. . .] Un rapporto simile, ma rovesciato, si riscontra fra la Settima Giornata, dedicata alle beffe «le quali, o per amore o per salvamento di loro, le donne hanno già fatte a' lor mariti», e l'Ottava, in cui il tema delle beffe viene volutamente generalizzato ed esteso ad una più larga varietà di rapporti umani. (38)

> The first part, Days 2, 3, and 5, deals with the enterprises and adventures (amorous and otherwise) that end happily—Day 4 treating the subject of unhappy love stories. In the second part, Days 6 and 7 contain acts of trickery while the tenth holds just the opposite, namely liberality in "affairs of the heart or other matters." Each of the two parts therefore presents a dominant theme as well as a day dedicated to its overturning. The third day, moreover, takes up and continues the theme of the second in a more focused way. A comparable, albeit opposite, relation exists in the seventh day, dedicated to the tricks "that, either out of love or for their own self-preservation, wives have played on their husbands," and the eighth in which the theme of trickery is intentionally generalized and expanded to comprise a wider variety of human relationships.

In other words, Days 2, 3, and 5 form a single group (tales of adventure with happy endings), as do Days 7, 8, and 10 (insofar as Days 7 and 8 deal with trickery and Day 10 showcases trickery's antithesis). Days 4 and 9 interrupt the continuity of each half, and Days 1 and 6, as mentioned above, should each be read by the light of the other since they both deal with quickness of wit. What the system lacks in clarity is recuperated in Stewart's summation: "ma quel che importava sottolineare è l'intrecciarsi in tutta la struttura del *Decameron*, attraverso una serie di analogie, simmetrie, rovesciamenti e differenze, dell'ideale della varietà con quello dell'unità" (39) ("but what mattered most is the interrelatedness of the whole of the *Decameron*'s structure, the presentation of a series of analogies, symmetries, inversions, and differences between the ideals of variety and unity").

At this point, one may rightly wonder to what degree it is profitable, especially in the light of the crystalline analyses of Neri and Branca, to engage one's students in the more complicated and not immediately intuitive theories of others. The answer, of course, is that it can be very profitable indeed whenever the patience and concentration required to follow the theories permits a deeper understanding of what our author may have had in mind. And with this said, let us turn our attention to the work of Janet Smarr, who has demonstrated two distinct narrative systems at work in the *Decameron*: symmetry and the "nine plus one pattern" ("Symmetry" 160). Both of these principles, while not necessarily to be taken for granted, should be readily accessible to any student who has read Augustine, Aquinas, or Dante. The medieval fascination with *claritas*, with an orderly organization of components based on perceived intrinsic value, is at the very heart of studies of this kind and would certainly not have rung hollow to Boccaccio's contemporaries. When applied to the *Decameron*, the nine-plus-one pattern is evident in Dioneo's position as tenth storyteller, exempted from the established topic and, Smarr suggests, can be used to disassemble the work into nine days plus one (171).

Once the tenth day has been momentarily detached from the others, the remaining nine can be seen as a neatly planned, symmetrical system with Fiammetta's day, the fifth, at the center. A great advantage gained by this proposal is the ease of incorporation of Day 9 into the model. Neri simply discarded it from his two-part structure; Branca called it a "tapestry of mixed themes"; Stewart saw it as a themeless separator between tales of *beffe* and tales of anti-*beffe*. Smarr, however, integrates it as a counterpart of the first and thus opens the door to a symmetrical design of pairs (the two days of Fortune, the second and the third, counterbalanced by the two days of *beffe*, the seventh and the eighth). Even more convincing are her observations regarding the order in which the members of the *brigata* sing together. On Days 3, 5, and 7 Dioneo sings at the close of storytelling. At the center of the nine-day array he sings alone, but on the other two occasions, he sings with Fiammetta; this produces a triangular arrangement that sets Days 4 and 6 in opposition with each other. Smarr is quick to point out that these are the very days on which the otherwise regular cycles of storytelling are interrupted, first by the narrator's introduction to Day 4 and then by the intrusion of Licisca and Tindaro (introduction to Day 6), the servants whose quarrel is not too distant in tone from the half-tale of Filippo Balducci and the "papere" ("goslings"). This overall organization strengthens the moral reading of the text, Smarr believes, because it displays a coherent system of narration, one that is concerned in several passages with the utility and beauty of the individual *novelle* that make up, in due measure, the whole. All things considered, the approach tends to obscure somewhat the fact that the pivotal fifth day, which one would imagine to be the proverbial roots of the tree, is more closely related to the fourth, of which it is a correction of sorts, than to the sixth. Similarly, Day 6 either prepares the reader for the two days that follow it (as we have seen in Neri and Branca) or can be meaningfully related to the first day (as we have seen in Stewart), but it does not have many parallels with the fourth day aside from the interruptions mentioned above.

As all teachers of Boccaccio know, there is no such thing as a completely air-tight generalization. Just as we make a pronouncement regarding the work in its entirety, a small voice of warning sounds (or should be sounding) in our ears. Nevertheless, some of our students are fastidiously curious about how all these tales go together and they want to learn the way that makes sense from all directions. For this group, we would do well to suggest the reading of Joan Ferrante ("Patterns"), to whom this essay owes in part its title. Hers is a straightforward overview that is deceptively clear in its outlines and exceptionally functional in its details. Like other scholars, she emphasizes the division between Days 5 and 6 in order to indicate the *Decameron's* symmetry, but rather than consider each half as a part of the same linear structure, she sets the second against the first in reverse order. Neri and Branca had already pointed out that Day 10 could be read as a correction of the first; Ferrante follows up on this notion by juxtaposing the second with the ninth, the third with the eighth, and so on. This arrangement re-creates the same uniformity that Smarr had proposed, losing the central *giornata* but recovering the tenth, and succeeds in attributing a theme to the seemingly elusive Day 9. Ferrante does not expect her theories to supplant those of all who came before her ("these comments are intended to be complementary, not antagonistic, to other studies of Boccaccio's style" [585]) and does not broach the larger thematic subjects such as fortune, love, and intelligence. What her study does give us is an intriguing contextual frame for each of the days and for many of the tales. "The existence of such patterns does not prove that Boccaccio had a tightly worked-out scheme for all the stories of the *Decameron*," she writes, but it does prove "that he had definite ideas in his mind, which he was consciously playing with" (587). Her ideas go a long way toward providing a convincing system into which to herd a good number of otherwise unclassifiable tales while not overturning the larger organizational proposals of previous scholars.

Though the system on the whole is complex and cannot be comprehensively summarized in the limited space here, it is worthwhile to reproduce Ferrante's general scheme of days below (586):

I. faults, particularly in high places;

II. fortune reverses man's situation;

III. man changes his situation by his own efforts, with the help of fortune, and gets what he wants;

IV. love is thwarted, the obstacle coming usually from the family;

V. love unites;

X. virtues, particularly in high places;

IX. man, by his faults, reverses his normal situation;

VIII. man's situation is changed by the efforts of others, aided by his faults, and he gets what he deserves;

VII. adultery is successful, the husband usually an ineffectual obstacle;

VI. wit corrects.

This arrangement, especially in its status of "complementary" proposal, is remarkably effective. It organizes on a secondary level an alternative structural pattern ("that Boccaccio was playing with") while preserving the fortune-love-intelligence progression which operates at the primary, linear level. Indeed, we could even go so far as to call Ferrante's patterns *sup*-plementary in that the lion's share of her analysis is directed at the organization of tales within their narrative days.

The novelle of Day 1, for example, are grouped by Ferrante according to patterns of "corruption in high places" (587): there are kings in tales 3, 5, and 9; members of the clergy in 1, 2, 4, and 7; women in 5, 9, and 10. In Day 2 (among other patterns), a hero falls in the first five tales through no fault of his own, and a woman is the victim of fate in four of the last five. Day 3 parallels the second day but emphasizes gain rather than loss: people get what they want through their own cleverness (tales 1 and 2), through the simplicity of another (3 and 4), despite another's trick (5 and 6), and often with unexpected boons (1, 7, 8, 9, and 10). Days 4 and 5, widely recognized as a thematic diptych, are broken down into individual tales that correspond to one another across *giornata* boundaries (e.g., eloping couples in 4.3 and 5.3, separation and reunion of lovers in 4.8 and 5.8, husband unable to satisfy his wife in 4.10 and 5.10). The analysis continues through the remaining days in equally detailed fashion and comes to a close with a look at Day 10 as the counterexample of the first.

The organizational interpretations we have seen thus far have differed substantially in many respects but are fundamentally comparable insofar as all tend to isolate parts of the *Decameron* and then categorize, juxtapose, and extrapolate. Teodolina Barolini ("Wheel"), however, pursues a somewhat different approach. Instead of subjecting only selections of the text to comprehensive analysis, she considers the whole of the work according to generalized themes. Here, too, the first and the tenth days are presented in a meaningful relation to each other. What distinguishes Barolini's study from those of others who see the two days as terminuses of an "ideal journey" or as cornerstones of a framework that rises to a central climax is her notion that the *Decameron*'s underlying form is not a linear spectrum but a "circular frame structure" or "wheel" (521). Barolini's analysis begins in the introduction of the text, what she calls the "catalyst of the rest of the *Decameron* in that it defines the text's narrative pole, the level of loss from which the *brigata* must recover. The reduction of Florentine society to grade zero," she explains, "is accomplished rhetorically through the Introduction's portrayal of two discrete stages of loss which together bring about total collapse; the narrator concentrates first on the loss of *ingegno* and secondly on the loss of *compassione*" (522). From this space of loss begins the *brigata*'s circular journey of experience. Barolini explains, "The *Decameron* could be pictured as a wheel—Fortune's wheel, the wheel of life—on which the *brigata* turns, coming back transformed to the point of departure. In Days I through V they move steadily away from the city as they are renewed in *ingegno* and *compassione*, i.e., intellectually and ethically. The outward turn of the wheel is completed with their arrival at the Valley of the Ladies" (534).

In the first five days of their storytelling, the company of young men and women engage in a process of recovery. Their first cathartic reclamation comes in Days 1–3 in which they manage to regain the property of intelligence. In the two *giornate* that follow, the narrators regain compassion through the tales of unhappy love. At this stage the *brigata* is at a sort of apogee in the circular journey that begins and ends in Florence.

The movement back is signaled by a repetition of motifs from Day 1 (those cited by Stewart in her study as well) and is characterized by the establishment of a new "primary mission": "*ristorare*/restoration" (527). This mission can be described as edification produced in conjunction with desensitization. Barolini sees the second half of the *Decameron* as a "return to reality" and locates the turning point at the appearance of Licisca, who "operates as a kind of reality principle, whose function it is to introduce aperture where there was closure, reversing the *brigata*'s isolationism and turning them back toward Florence" (528–29). From this moment to the end of Day 9, the storytellers engage in "lessons of survival" (532); it is interesting to note that it is at about this time that the first mention of the plague occurs since their departure from the city and that Dioneo attempts then to indulge in bawdy songs rather than the courtly music preferred by the ladies. Not surprisingly, the following tales take on more heavily sensual overtones, and Tuscany dominates the fictional settings. Gone for the most part are tales of adventure and distant lands. Instead, the *giornate* are given over to the *beffa* and to typically Florentine characters such as Calandrino and his companions. By the close of Day 9, the return cycle is nearly complete. Barolini writes, "Only when the *brigata* is fully coached in the lessons of survival does it complete its turn toward Florence, with Day X, which shows men and women practicing generosity and renunciation, the very social virtues required for the *brigata*'s reintegration into society" (532). Day 10 not only advocates self-discipline, sexual renunciation, and tolerance but also provides the completion of the wheel's turn, the closure of a moral journey at the level of the fictional narrators no less than at that of the reader. Barolini's perspective is seductively convincing and well argued, two qualities that tend to produce positive results with students.

Although it is impossible to reconcile the often incompatible positions of scholars (indeed, why try?), we as teachers are frequently faced with the task of presenting a coherent, comprehensive answer in regard to the patterns of meaning in the *Decameron*. As satisfying as success in this endeavor would be, however, it is simply not possible. Most helpful in responding to the need to elucidate Boccaccio's tendency to embrace multiple patterns of meaning (that are not always in harmony with one another) is the permissive structural interpretation of Franco Fido. Rather than privilege a single organizational scheme, Fido intelligently proposes that we see the *Decameron* as an organic unity, symmetrical in its entirety yet somewhat irregular and misshapen in its individuality. Key to this perspective is his notion of *simmetrie imperfette* ("imperfect symmetries"), coherent patterns such as 9 and 1 or 7 and 3 that, when repeated and elaborated on, help create meaning for the reader when seen against the dominant design based on tens. He explains, "[P]roduce uno straordinario effetto di vivente armonia che è peculiare al *Decameron* e ricorda quello che proviamo davanti a certe forme vegetali o biologiche, una foglia, una conchiglia" ("Architettura" 32) ("it produces an extraordinary effect of living harmony that is particular to the *Decameron* and brings to mind the sensation one gets when observing certain plant or biological forms, a leaf or seashell"). The overriding advantage of this notion is twofold; on the one hand, this "imperfect" system of parallelisms and allusions gives the impression of perfection without sacrificing artistry to geometry and, on the other, helps us attenuate the often oppressive tendency of scholars to reduce Boccaccio's masterpiece to a "narratological machine" (*Regime* 7–9). In accordance with Fido's perspective, teachers and students alike—as much as the unhurried pleasure reader—are encouraged to delight in the suggestive elegance of near mirror images and approximate repetitions, immune to the burden of mathematical exactness (cf. Potter, *Five Frames* 118). The fullest enjoyment of the *Decameron* lies in the almost Barthesian play of suggested patterns, the unevenly assembled structures that hint at completeness but stop short of obliging us to demonstrate the author's hidden intentions. "Nor does it make good sense to me," writes Charles Singleton, "when by exegetical hook and crook we have done our best to carry out this obligation, to call what we have found the meaning and real significance of the *Decameron*" (122). Just as successful teachers of Boccaccio's masterpiece must be aware of the principal theories put forward to explain the work's organization, they must also permit their students to accept and reject them much as Boccaccio allowed his ladies to choose their tales in the hope that "potranno cognoscere quello che sia da fuggire e che sia similmente da seguitare [. . .]" (5) ("they will recognize what should be avoided and what should be sought after" [3]). And in those situations in which students suggest new patterns of their own? Then we may simply respond as Jorge Luis Borges once did: "Two is a mere coincidence; three is a confirmation" (110).

NOTE

[1] All English translations of Italian-language quotations in this essay have been provided by the author.

APPENDIX
POSSIBLE PATTERNS OF MEANING IN THE DECAMERON

	1	2	3	4	5	6	7	8	9	10
Neri	"Aggressive"	Fortune and *Industria*	(span →)	Unhappy endings	Happy endings	*Ingegno*	*Beffa*	(span →)	Miscellany	"Exemplary"
Branca	Vices	Fortune	(span →)	Love	(span →)	*Ingegno*	(span →)	(span →)	"Tapestry of mixed themes"	Virtues
Stewart	The bon mot	Happy adventure	(span →)	[Interruption]	Happy conclusion	The bon mot	*Beffa*	(span →)	[Interruption]	Anti-*beffa*
Smarr	Free topic	Linked to next day —>	Fiammetta and Dioneo sing together	[Interruption] Filostrato is king and sings	Fiammetta is queen, Dioneo sings	[Interruption] Elissa is queen and sings	Fiammetta and Dioneo sing together	Linked to previous day <—	Free topic	The "one" in the "nine plus one" pattern
Ferrante	Faults	Fortune makes reversal	Human beings get what they want	Family thwarts Love	Love unites	Wit corrects	Adultery thwarts family	Human beings get what they deserve	Human beings make reversal	Virtues
Barolini	Intellect affirmed	Fortune wins	Humankind wins	Fortune wins	Love wins	Through words	——	Through deeds	——	Return to Florence
	Intellect versus Fortune	(span →)	Love versus Fortune	(span →)	(span →)	Survival in "real life"	(span →)	(span →)	(span →)	(span →)

Teaching the *Decameron* in a Historical Context

Steven M. Grossvogel

That the *Decameron* begins with a detailed account of the black death of 1348, an account that is referred to in practically every historical study on the bubonic plague, suggests that history plays a significant role in Boccaccio's masterpiece.[1] It is clear from the remarks he makes in the proem that Boccaccio wanted to represent an event in human history whose reality could not be contested and whose cataclysmic effect on fourteenth-century Florence had to be confronted by his readers as well as by his ten narrators. Boccaccio's account of the plague, therefore, should be a point of departure for every teacher of the *Decameron*. Students cannot ignore this dramatic moment in history, just as the *brigata* and their *novelle* can never truly escape it.

I like to discuss the plague with my students in terms of what Vittore Branca has written about it. I introduce students not only to one of the best cultural and literary interpretations of the plague in the *Decameron* but also to the ideas of the world's foremost authority on Boccaccio.

As Branca points out in his seminal study *Boccaccio medievale*, the structural plan of the *Decameron* is anchored in reality and history by way of the plague. The black death marks both the end and the renovation of an age condemned and consumed by its own avarice (34). Historical validity resides not just in the description of the plague, as Branca states, but also in the portrait of a society that has reached an important turning point: the economic success and prestige of Florence, the largest and wealthiest city in fourteenth-century Europe, is shaken to the ground by the plague and in need of *renovatio* ("renewal" both spiritual and material). History is thus seen as a series of Vichian *corsi e ricorsi* ("occurrences and recurrences") whereby the characters rise and fall on the wheel of Fortuna, the Boethian goddess who dominates so much of the world of the *Decameron*.

Since few students associate a powerful middle class with the late Middle Ages, I like to give them a brief socioeconomic history of Florence in the decades leading up to the black death.[2] The economic and social milieu of the merchants adds to the verisimilitude of the narrative. As Branca has shown, the harsh mercantile world often serves as a backdrop against which the lives of unhappy lovers play themselves out in the *Decameron* (151). The pathos of the tragic *novelle* is heightened by the insensitive world of calculating merchants (154–55). Even the plague becomes a metaphor for the avarice of merchants (162).

Since half of the *novelle* are about merchants and all of the earliest manuscripts of the *Decameron* were owned by merchants, the popularity of the *Decameron* among merchants in medieval Florence is not surprising. It is the first time in European literature, Branca notes, that this class and its way of life have been given such prominence (135). In "L'epopea dei mercanti," one of the best-known chapters of *Boccaccio medievale*, Branca reveals how power-ful and influential Florentine merchants and bankers were in the fourteenth century.[3] The age of chivalry, which played an important role in Boccaccio's ear-lier works, is just a nostalgic memory in the *Decameron*. The people who must now contend with the forces of love, fortune, and *ingegno* are the merchants: they are the new knights who must test their mettle on completely different, but equally dangerous, battlefields.

If the realism of the *Decameron* is anchored in time and space by the plague and the mercantile world of fourteenth-century Tuscany, so are most of the characters. According to Branca, ninety percent of the characters and the events narrated in the *Decameron* belong to the age immediately preceding 1348. Boccaccio also includes, among his characters, people who were still alive or had recently died (348, 349). Even some stock characters in the *Decameron*, including several cuckolds, were people whom Boccaccio either knew person-ally or knew something about. That most of the characters in the *Decameron* were based on Boccaccio's contemporaries makes this work one of the earliest examples of testimonial literature. The black death heightens the testimonial nature of the *Decameron* since it marks the end of the epoch in which most of these characters lived.

After discussing the introduction to the *Decameron*, I ask my students to compare Boccaccio's Ser Ciappelletto (tale 1.1) with the historical Cepparello da Prato. They can do this either by using the footnotes in any of Branca's an-notated editions of the *Decameron* or by reading the second chapter of Luigi Fassò's *Saggi e ricerche di storia letteraria*.[4] Students soon realize that there are discrepancies between historic reality and Boccaccio's rendition of it. Branca demonstrates Boccaccio deliberately altered his own personal experiences and those of others when he wrote about them in his works, and he did this accord-ing to paradigms of medieval culture (243). It is important for students to real-ize that Boccaccio, like many medieval authors, had a different understanding of what history was and of how it could be used. For Boccaccio, history has a subjective and moral dimension quite unlike the rationalistic and objective his-tories most students are familiar with. Since the description of the plague was borrowed, in part, from Paul the Deacon's *Historia Langobardorum*, as Branca points out (381–87), we can see that for Boccaccio history is not limited to first- or secondhand accounts of the actual events but is also patterned after similar events that occurred centuries before. Therefore, the concept of *auctoritas* is as important to the narration of history as it is to the narration of fiction.

Boccaccio's understanding of history determines not only the way it is used in the *Decameron* but also the way in which events and characters can be inter-preted as exempla. Using Ernst Curtius's definition of *exemplum* as both an " 'exemplary figure' (*eikon*, *imago*), i.e., 'the incarnation of a quality' " and "an interpolated anecdote serving as an example" (59–60, 1963 ed.), I try to illus-trate how the exempla Boccaccio used are both literary sources for his *novelle* and historic anecdotes that serve, among other things, as models of appropriate or inappropriate behavior. Students, however, should be made aware that even though Boccaccio is using history within the tradition of the exemplum, he is also aware of the genre's subjectivity. As Millicent Marcus has shown, the *Decameron* can be read as a work that subverts the exemplary tradition (*Allegory* 20–25).

When teaching the first novella of Day 1 in relation to the introduction, one should mention the apparent dichotomy between the historically accurate and vivid descriptions of the black death and Ser Ciappelletto's world of fiction, hyperbole, and subterfuge. This transition from the graphically real world of the introduction to the surreal world of the first novella is Boccaccio's way of introducing his readers to the worlds of *istoria* (history) and *fabula* (fiction), and to the points where these two worlds intersect. By juxtaposing Florence during the black death with the novella of Ser Ciappelletto, Boccaccio shows how history is the product of not only unquestionable cataclysmic events but also of questionable and often contradictory accounts of an individual's *vita, morte e miracoli* ("life, death, and miracles").[5]

When analyzing the first novella, I discuss the distinction Boccaccio himself made between *istoria* and *fabula* by having students read Charles Osgood's *Boccaccio on Poetry: Being the Preface and the Fourteenth and Fifteenth Books of Boccaccio's* Genealogia Deorum Gentilium. Besides providing students with an excellent introduction to Boccaccio's poetics, this work sheds light on how Boccaccio saw history and fiction intertwine. For Boccaccio, history is associated with the literal truth and is often sacrificed in invention by poets (64). Whereas historians "begin their account at some convenient beginning and describe events in the unbroken order of their occurrence to the end," poets are not constrained by chronology and "begin their proposed narrative in the midst of events, or sometimes even near the end; and thus they find excuse for telling preceding events which seem to have been omitted" (67, 68). Furthermore, poets do not have to portray historic figures the way history has depicted them: Boccaccio notes that there are discrepancies between Vergil's portrayal of Dido and the way history depicted her and gives several compelling reasons for these discrepancies.[6] Altering chronologies and representing historic figures as allegories of human passions are liberties that Boccaccio takes in many of his works, including the *Decameron*; his reasons for doing so are often similar to those he attributes to Vergil.[7]

Teachers of the *Decameron* may emphasize the predominance of *fabula* over *istoria* or vice versa, but they should also encourage students to see where the two overlap. If students learn to read the *Decameron* without completely separating *istoria* from *fabula*, they can better appreciate the limitations of critical interpretations that regard the novella of Ser Ciappelletto as pure fiction or metafiction and the similar limitations of historical studies that ignore the metaphoric significance of the black death. In short, if students are reminded that *fabula* and *istoria* are, for the most part, mutually inclusive, they will have a better appreciation and understanding of the *Decameron*.

After presenting students with Boccaccio's views of history and its relation to fiction, I give them a historic perspective of this issue. The question of the no-velle's historicity was first raised by Petrarch in his last letters to Boccaccio, *Rerum senilium* 17 (qtd. in *Boccaccio medievale* 166–67). These letters, readily available in English translation, are also worth assigning to students because they include Petrarch's influential Latin translation of the last novella in the *Decameron*.[8] Petrarch becomes the first in a long line of critics to question whether Boccaccio's novelle are *istoria* or *fabula*.

As Branca has shown in *Linee di una storia della critica al* Decameron, a work that provides students with an excellent survey of the critical reception of the *Decameron*, the issue of the *Decameron*'s historicity was widely debated in the eighteenth century (31–37).[9] F. Bottari believed that even though Boccaccio often relied on reality for the writing of his novelle, he used *inven-zione* for most of the *Decameron* (30–31).[10] D. M. Manni, by contrast, wanted to show that the *Decameron* was all history (32). The study of sources and ana-logues was important because they proved, for Manni, that Boccaccio did not invent the novelle but based them on something real.[11] As Branca points out, Manni's historical readings of the novelle were meant to purge Boccaccio of the accusation of immorality and to show that the *Decameron* was worthy of high praise because it represented real people and events rather than invented ones (32).

In the nineteenth century, Boccaccio scholars fell under the influence of Romanticism and viewed history in relation to the artistic qualities of the *Decameron* (*Linee* 38–39). Ugo Foscolo looked at the spiritual and historic cli-mate of fourteenth-century Italy to clarify textual and linguistic difficulties in the *Decameron* (*Linee* 39). Other scholars during that century saw the value of reading the *Decameron* in terms of its historic context but tended to view the work as the expression of the interests and tendencies of the trecento (40). The anticlerical positions of several Boccaccio scholars in the nineteenth century, coupled with the anticlerical novelle of the *Decameron*, fostered the idea that it was a work that marked the end of the Dark Ages, viewed as a period of primi-tive and religious vigor, and the beginning of the modern era, viewed as a pe-riod of unbridled joy and a hedonistic sense of life. According to Branca, such interpretations distorted not only the *Decameron* but history itself (40–44).

Once students know something about the critical history of the *Decameron* and are aware of some of the pitfalls of reading Boccaccio's masterpiece from a purely historical perspective, they are in a better position to appreciate Branca's balanced, historical, and literary studies. Branca began writing the articles that would become *Boccaccio medievale* at a time when the study of medieval litera-ture and culture was undergoing significant change (*Boccaccio medievale* ix). Since modern scholars no longer viewed the Middle Ages as the Dark Ages, their perception of the relation of the Middle Ages to the Renaissance differed from that of writers in the eighteenth and nineteenth centuries (ix–xii). Branca, the first scholar to look at Boccaccio's works in terms of this new understanding of the Middle Ages, interpreted the *Decameron* in relation to the numerous facets of medieval culture that imbue the text. Branca's work would become a precursor to several trends now popular in cultural studies. In fact, when teaching the *Decameron* from a historical perspective, one should examine not only the roles of *istoria* and *fabula* but also the various aspects of medieval culture that permeate the work (e.g., the status of women in medieval society, the role of canon law in determining the restrictions on human sexuality, etc.). In short, the *Decameron* has much to offer to the field of cultural studies.

Finally, to complement Branca's scholarship, I introduce students to Lee Patterson's discussion of the relation between history and self. As Patterson points out in *Chaucer and the Subject of History*, the historical communities of the medieval world establish the social identity, or persona, of Christians, while at the same time creating impediments in the Christian's journey to God (8). (An example of this could be the false confession that Ciappelletto justifies on the grounds that he could never be absolved of his sins if he confessed them truthfully.) According to Patterson, the "medieval conception of selfhood is typically understood as a dialectic between the Christian subject and this objectified historical identity." The tension between the subject and history, "between the inner self of desire and its external mode of self-articulation as a singular individual who traces a specific worldly career," is best seen in Dante's *Commedia* (8, 10). The same thing can be said of the first novella in the *Decameron*. Ciappelletto's identity is determined by two contradictory and radically different accounts of his life: a negative account, created by Ciappelletto to survive in the cutthroat world of merchants and moneylenders and promulgated by the Italians who claim to know him (Panfilo, Messer Musciatto, and Ciappelletto's two Lombard hosts), and a positive account, created by Ciappelletto to get a Christian burial and promulgated by the friar and the Burgundians who revere him after his death. Ciappelletto's self-portrayal in both accounts is "the product of a dialectical movement between a socially undefined subjectivity [. . .] and a historically determined role" (28).

What Patterson says about the characters in the *Canterbury Tales* can also be said about most of the characters in the *Decameron*: the various estates created by history have imposed on the characters certain roles and functions that they, as individuals, relate to in different ways: "character is not an object to be described [. . .]. Character is what emerges from the transactions between the given world outside (history) and the unspecified world within (the subject)" (28–29). Ciappelletto can serve as an example of this interplay: his true self is always a mystery because he is constantly reinventing it in the light of social and historical dictates. The same can be said of many other characters in the *Decameron*.

That scholars are reevaluating and redefining the role of history in fourteenth-century vernacular literature clearly indicates that history itself is too important to be ignored in the *Decameron*.[12] Besides considering the relative merits and shortcomings of reading the *Decameron* in a historical context, students and teachers should examine the multifaceted role and complex significance of history in this work for a deeper appreciation of Boccaccio's masterpiece.

NOTES

[1] Historical studies of the black death regard Boccaccio's account of the plague as both historically and medically accurate.

[2] Besides chapter 5 of *Boccaccio medievale*, students may benefit by reading Gene Brucker's *Florentine Politics and Society, 1343–1378*. Other works in English that can provide students with a cultural and historical background of fourteenth-century Florence are Marvin B. Becker's *Florence in Transition* and *Medieval Italy: Constraints and Creativity* and Ferdinand Schevill's *Medieval and Renaissance Florence*.

[3] Teachers should also consult the first part of Christian Bec's *Les marchands écrivains* and especially chapter 7 of Lee Patterson's *Chaucer and the Subject of History* ("Chaucerian Commerce: Bourgeois Ideology and Poetic Exchange in the *Merchant's* and *Shipman's Tales*" [322–66]), which illustrates how the economic system of the time is dramatized by Chaucer in two tales that have sources or analogues in the *Decameron*.

[4] Luigi Fassò's "La prima novella del *Decamerone* e la sua fortuna" (31–90) summarizes and evaluates the historical research done by Giulio Giani and others.

[5] I have tried to elaborate on this in an article entitled "What Do We Really Know of Ser Ciappelletto?"

[6] First, Vergil "desired to bring his hero to somebody worthy of regard who might receive him and urge him to tell of his own fate and that of the Trojans. Such a one above all he found in Dido, who, to be sure, is supposed to have dwelt there not then, but many generations later" (Osgood 67–68). Second, Vergil wished "to show with what passions human frailty is infested, and the strength with which a steady man subdues them [. . .]. So he represents in Dido the attracting power of the passion of love, prepared for every opportunity, and in Aeneas one who is readily disposed in that way and at length readily overcome" (68–69). Third, Vergil wished "to extol, through his praise of Aeneas, the *gens Julia* in honor of Octavius" and, fourth, "to exhalt the glory of the name of Rome. This he accomplishes through Dido's execrations at her death; for they imply the wars between Carthage and Rome, and prefigure the triumphs which the Romans gained thereby" (69).

[7] Boccaccio's remarks about history and fiction appear in the second redaction of the *Trattatello in laude di Dante*, as Pier Giorgio Ricci has shown (434–35); and similar remarks appear in the introductions to *De casibus virorum illustrium* and *De mulieribus claris*, as Branca has shown (*Boccaccio medievale* 167). These three works by Boccaccio are historical narratives that, despite their differences in content and language, share an intermingling of *fabula* and *istoria* similar to what we find in the *Decameron*. Selections from all three works could be included in a course on Boccaccio because these works reflect the author's continued interest in the relation between history and poetic invention even after the *Decameron* and because they tend to favor *istoria* over *fabula*, unlike many of Boccaccio's earlier works.

[8] Petrarch's translation was itself translated into Old French by his friend Philippe de Mézières, whose translation became the source of the miracle play *L'estoire de Griseldis*. Chaucer attributed to Petrarch the source of The Clerk's Tale.

[9]A shorter and more accessible survey of the critical history of the *Decameron* may be found in Branca's 1980 Einaudi edition of that work (lxiii–lxxvi).

[10]Bottari's research focused on identifying numerous sources and analogues of the *Decameron* while trying to reconstruct the historical and social context of the individual novelle. Bottari views the *Decameron* as a work that freed itself from the superstition and credulity of the Middle Ages (Branca, *Linee* 31, 30).

[11]Manni concluded that if Boccaccio narrated real events, he did not persuade others to do evil with his licentious novelle any more than he persuaded them to do good with his virtuous ones (Branca, *Linee* 32).

[12]Giuseppe Mazzotta, too, has several compelling thoughts on how Boccaccio used history in the *Decameron* (*World* 51–53, 80).

Reflections on the Criticism of the *Decameron*

Giuseppe Mazzotta

Readers of the *Decameron* and other works of Boccaccio know how sustained is Boccaccio's concern with the act of reading and with his critics' reaction to his works. His theoretical musings on allegory, his commentary on Dante, and his autocommentary on the *Teseida* show Boccaccio's awareness of the complexities and high stakes that are always involved in the reading of literature.[1] In the *Decameron* the reflection on critics and readers (and the two terms are by no means identical) figures, first, in his dedication of the novelle to the "women of leisure" and, second, in the extensive polemic with his critics staged in the introduction to Day 4. The women of leisure, for all the irony entailed by "ozio" ("leisure") in a text of mercantile activities, constitute the ideal circle of readership. Nevertheless, in this introduction (and later in the conclusion to the *Decameron*) Boccaccio berates those critics who have misunderstood his art. Keeping them at a distance appropriate for polemics, he views the critics as detractors who reproach him for what they perceive to be an indecorous love of women and an equally indecorous manipulation of language. He also charges that their criticism amounts to an act of violence in that they tear apart the sense of his tales, and to their violence Boccaccio contrasts the softness and charms of women's love.

There can hardly be any doubt that the *Decameron* displays a deep entanglement with both critics and women or with violence and love. But the core of Boccaccio's polemical response to the critics' violence is also a parable directed to all readers about the uneasy relation, indeed about the misunderstanding, that exists between texts and critics and about the gulf yawning between literature and criticism. Nonetheless, Boccaccio fully grasps the profound links and even complicity binding literature and criticism. In fact, the distance between these two rhetorical modes of discourse is not as wide as is commonly presumed. What exactly is the nature of the link? And how is one to account for the critics' alleged misunderstanding of the *Decameron*? Is this misunderstanding a form of literary irony, the unavoidably impenetrable residue of opaqueness of all language? Or is it triggered by a question of ethics (say, as Boccaccio charges, envy blinding the faculty of judgment) and by a likely antithetical view critics have of literature (and of women, love, values, etc.) or by their divergence from Boccaccio's own assumptions? A possible answer to these questions can only emerge from an analysis, however brief, of some elements of the structure of the *Decameron*.

The fundamental component in the metaphoric design of the *Decameron* is the conversation that unfolds among and binds the ten young people who retreat to a natural *locus amoenus* to escape the threatening horror of the plague. There is an oblique link between the open, conversational mode and the naturalist, pastoral landscape of the frame in which the storytelling takes place. The quasi-Edenic locale casts its transparent light on Boccaccio's rhetoric: it is as if the language of the garden had a natural, direct, and univocal signification. Further, in the harmonious, aristocratic, and even utopian world of the garden the elegant conversation and the exchange of stories that make up the text are the unequivocal mark of the sovereignty of order. The young people communicate with one another and observe the rational rules that the queen has imposed on all of them.

Boccaccio's narrative, however, moves beyond the illusory fictions of the pastoral world and unveils the wishful thinking lying beyond rational constructions of reality. Regrettably, critics lapse into a far too common fallacy and construe a subtle literary text such as the *Decameron* as if it were simply reducible to univocal senses (which they variously take to be nature, reason, love, reality, etc.). A careful close reading of the language of the novelle shows that the myth of a natural, transparent signification, for all its powerful pull, is ceaselessly countered by disruptive ironies, contradictory meanings, and metaphoric ambiguities that all together draw the *Decameron* into the equivocal and elusive space where interpretations are not a priori given by abstract rules. In this ambiguous space, which is the space of literature, the possibility of criticism, an activity that Boccaccio highly values and is to be understood as an exercise of judgment and choice, becomes problematical. Why is this so?

The clarification must be brief. The imaginative model that sustains the vagaries and mobility of the text is essentially economic and temporal (plainly, even the metaphor of the conversation, which designates the exchange of language, is ruled by this model). Through the central shifty figurations of merchants and time (and their numberless disguises and variants) the *Decameron* dismantles all complacent, self-serving readings (though it warns us that all readings are always also self-serving). It invites us to be suspicious of moralizers and other ideological despots (be they Tancredi or Gualtieri, or even a libertine such as Dioneo, for a libertine, in the pursuit of pleasure, is nothing more than a masked tyrant). Like the critics, these characters are authoritative figures, who read with fixed categories and tyrannical, one-dimensional, or self-centered senses in mind. To put it in rhetorical terms that apply to characters and critics alike, these moralizers, who in the present-day scholarly scene are identifiable as the delirious panallegorists of medieval texts, mistake parts for the whole, disrupt the free flow of language, simplify complexities, and in their anger cripple and are blind to the extraordinary energy of this text. Moreover, the *Decameron* dramatizes the unavoidable complicity and the endless series of exchanges between seemingly contrasting categories (reason and love, friendship and rivalry, intelligence and naïveté, saintliness and blasphemy, critics and women, different rhetorical tropes such as the literal and the allegorical, etc.).

It is not immediately evident that the implications of Boccaccio's hermeneutical-polemical caveat in the introduction to Day 4 and the conclusion to the *Decameron* have been adequately grasped by contemporary critics. In fact, one cannot but be surprised by the apparent lack of self-awareness in several modern critical readings of the *Decameron* about the relation between text and criticism. To be sure, there have recently been many debates on medieval allegory, a term that describes a mode of expression as well as techniques of textual interpretation, but these debates have mainly been circumscribed to Boccaccio's romances and have steered clear of the *Decameron*.

This lack of theoretical interest in how to read a classic of Italian literature has causes and consequences that are too complex for me to go into in this context. Nonetheless, a few speculations are in order. One can speculate that a false assumption governs the practice of many critics. As I said earlier, most critics' beliefs are shaped by the assumption that the meaning of the *Decameron* is transparent, and, despite Boccaccio's difficulties with his critics, its meaning has been established once and for all by the critical tradition. Further, since a classic is by definition a text that has been canonized by tradition, it would seem that it is wrapped in a special aura that makes it sacrosanct and inviolable. And as happens with all canonized texts, such as the Bible, which unavoidably generates self-same, self-repetitive glosses, each reading of the *Decameron* limits itself to merely confirming the authority of its traditional reception. In the light of these assumptions, it follows that the critics view their role as map makers, as it were, of the text's cultural lines of force. Thus criticism is reduced to a perfunctory gesture that ends up deadening the text's vital imaginative powers. The interpretive predicament of current criticism of the *Decameron* is perplexing (though, paradoxically, it is, at the same time, unquestionably attractive) because it goes against the grain of the fashionable theorizing and critical self-reflexivity that is rampant in the current American academic scene.

The scholars' resistance to critical fashion is certainly attractive even if it is only a (largely involuntary) sign of the insight into what I call the untimeliness of literature. What does this term mean? It means that, for all its mimetic reflection of reality, literature's distinctive trait lies in its power to transcend and counter the lure of immediacy and the domain of contingencies it nonetheless seeks to celebrate. No text in Italian literature possibly embodies this simultaneous dual impulse more eminently than the *Decameron*. Unquestionably, however, the resistance of the critics to newfangled practices, for all its attractiveness, becomes a symptom of what must be called the crisis of Italian literature. The word *crisis* is in many ways synonymous with literature, for literature is centrally the critical language of radically decisive experiences.

As the *Decameron* hedges between the multiple elusive demands of, say, literal naturalism and the free play of the imagination, playful evasion and utopian order, ironic displacements and contingent humor, eutrapelia and simulation, desire and politics, and so on, it carries within itself both a desire to represent the play of the world and the equally irreducible desire for closure. The relation between literature and criticism persistently reenacts this tension, and the text draws its inexhaustible, seductive energy from polarities of thought that feed on each other. Nonetheless, the crisis investing Italian literary studies at present has less exalted causes and forms of expression. It may well have to do, I suggest, with critical stances that encourage modes of reading aiming at closing off, dismembering, and doing violence to a text such as the *Decameron* that forever checkmates the critics' will to power.

How does the exercise of interpretive closure translate into a concrete institutional practice? It is a fact that, with a few notable exceptions, Italian literary studies have traditionally been and continue to be marginal (and self-marginalized) in the topography of American intellectual life. There are many historical and political reasons for this marginal status of literature in general and Italian literature in particular in American universities. Lest one fall into some deluded nationalistic narcissism, let me quickly add that this crisis of Italian studies is not only an American phenomenon. Incredible as it may seem, the crisis involves, in all its gravity, literature departments in Italian universities. Fossilized, unexamined critical styles; views of literature as formal self-enclosures rather than as texts involved with all forms of knowledge and experience; didactic practices that perpetuate old canons of literature—these are, no doubt, only some of the elements that bear a significant responsibility for the present realities. It is evident, therefore, that to reflect on the language and on the questions raised by the criticism on the *Decameron* is more than an innocent academic exercise. It is a professional necessity.

A general glance at the outline and contours of the current critical perspectives on the *Decameron* brings us back to the nineteenth-century foundation of literary criticism. It is customary for critical anthologies on the *Decameron* to mark the beginning of a typically modern thinking about literature with the essay originally published by Ugo Foscolo in 1826 in the *London Magazine*. Over and against eighteenth-century aesthetics that valorizes the question of taste, Foscolo casts his account of the *Decameron* in terms of Boccaccio's whole life and works. But the real founder of modern Italian literary criticism is Francesco De Sanctis, who wrote some immensely influential and still vital pages on the *Decameron*, as on a number of other texts, in his *Storia della letteratura italiana* (1870–71).

Shaped by a Hegelian historiographic paradigm, whereby texts and events unfold in a pattern of antithetical disjunction within themselves and from each other, the *Storia della letteratura italiana* presents the *Decameron* as an epochal text ushering in what De Sanctis calls, in a highly exalted Romantic rhetoric, a "cataclysm, or, at least a revolution" in literary history (254). From this standpoint, the primary aim of the essay is to document the occurrence of a historical periodization, and the *Decameron* serves as the original focus for a historic shift from the Middle Ages to the period we call the Renaissance. Drastic divisions are drawn between the two broad periods. In effect, the portrait of the Middle Ages that De Sanctis etches betrays typically nineteenth-century (and belated Enlightenment) prejudices about the Middle Ages. The Italian risorgimento, which is the background against which De Sanctis writes his narrative of Italian literature, can only justify itself by rethinking the traditions of the past and peddling new myths for the present. As happened in many Italian historical novels of the nineteenth century that idealized or punctured the Middle Ages, the *Storia della letteratura italiana* gives an imaginary construction of the past so that the present can justify itself.

In this imaginary reconstruction, the Middle Ages is viewed as a time whose essential quality is transcendence, or the denial of the reality of nature and of humanity and the displacing of all perfection and virtue outside of life. What we are given is, doubtless, a Manichaean view of the Middle Ages, which De Sanctis supports by evoking the belief in the division of body and soul, the break between consciousness and law, and, more generally, the rupture between life and its ultimate purposes. Such a view is extended to cover the political, moral, and philosophical map of the times. Medieval philosophy is thus reduced to a univocal struggle between nominalists and universalists and, what is more, to a futile exercise of abstractions and sophistry. With only scant attention to nuances, moral values are said to be under the sway of an ascetic rigorism; politics is decried as merely theocratic; literature is dismissed for its overindulgence in allegorizations and as a morally suspect activity. Nothing is said about literature's fictional status and its power to breach the claims at sovereignty of logical truth. With sharper accuracy, however, medieval poetics is said to seek to subdue the domain of the passions.

This intellectual portrait of the times is clearly tendentious, and this tendentiousness impinges on the validity of the real intent of De Sanctis's project: establishing bonds between the reality of history and the text, so that the text can no longer be viewed as an autotelic construct. Despite his ideologically slanted perspective and because he is too refined an aesthetician, De Sanctis's account of the *Decameron* is not really affected by his all too general, if vigorous, description of the cultural temper of the Middle Ages. What rescues the essay from being a chronicle of demonstrably inaccurate generalities is De Sanctis's extraordinary (Romantic) sense of the text's inner dramatic form.

The real point of departure for his analysis is the formal question of Boccaccio's narrative. De Sanctis begins by emphasizing the *Decameron*'s systematic reelaboration of traditional rhetorical genres, from romances to legends, from fables to songs. In turn, the remark on the formal aspects of the *Decameron* introduces the key issue of De Sanctis's broad and far-ranging interpretation: the aim of Boccaccio's art in the *Decameron* is the creation of a harmonious world, a world of art. But De Sanctis pays no attention to the dissonant components of this aesthetically harmonious construction. Deploying a central epistemological category, he stresses that this imaginary world is not viewed from a transcendent perspective; he characterizes it, rather, as a superficial world. The term, which designates a universe without depths, without hidden sense, and without hierarchies, reduces the text to a play of appearances, a theater of spectacles, which De Sanctis, whose thought is circumscribed within a Hegelian vocabulary, cannot quite probe. The adjective *superficial* is understood in both ethical and aesthetic senses, and De Sanctis invests these senses with the meaning that is essentially Hegelian but also approximates the one that Kierkegaard gives them in his anti-Hegelian polemic. Aesthetics and ethics for De Sanctis are not actually separate stages of life, but they are activities distinct from each other and yet involving each other.

From a moral and aesthetic viewpoint, the imaginative world of the *Decameron* denies all internal and spiritual energy. It is a world inhabited, as we are told, by a happy group of people trying to forget the evils of life and of the plague by passing time listening to stories. Yet play never becomes a central aesthetic category or a metaphor of the text, nor is it connected to the Franciscan or goliardic tradition of play. In pursuing an all-encompassing definition of Boccaccio's vision, De Sanctis shifts to the dubious assertion that the art world of the *Decameron* is not moved by God or by Providence. Even more dubiously, and in the obvious though unstated effort to align Boccaccio with Ockham, these theological terms are said to have a merely nominal, but not substantial existence for Boccaccio. De Sanctis concludes that if there is a privileged point of view around which the narrative landscape of the *Decameron* is organized, it is humanity's viewpoint and humanity's free will. What matters in the depiction of humankind is the power of the instinct and of natural inclination, and it does not seem to matter to Boccaccio that this sort of naturalism enslaves human beings to a mechanical idea of nature.

The general thrust of the essay is to argue that because of all the above formal and moral concerns, the *Decameron* breaks with traditional morality and opens a new world. Taking on what from an Anglo-American perspective strikes one as an anti-Victorian stance, De Sanctis defines Boccaccio's polemics in terms of a morality that celebrates the reaction of the flesh against the abstract moralism imposed by the clergy. If the text has any hold on the reader's imagination (which, after all, Boccaccio announces in the proem by referring to the melancholy—the imaginative self-absorption—of his women of leisure and the problematical status of the text in arousing desire), we are never told. Nonetheless, by the end of the chapter De Sanctis introduces an element of dissonance in his narrative, which threatens to undo the complexity of his elaborate tour de force. As stated above, he suggests that the ultimate achievement of Boccaccio is to bring about an imaginative retrieval of the spectacle of life and to represent the visible surface of the world. One must insist that Boccaccio's concern with visibility is steadily countered by his absorption with the hidden and the invisible. Yet, bypassing questions of formal symmetries and exhibiting brilliant intuition, which if fully articulated would put him ahead of his time, De Sanctis comes close to identifying Boccaccio's play of appearances as the figuration of the new morality the *Decameron* symbolizes. Using a terminology that betrays a degree of hesitation, he states that the aesthetic aim of Boccaccio's storytelling is not moral; rather, it parodies the *Divine Comedy* and, in the process, it creates an all too human comedy. From this standpoint, the *Decameron*'s preeminent quality is joy, and as such it adumbrates the works of Angelo Poliziano and Lodovico Ariosto.

The power of De Sanctis's interpretation of the *Decameron* is evident from the impact it has had on the successive readings elaborated by scholars such as Erich Auerbach and Natalino Sapegno and on a critic of a different temper, Aldo Scaglione. I cannot go into a detailed discussion of each of these signal critical contributions. There is no doubt that they have come into being in the shadow of De Sanctis's theoretical concerns and practical criticism, and they all share with De Sanctis the conviction in the critical potential of literature, its power to enter history and to subvert existing cultural codes. De Sanctis's Hegelian sense of a direct, mimetic continuity between literature and history still shapes the work of the most authoritative scholar on Boccaccio in recent times. I refer to Vittore Branca, who has managed to present a highly original picture of Boccaccio and especially of the *Decameron* that sharply diverges from the general interpretive lines of De Sanctis and his more immediate followers. Driven by a rigorously philological sense of the specificities of the medieval social, cultural, and intellectual context, Branca's now classic *Boccaccio medievale* persuasively argues that the novelty of the *Decameron* lies in its supplanting of the old chivalric code with a bourgeois mythology of profit.

Undeniably, even the scholars who avowedly work in De Sanctis's line of vision have somewhat departed from his general interpretation. One should mention, even if in passing, the genuinely new critical perspective contributed to Boccaccio studies by Auerbach. His *Mimesis*, which is written from the unusual standpoint of a Vichian who was reared in Hegelian philosophy, consistently echoes, especially in the chapters on Dante and Boccaccio, De Sanctis's critical insights about literature's effort to give an adequate representation of a problematical and ever-elusive, time-bound reality. Unlike De Sanctis, however, whose focus is the large historical definition of Boccaccio's art, Auerbach refreshingly goes into a stylistic-ideological reading of the text. Style, as his analytical probing into the linguistic stratifications of the novella of Frate Alberto (4.2) shows, is the locus of Boccaccio's art, the privileged point of intersection between literature and society. Even so, Auerbach cannot get away from the powerful pull of De Sanctis's secular reading of the *Decameron*. The latter's claim about Boccaccio's purely aesthetic aims finds a direct extension in Auerbach's equally dubious argument that the *Decameron* articulates a new ethics of love that is radically anti-Christian.

In the same subversive spirit as Auerbach, but with a thorough control of the disparate facets of the complex cultural context of medieval naturalism that exceeds Auerbach's hasty delineation, Scaglione's *Nature and Love in the Late Middle Ages* shows how medieval theories of love (e.g., Andreas Capellanus's

The Art of Courtly Love and Jean De Meung's *Romance of the Rose*), naturalistic-medical philosophies (e.g., Dino del Garbo's), and literary texts (Cavalcanti's "Donna me prega") all converge to cast love as a ravishing disease of the appetite. Boccaccio departs, however, from the view of love as a mishap darkening the mind and sickening the body. By contrast to the anguished sense of life voiced by his predecessors and seemingly justified by the tragic occurrence of the plague, Boccaccio summons the readers to a sort of Horatian carpe diem, to an enjoyment (a term that echoes De Sanctis's joy) of the world in all its manifestations. In this new ethics of love and of life, which manifestly reelaborates and updates De Sanctis's interpretation, Boccaccio is the humanist who unconditionally supports the idea of humankind's freedom against all conventional morality.

No doubt, there is a common thread between the theories of realism and naturalism running through the readings of De Sanctis, Auerbach, and Branca. In their different critical voices they all stress the ideological thrust of the *Decameron*, but they never focus on the problematical question of literary representation and mediation. Such a charge may seem ludicrous when one thinks that Auerbach's subtitle of *Mimesis* is *The Representation of Reality in Western Literature*. Representation, however, is not simply the mimetic reflection or copy of reality, no more than imagination is the threshold of rationality. As much as imagination—which as desire, memory, and madness questions the assumption of neat, easily definable division between the imaginary and the rational—mimesis comes forth as the metaphoric displacement and as a fictive otherness in relation to the real world. More precisely, it is as a simulacrum, as a work of the imagination and not as a mere copy or mirror of reality, that the literary text puts into discussion the objective, solid conventions of the real. Few authors have grasped the enigmatic ambivalence of literature—its simultaneously real and imaginary quality, its utopian and real bent—with the clarity and self-consciousness Boccaccio constantly displays even in his dramatization of the critics' response to some of his tales.

By focusing on what one can call the equivocality of a text such as the *Decameron*, one can understand Boccaccio's radical notion of literature. As I have shown in my book *The World at Play in Boccaccio's* Decameron, Boccaccio dramatizes his novel understanding of literature in a number of ways. He highlights, for instance, the text's marginality or liminality by placing the storytellers at the ambivalent edge of history, in an enclosed garden that is, nonetheless, in time. This perception of ambivalence of the *Decameron* cannot be an end in itself. Rather, the notion of ambivalence reveals the imaginary space opened by the *Decameron* as a playful world in which all discourses of the tradition are rethought and are reinscribed in the utopian world of the imagination. In this reading, play (a category that De Sanctis adumbrates in his musings on joy) is both an aesthetic and an ethical mode. It is, more precisely, an optic or a way of seeing in wonder and with a critical eye the world and ourselves in it. The future possibilities of Boccaccio studies will depend on the willingness to think anew the relation between literature and criticism. The *Decameron* has shown us the way to take in this future common endeavor.

NOTE

[1]Sherry Roush, a Yale graduate, examines the problematic relation between literature and criticism in her brilliant dissertation, "Renaissance Modes of Italian Poetic Self-Commentary."

Women in the *Decameron*

F. Regina Psaki

A teacher who reads gender as central to the *Decameron* does well to introduce students to Boccaccio's thematization of gender difference without making totalizing claims that the work is pro- or antifeminist (Migiel). This protean text—fragmentary, experimental, plurivocal—will not support a programmatic reading; its many stances are contingent and contradictory, and unlike the *Divine Comedy*, it assumes no ultimate truth to which the others can be subordinated (F. Bruni 263). A feminist examination of the *Decameron* need not be the sole purpose of a course; it can emerge from a study of the book's structures, rhetoric, linguistic registers, component genres, and sources; it can even emerge from a reading that gives gender issues no priority over such categories as the church, early capitalism, social hierarchies, literary genres, morality, obscenity, or violence. I therefore propose approaches to the book that I have found both likely to elicit reflections on its treatment of gender and portable from one kind of course to another.

Voicing

The *Decameron* is a densely woven polyphony of voices, which purport to originate in different classes, types, estates, and genders. The historical author has assigned the utterances that constitute the book to various levels: a persona we can call the primary narrator, his readers and critics, the ten narrative personae, their servants, and the speakers inside the tales make competing declarations and implications regarding the experience of women (NB, not of men per se). We must alert our students early on to differentiate among speakers and contexts or risk reading in a student essay that Boccaccio (rather than Filomena) describes women as "fickle, quarrelsome, suspicious, timid, and fearful" (*Dec.*, trans. Musa and Bondanella 15), the quotation produced as incontrovertible evidence of the author's opinion of women. No single pronouncement is definitive, even when we might want it to be; each will be contradicted sooner or later, tacitly or explicitly.

One good way to begin a discussion of gender in the text, and a useful shortcut to the commonplaces of medieval misogyny, is to survey the normative and prescriptive pronouncements on female nature that are found in the frame and in the tales. Such statements tend to catch students' eyes and to stand out from their context for the bland confidence with which they are uttered. The primary narrator makes explicit statements in the proem about women—his debt to them, their compassionate nature, the unfortunate restriction of their freedom of movement, their pleasing characteristics—that mark him as a very partisan speaker and a far from disinterested one. He clearly hopes to be the consoling suitor who benefits from his ostentatious recognition of their sufferings, merits, and virtues. In addition, the speeches of the ten inset narrators and their servants reflect a myriad of opinions and moments and should also be examined for how they can illuminate one another. Elissa's claim in the introduction that "Veramente gli uomini sono delle femine capo, e senza l'ordine loro rade volte riesce alcuna nostra opera a laudevole fine [. . .]" (24) ("Men are truly the leaders of women, and without their guidance, our actions rarely end successfully" [5]) should be juxtaposed with Dioneo's acknowledgment that "Donne, il vostro senno più che il nostro avvedimento ci ha qui guidati" (27) ("Ladies, more than our preparations, it was your intelligence that guided us here" [18]). Within the tales themselves, the statements the characters make about women range from rather generic accusations of garrulousness (8.7, 7.2) and sexual voracity (2.7, 5.10, 3.1) to the praise Griselda receives from her husband and people for her inhuman perfection (10.10).

Not all the book's communications about gender roles are explicit, however. Parts of the *Decameron* grant to women, without editorial commentary, the right to speech, to sexual self-determination, to economic autonomy, and so on. The right to speech, for example, is assumed rather than explicitly defended in Ghismonda's long declaration of independence from her father (4.1); in Bartolomea's and Pietro's wife's spirited claims to the right to satisfying sex (2.10, 5.10); and in the many tales in which a woman's witty riposte resolves a situation grown dangerously unstable (e.g., 1.5, 1.9, 6.1, 6.3, 9.2). Women's right to *public* speech, while less evident, is upheld in Madonna Filippa's magisterial defense of her sexual autonomy and in her condemnation of an unjust law (6.7). Women's right to representation and to self-representation is often staged in this text as self-evident—just as it is often contested by narrators and personae alike (e.g., 1.10).

The right of women to direct or to evade the sexual economy of their culture is the subtext of many tales that students may profitably read as a cluster.

Women manage to liberate themselves from unwanted attentions through re-proof, ruse, or outright refusal (1.5, 5.9, 6.3, 8.4, 9.1, 10.5). They succeed in en-gineering their own erotic satisfaction in many more tales, though they are sometimes punished or defeated afterward (2.10, 3.3, 3.9, 4.1, 4.5, 4.9, 5.4, 5.10, 6.7, 7.1, 7.2, 7.4–7.9, 9.2). Students may also be assigned a group of tales in which women try to outdo men financially; in this they succeed less often (2.5, overturned by 8.10; 8.1; 8.2, etc.). The extent to which sexual autonomy is a figure for, a substitute for, or a subset of a more broadly defined personal lib-erty or for economic supremacy is an area of inquiry that students typically find both legitimate for this text and relevant today (Potter, "Woman"; Barolini, "Parole").

I have students record the explicit statements about female nature they find in the frame narrative. I ask them to identify the speaker and context of each declaration and to present the contradictory views and their reception within the text (e.g., Tindaro's defense of women's chastity compared with Licisca's de-fense of women's sexual autonomy [introduction to Day 6] or the primary nar-rator's description of women as delightful compared with his critics' claim that they are dangerous and trivial [introduction to Day 4 and author's conclusion]). I also have them locate and juxtapose verbal echoes and parallel claims within the tales (such as the comparison of male and female potential in 5.10 and 8.7 or of male and female sexual stamina in 3.10 and 5.10). This exercise helps them recognize the background noise of medieval misogynist and misogamist clichés. Students discuss what is gained by the book's sweeping and contradic-tory statements and how these speeches characterize and delimit their speak-ers. Usually they conclude that neither the philogynous nor the misogynist pole constitutes a reliable index of either the author's intention or a medieval audi-ence's understanding of the book.

Genres

Millicent Marcus in her book *An Allegory of Form* argues that the *Decameron* uses its mosaic of genres to interrogate accepted conventions of storytelling and to make a space for a new, secular storytelling with no pretensions to transcen-dent truth. An implicit corollary to this thesis is that the women of the *Decameron* are not intended to resemble "real" women in the author's physical world; they behave like women *in a particular genre*. They reflect, in other words, the genre conventions of the tale they appear in, though not always strictly. This accounts for such enigmatic characters as Griselda, whose forti-tude is entirely consistent with a saint's life but notoriously problematic in al-most any other context. It also accounts for the measurably different status of the women in the frame narrative: they embody but also elude the clichés of their gender, in part because Boccaccio is constituting a new order of genre as he goes along. Exemplum, fabliau, romance, lay, dream vision, sermon, *motto*, confession, misogynist diatribe, hagiography, lyric, and many others are invoked (and sometimes exploded) as Boccaccio sardonically revisits the narrative categories of his time.

Students naturally lack a sense of the generic repertory available to Boccaccio and his contemporaries, and a certain amount of background is needed to help them understand Boccaccio's variations on it. Pairing a tale or a *giornata* with a straight example of the genre it explores can help students appreciate resonances they would otherwise miss, resonances that could make all the difference to an understanding of gender functions. A saint's legend makes a useful gloss (though for opposite reasons) on 1.1 and 10.10. The tragic love stories of Day 4 can be illuminated by a reading of the *Châtelaine de Vergi* (*The Lady of Vergi*) or the *Lai de Laüstic* (from Marie de France, the *Lais*). The *Lai d'Aristote* (Henri d'Andeli), Juvenal's *Sixth Satire*, or the anonymous *De coniuge non ducenda* (Rigg) can all shed light on the misogynist conventions of 8.7. A sampling of fabliaux can improvise a background for the marital *beffe* of Days 7 and 8. A sample of vernacular preaching will gloss 6.10, and so on. The potential intertexts are infinite, but one other merits particular mention. Reading the purported visits to or visitations from the underworld (e.g., 3.8, 5.8, 7.10) in tandem with Dante's portrayals of divine punishment in the *Divine Comedy* yields some unexpectedly irreverent implications about the latter and about the role of women in a masculine economy of guilt.

The Body as Spectacle and the Specular Corpus

Michel David claims that fully thirty-five *Decameron* tales involve "pure voyeurism" and that fifty-four "are in some way contaminated by the impulse to see (or to hear) without being seen," "to the point of making [voyeurism] one of the essential elements of [Boccaccio's] narrative tension" (239, 241). The *Decameron* offers the body as a spectacle, overwhelmingly female and frequently nude, centering the reader's gaze on it: to what end? The female object of aggressive or transgressive vision is deployed so conspicuously in this text that it merits a category to itself, and it is deployed as a stand-in for the *Decameron*, its author, and its audience in a sophisticated project of textual self-referentiality that finds few rivals in medieval narrative.

The *Decameron* introduction, describing how the plague had broken down all shame (*vergogna*) among ladies, sets up female nudity as a powerful taboo, at least in a certain social milieu:

> E da questo essere abbandonati gl'infermi da' vicini, da' parenti e dagli amici e avere scarsità di serventi, discorse uno uso quasi davanti mai non udito: che niuna, quantunque leggiadra o bella o gentil donna fosse, infermando non curava d'avere a' suoi servigi uomo, qual che egli si fosse o giovane o altro, e a lui senza alcuna vergogna ogni parte del corpo aprire non altramenti che a una femina avrebbe fatto, solo che la necessità della sua infermità il richiedesse [. . .].   (15)

And since the sick were abandoned by their neighbors, their parents, and their friends and there was a scarcity of servants, a practice that was previously almost unheard of spread through the city: when a woman fell sick, no matter how attractive or beautiful or noble she might be, she did not mind having a manservant (whoever he might be, no matter how young or old he was), and she had no shame whatsoever in revealing any part of her body to him—the way she would have done to a woman— when necessity of her sickness required her to do so.   (9)

This passage alerts us to the powerful impact of nudity in the work that follows, and students can be asked to analyze how nudity functions in specific textual moments. The scenes that voyeuristically stage spectacles of female nudity can be assigned in groups according to their function, observer, object, tone, and narrative context.

I assign those passages in which we see the female nude as the unwitting object of a rapt, desiring male gaze (2.7, 2.9, 5.1, the conclusion to Day 6, 8.7, 10.4, 10.6). We examine the alignment of the reader with that gaze, especially in light of the text's explicit dedication to a female audience. In addition, I assign or summarize articles that examine that dynamic (David; Stillinger; Marcus, "Misogyny").

In another subset of tales (e.g., the introduction to Day 4; the metanarratives of 6.1, 6.8, 6.7; and the conclusion to Day 6) the female body serves as an inset mirror of the text itself. The primary narrator's fragmentary tale of the goslings encapsulates the *Decameron*'s poetics of partial pattern I alluded to above: it seems to open a discourse that it then pointedly suspends. Day 6 contains several well-known metanovelle, tales that seem to allude to the *Decameron*'s own project. The jumbled tale incompetently told to Madonna Oretta (6.1) is a sly compliment to the formal competence, artistry even, of the *Decameron*; Madonna Oretta, jounced and jostled, sweating and nauseated, is a stand-in for the *Decameron*'s female audience, ill-treated by raconteurs (lovers) less expert and amiable than the narrator. The petulant Cesca (6.8), who hates to see ugly and unpleasant people, is a figure for those *Decameron* critics of whom the narrator complains in his apologies. If you do not like to see what you deplore, he tells them, take care not to look in the mirror—that is, of his text, in which they will see only a reflection of their own ugliness and prurience. Madonna Filippa (6.7), whose beauty makes as compelling a plea as her rhetoric and her logic, represents the formal beauty and seductiveness of the *Decameron*; like Filippa, the text woos and wins its judges with its surface beauty, then answers its accusers with their own logic, refusing to be judged by criteria to which it never agreed.[1] The ladies' escape to the *valle delle donne*, a brief retreat from society to nature, "looks like a microcosm of the entire *Decameron*," and their nude bodies "a metaphor for metaphor" (Stillinger 303, 319). Again, what is implied by the multiple significations of the specifically female form in this text, and why is it such an apt vehicle for self-reference?

The sexualized body functions as at once the object and subject of mutual pleasure and intersubjective gratification in frame and tales alike (2.3, 3.10, the introduction to Day 4, 5.10, 6.7, 7.2, 8.10). More evenhanded in portraying the eroticized body, these moments lead up to and culminate in the astonishing revelation in the author's conclusion of the primary narrator as a successful lover, in fact an erotic subject and an object of erotic speculation for the readers. The fanciful logic with which he refutes his critics dissolves into a suggestive riff on the lightness of his body and the sweetness of his tongue, attested to in an evocation of a love scene with a "vicina" (964) ("neighbor lady") who stands in for the female audience ("all'oziose e non all'altre" [962] ["idle ladies and no others"]), who, he implies, may yet have the chance to "weigh" ("pesare") (963) him. The lush pleasure the narrating voice takes in linguistic and erotic play in this passage closes the book with a note of naturalism that has been read as its center of positive value (Scaglione, *Nature*), though this too is a partial reading.

Finally, in many scenes the nude body is the occasion of either a voyeuristic discovery of illicit sexual activity (1.4, 4.1, 4.5, 4.9, 5.6, 6.7, 7.9, 9.2, etc.) or a deeply disturbing vision of violence (5.8, 8.7, 10.7, 10.10). In the former, we as readers are invited to identify with the sympathetic protagonists who are spied on, yet the narration positions us to share the visual perspective of the voyeur. This fragmented perspective promotes the same perplexed suspension of judgment as do the scenes of sexual violence, which act in this text as an open call to interpretation. The tales of Nastagio (5.8) and Rinieri (8.7), Durling notes, "invite the reader to share in intense fantasies of violence done to women" ("Long Day" 274), as do also 9.9 and 10.10. These most troubling tales, moreover, dramatize their problematic status by attributing interpretative disagreement and dissatisfaction to their inscribed audience. Gualtieri's interminable torture of Griselda, already condemned by Dioneo's asides, is also thoroughly talked over by his listeners:

> [A]ssai le donne, chi d'una parte e chi d'altra tirando, chi biasimando una cosa, un'altra intorno a essa lodandone, n'avevan favellato [. . .].   (955)

> [T]he ladies, some taking one side and some taking the other, some criticizing one thing about it and some praising another, had discussed the story at great length [. . .].   (682)

The audience is equally divided on Rinieri's revenge:

> Gravi e noiosi erano stati i casi d'Elena a ascoltare alle donne, ma per ciò che in parte giustamente avvenutigli gli estimavano, con più moderata compassione gli avean trapassati, quantunque rigido e constante fieramente, anzi crudele, reputassero lo scolare.   (738)

Grievous and painful as Elena's misfortunes were for the ladies to hear, they listened to them with restrained pity, since they felt she had in part deserved them, although at the same time they did consider the scholar to have been somewhat rigid, and fiercely relentless, not to mention cruel.   (525)

Giosefo's sadistic beating of his wife, however, elicits a clear gender split:

Questa novella dalla reina detta diede un poco da mormorare alle donne e da ridere a' giovani [. . .].   (838)

This tale told by the Queen caused some murmuring among the ladies and some laughter from the young men.   (596)

These inscribed debates dramatize the entire problematic of this text's complex gender dynamics: what is the relation between textual misogyny or philogyny and the real world in which the Decameron was written, was originally read, or is read now? I ask students to consider what is at stake in these several uses of the body and what is suggested by the demonstrable disparity between episodes and tone of male and female spectacle, but I emphasize that we cannot assign an unequivocal value to them. Again, the Decameron refuses to be systematized, as students find that these images can represent various figures and functions in the extratextual world in which the artifact is "consumed."

Why does the Decameron direct our attention to women or femaleness as an object of inquiry and not to men or maleness? I have insisted on the plurivocality of the work, the multiplication of its putative narrators, perspectives, and positions. These multiple matrices of narrative speech preclude any definitive statement of the Decameron's (let alone its author's) stance on women. If the Decameron is neither programmatically feminist nor complicit with an assumed cultural misogyny, exactly how do we understand its marked focus on women? Claude Cazalé-Bérard, interpreting the text as a manual for a mature and reasoned "wise use" of literature, considers its author's de facto alignment with the masculine pole of learning, philosophy, poetry, and literature. Boccaccio's project is to interrogate and destabilize accepted cultural models "by bringing into focus their most burning problematic, that of the configuration, cataloging, and interpretation of female roles" (123).

Because erudition, ratiocination, and writing are gendered masculine in Boccaccio's time, then, their object will, a priori, be gendered feminine. A recent work on misogyny complicates this alignment by noting that the writer is intrinsically implicated in femaleness by virtue of his very loquacity ("verbal transgression, indiscretion, and contradiction" [Bloch, Misogyny 56]); the nature of femaleness could thus be a crux to which he must always return.

I try to argue that questions of gender characteristics and roles, abilities and limits, and rights and privileges are fundamental to the text's exploration of the entire spectrum of humanity. Robert Hollander wisely notes that "Boccaccio's purpose was never to praise nor to blame the female sex, but to explore the effects of our sexual identities and desires upon women and men alike" (*Fiction* 29).

Women, as the nondefault gender, receive a specific kind of attention in this text, but it is the humanity shared by men and women, our virtues and vices alike, that this author pursues with great subtlety and with little certainty. Just as Boccaccio's inquiry is not conclusive, moreover, it is not exhaustive; he gives relatively little attention to male homosexuality and no explicit attention to female, making it difficult to extrapolate even a range of positions on this crucial area of gender studies. What we can conclude from the *Decameron*'s polyphony, however, is that its author meant to pose more questions than he answered, to open up a cultural debate rather than to close it off with a position paper. If our students can recognize that this text deliberately stages some of the debates on gender that preoccupy us today, they will have begun to nuance the myth of absolute alterity that can so alienate them from the study of the past.

NOTES

I would like to dedicate this essay to the memory of Joy Hambuechen Potter.

[1]I owe these readings of 6.7 and 6.8 to former students Frédéric Canovas and Rome Cusimano, who elaborated them in seminar papers.

Medieval Fantasies: Other Worlds and the Role of the Other in the *Decameron*

Marga Cottino-Jones

The medieval world is often referred to as a highly autocratic system that aimed to control the social and personal life of its subjects with traditionally set rules. In medieval art and literature this system is often represented quite faithfully, even if some literary and artistic works of those times appear to suggest clever ways of questioning its mechanisms for control. The *Decameron* in particular provides significant social insights in this respect. It clearly analyzes the social system of medieval times by confronting its rules and regulations with other worlds. Indeed, besides the social world of medieval life, the text contemplates two additional worlds, that is, the supernatural world of the Christian afterlife and the magic world of popular superstition. Because of space limitations prescribed for this essay, I limit my discussion to pointing out some of the narrative effects that the interaction of the medieval social world and the Christian supernatural world produces in the *Decameron* at the level of meaning.

The social world of medieval life, often a communal world, represents the values held by the society within the text while reflecting those of the social system outside it. These values are mirrored in the laws and rules that, within the patriarchal system so ingrained in medieval society, aim at controlling individuals and their drives for self-assertion and at imposing interdictions and punishments to be enforced whenever transgression takes place. Consequently, all the linguistic, sexual, and social relations of that system are formulated through the dynamics of the conflict between authoritarian control and individual self-assertion.

The supernatural and magic worlds reflect the same system of values governing the social system, but at the same time, they provide the proper ground for questioning the value system from a perspective directed from outside the human world, either from an afterlife world or from a magical one.

Instead of dealing with each of these worlds separately in different novelle, the *Decameron* strategy of narration often combines them within the texture of a single novella. In this way, their interaction projects a conceptual reality hardly confined to medieval standards. The manner in which the supernatural and the magic worlds question the medieval social system is connected to the roles that self-assertive persons—often women—play within the authoritarian system. By setting them within a supernatural or magic context, the narrative places these persons in juxtaposition with the dominant ideology and turns them into a disturbing and often disruptive presence, in other words, into the *other*.

A closer reading of a few novelle may help illustrate this point concerning the

Christan supernatural world. The first one I analyze is the little-known novella of Meuccio and Tingoccio (7.10), where the communal world of Siena opens up to the Christian afterlife world. In connection with this novella, I consider another tale of the same day (7.3), since it sheds additional light on the interpretation of 7.10. A critical reading of these novelle provides insight into the *Decameron's* unusual strategies of narration, particularly in the area of gender role-playing.

According to Dioneo, the narrator of 7.10, inspiration for this particular story came to him from 7.3, which deals with the same main themes: "the stupidity of the Sienese" (468) and the Christian code that controls the kinship between godparents, called *comparatico*. In 7.10, the text uses this relationship strategically to construct a complex narrative discourse around the representation of the communal world of Siena and its interaction with the world of the Christian afterlife. Furthermore, the characterization of woman as disturbing presence, or as other, adds to the narrative complexity that develops out of the superimposition of different meanings. As part of Day 7, novella 7.10 is expected to deal with the storytelling topic of the day, that is, with the "tricks which [. . .] wives have played on their husbands" (410–11). But since Dioneo, the narrator, is also king for this day and only he enjoys the privilege of being exempt from complying with the storytelling rule, we expect Dioneo to choose a different topic. That is just what he does, but he also explains at length why he intends to transgress from the topic he has established as law at the beginning of that day. In doing so, Dioneo formulates an interesting set of rules regulating storytelling in terms similar to those governing the social system of the storytellers' own world. He sets up a clear comparison between a real king and himself (a king within a narrative environment) by stating:

> [E]very [. . .] king must be the first to follow the laws he himself has set down, and if he does otherwise, he should be considered a servant deserving of punishment rather than a king [. . .]. I, your King, am almost forced to fall into this very error, thus incurring your disapproval. [. . .] And [. . .] since I am forced to break the very law I myself established, I confess to be deserving of punishment and am prepared [. . .] to make any amends which may be demanded of me [. . .].   (467–68)

> [O]gni giusto re primo servatore dee essere delle leggi fatte da lui, e se altro ne fa, servo degno di punizione e non re si dee giudicare [. . .] dovendo peccare nella legge da me medesimo fatta, sí come degno di punizione, infino a ora a ogni ammenda che comandata mi fia mi proffero apparecchiato [. . .].   (657; partial text)

Dioneo's introductory remarks thus construct a careful social backdrop for the story to come, inasmuch as they articulate a system of rules, transgressions, and punishments that reproduces the patriarchal system of the law of the father or king, regulating all the linguistic, social, and sexual relations of the society within as well as outside the text.

The story opens with the exclusively male world of the two Sienese friends, Tingoccio and Meuccio, whose stupidity is hinted at in their excessive concern for the Christian system of rewards and punishments that regulates life on earth as well as after death. Although the friends learned about this belief system through sermons at their church, they wanted to obtain proof of its validity. The promise the two friends make to each other "that whichever of them died first would return to the one who remained alive, [. . .] and would tell him whatever he wanted to know" (468) provides an explicit connection between the Christian afterlife world and the social world of communal Siena. "[I]nsieme si promisero che qual prima di lor morisse, a colui che vivo fosse rimaso, se potesse, ritornerebbe, e direbbegli novelle di quello che egli desiderava [. . .]" (658).

The topic of the kinship between godparents, or *comparatico*, is introduced through the character of Tingoccio within the general context of male friendship created at the beginning of the story. His new *compare* relationship is due to his role as godfather of Ambruogio and Mita's son at the time of his baptism. Once Mita, "a beautiful and charming woman" (468), enters the picture as *comare* to Tingoccio, she arouses the amorous desire of both Tingoccio and Meuccio and consequently becomes a divisive force between them. Indeed, notwithstanding their earlier friendship and devotion, "each one avoided speaking about his love to the other [. . .]" (468). As soon as she enters the narrative discourse, woman is projected as a disrupter of male friendship and a source of disturbance. This representation fits the traditional Christian and patriarchal view of woman as a transgressive force within the social order.

Sex with a *comare* is forbidden in Christian society because of the family ties symbolized in the *comparatico*. Sexual relationships between *comari* and *compari* were subject to all kinds of interdictions as acts not to be performed or talked about. Well aware of such interdictions, Tingoccio "kept from revealing [his love] to Meuccio because of the wickedness he himself saw in loving his own godchild's mother [. . .]" (468). This awareness, however, does not keep him from revealing his passion to Monna Mita and having his way with her: "Tingoccio [. . .] was so clever in word and deed that he had his pleasure of her [. . .]" (469). Woman is also introduced here as the cause of men's infractions of the interdictions regulating the *comparatico*, thus accentuating the transgressive nature of her role within the Christian system.

Dioneo's storytelling is inspired by a similar tale, about Frate Rinaldo's affair with his *comare*, in another novella of the same day (7.3). While Tingoccio's seduction tactics are simply hinted at in the laconic phrase "was so clever in word and deed," Frate Rinaldo's are described with detailed reference to his captivating eloquence aimed at dispelling his *comare*'s reservations, which are based on the traditional Christian view of the *comparatico*: "You are the godfather of my son [. . .]. It would be terribly wicked, and I have always been told that it is a very serious sin [. . .]" (7.3, 427). Frate Rinaldo counters this view with amusingly persuasive arguments that affirm his rights to her bed because of his close connection to her son, a connection second only to her husband's. Frate Rinaldo further argues that since her husband, who is a "closer relative" to her son than he is, normally sleeps with her, Frate Rinaldo, "less closely related" to her son, "should also be able to sleep with [her]" (427–28). This argument, promptly accepted by the woman, "who was unskilled at logic" (428), claims a *compare*'s sexual rights on the grounds of the father's and godfather's kinship with the son/godson.

As source and primary subtext of our story, 7.3 plays a significant role here. Indeed, it makes present-day readers aware of the oedipal connotation of the relationship between Monna Mita, the *comare*, and Tingoccio, her son's godfather. In the baptism ritual, the godfather's role is to stand for his godchild and lend it his voice in replying to the questions posed by the priest and vouching for its Christian faith. In other words, the godfather impersonates the child, becoming one with it. Tingoccio in his role as godfather impersonates Monna Mita's son, and his sleeping with her creates an oedipal situation. As such, the situation is transgressive not only within the Christian system but also within the patriarchal one, controlled by the law of the father.

Moreover, this situation, especially because of its ending, seems also to fit, even if ironically, within a Lacanian reading. Tingoccio's total fulfillment of his sexual desire for the *comare*, enjoyed in silence, creates for him a condition of plenitude closely related to the Lacanian imaginary. This status is known to last very briefly in the early life of a person and is doomed to disappear as soon as the symbolic order introduced by the law of the father is established also through language.

As Terry Eagleton aptly states in his considerations of Lacan and his theories, "language is in a way 'metaphorical,' in that it substitutes itself for some direct wordless possession of the object itself" (166). According to Lacanian theory, "desire springs from a lack, which it strives continually to fill. Human language works by such a lack, by absence of the real objects which signs designate, [and] the fact that words have meaning only by virtue of the absence and exclusion of others. To enter language, then, is to become a prey to desire"(167).

Tingoccio had achieved a status of perfect bliss through the "wordless possession of the object" of his sexual desire; thus he had no use for language, since language "works by [. . .] lack, by absence of the real object." Furthermore, according to Freud's theories, the pleasure drive in men is often closely linked to the "desire to scramble back to a place where we cannot be harmed, the inorganic existence which precedes all conscious life, which keeps us struggling forward" (Eagleton 185), in other words, to death. Tingoccio's death at this point of his pleasurable sexual experience may be viewed also in this light. Death represents the only way Tingoccio is able to maintain his status of pleasurable bliss produced by the "possessioni della comare" (659), that is, the total possession of his object of desire.

At the level of literal meaning, the novella text proposes a different interpretation of Tingoccio's death, presenting it as the direct result of excessive sexuality. This view reflects—even with some irony in the use of its sexual metaphors—society's Christian view of sex as harmful for the individual not only morally but also physically:

> Tingoccio found himself in possession of the lady's fertile terrain, and he so spaded and plowed it over that an illness struck him [. . .] and [. . .] he passed from this life. (469)

> [T]rovando Tingoccio nelle possessioni della comare il terren dolce [sweet], tanto vangò e tanto lavorò che una infermità ne gli sopravvenne [. . .] sí [. . .] che [. . .] trapassò di questa vita. (659)

The possession of the woman that brings death to Tingoccio becomes a referent for whatever can be harmful to the male body. And yet, the same imagery underlying the "*sweet* terrain" of the possession of the woman confirms the connection between pleasure and death and consequently undermines the negative view of woman suggested by the Christian context, while questioning the trustworthiness of such representation. Indeed the language of the text harps ambiguously on the woman as the sweet object of desire, that is, as the instrument by which Tingoccio achieves the highest possible status of sexual bliss, combining pleasure and death.

While the central part of the novella concentrates on the pleasurable fulfillment of desire and on death as its outcome, the ending introduces the afterlife world, already foreshadowed in the promise exchanged by the two friends at the beginning that whoever died first would come back to answer all his friend's questions. This world is usually handled with comic irony, especially through a reversal strategy that inserts into the narrative mood a parodic effect aimed at undermining the Christian context of the stories.[1] In this case, the narrative has been attentive, up to now, in maintaining a level of realistic representation of a communal society embedded in Christian traditions and customs, such as the *comparatico*. The usual practice that Tingoccio and Meuccio had of attending church and listening "to sermons which often dealt with the rewards and punishments of souls after death according to their merits" (468) was the source of their interest in the afterlife. The afterworld is introduced as a Christian system based on a strict correspondence between the "sins committed during this life on earth" and the "terrible punishment" (469) that the sinners are condemned to suffer for them.

Within this context of the afterlife world, another subtext, Dante's *Commedia*, surfaces. This literary presence is revealed first in the reference to the "perdute genti" (lost people) of *Inferno* 3 (3.3) when Meuccio asks if Tingoccio was lost; then in the statement on the importance of prayers and offerings for the dead made in *Purgatorio* 3, "che qui per quei di là molto s'avanza" (3.145), rendered in Tingoccio's "for such things helped them very much [there]" (469); and eventually in the reformulating of the character of Minos of *Inferno* 5, "E quel conoscitor delle peccata / Vede qual loco d'inferno è da esse" (5.9–10), given by Tingoccio's description of "someone who seemed to know every one of my sins by heart, and he ordered me to go to a place in which I lamented my sins in extreme pain [. . .]" (470) ("uno, il qual pareva che tutti i miei peccati sapesse a mente, il quale mi comandò che io andassi in quel luogo nel quale io piansi in grandissima pena le colpe mie [. . .]" [660]).

And yet, even within these obvious references to the *Commedia*, stressing the afterlife world's dimension of penitence and suffering, the text opens to humor and irony from the beginning of the episode, after Meuccio asks whether Tingoccio is lost, Tingoccio replies with a play on the term *perduto*, deconstructing its religious connotation by reproposing a more colloquial meaning and reinforcing its parodic overtone with the addition of an expression in Sienese dialect: "What is lost cannot be found; and if I stand here before you, how could I be lost?" (469). ("Perdute son le cose che non si ritruovano: e come sarei io in mei chi, se io fossi perduto?" [659].)

The tone becomes openly ironic when Meuccio's questioning introduces the topic of the *comparatico*: "for sleeping with your godchild's mother, what punishment did they give you?" (469). Tingoccio's reply is not a simple one; it starts with an elaborate description of his first encounter with Minos and goes on to describe his subsequent plunging into "a huge and very hot fire" (470) and his state of anxiety at the thought of the terrible penance he should be facing for his sin: "I trembled with fear [. . .] terrified of the judgment which I expect to be passed on me for a great sin that I have committed [. . .]. I slept with the mother of my godchild, and I made love to her so much that I wore it to the bone" (470). "[T]utto di paura tremava [. . .] del giudicio [del . . .] gran peccato che io feci già [. . .] che io mi giacveva con una mia comare, e giacquivi tanto che io me ne scorticai" (660–61). Eventually the reply to Meuccio's question surprisingly reveals that in the afterworld "they don't count the mother of a godchild for very much!" (470). This statement, through its unexpected reversal impact on characters and situation, opens the text to a clearly comic effect while affecting characters and readers in different ways.

Both Tingoccio and Meuccio react with a deep sense of relief, especially Meuccio, who "abandoning his ignorance [. . .] became wiser in such matters from that time on" (470). Presumably he means that he would now enjoy as many *comari* as he wants. We the readers, however, are faced with a whole series of new meanings that seem to add complexity to the representation of the novella's social system and of its view of woman as other. The revelation dismisses the sacredness of the *comparatico* and denies the sinfulness of any sexual relationship of that kind. Through it, the afterworld system undermines the Christian laws that control human sexuality on earth as well as the social system that imposes such laws on its members. At the same time, this message, as formulated through lower-class characters from Siena, on whose stupidity the narrator seems to be playing, makes the criticism much more relevant and influential for most lower- or middle-class people who are law-abiding citizens and good Christians. Viewed in this light, even Meuccio's decision to become wiser in the future suggests a reconsideration of his blind acceptance of the lessons he learned from the sermons in church.

Furthermore, the statement "they don't count the mother of a godchild for very much!," concentrating particularly on the *comari*, also brings up the role of woman in both worlds, the afterlife and the social world of medieval Italy. It may imply that all women in the afterlife are seen at the level of *co-mari*, thus subscribing to the patriarchal system's traditional view of woman exclusively as mother. Yet the statement also aims at dismissing the sacredness of the *comparatico* and denying the sinfulness of any sexual relationships involving *comari* ·as well as *compari*. Thus it seems to undermine or at least to question the previous, more obvious meaning. If sexual relations involving *co-mari* are not to be seen as sinful, women may express their sexuality even as *mari*, or mothers, and their sexual relations will be just as sinless as men's. Once this view is accepted, women will cease to be seen as disruptive forces, and the typical role as other, enforced on them as disturbers of the male order or as catalysts of men's spiritual and physical destruction, will no longer exist.

The last paragraph of the story, Dioneo's own commentary, humorously refers again to the character of Frate Rinaldo from novella 7.3, within the context of the revelation made by Tingoccio:

> If Brother Rinaldo had known these things, there would have been no need for him to go about dreaming up syllogisms when trying to convert the worthy mother of his godchild to his pleasures. (470)

> Le quali cose se frate Rinaldo avesse sapute, non gli sarebbe stato bisogno d'andare silogizzando quando convertì a' suoi piaceri la sua buona comare. (661)

By underlining the meaning of Tingoccio's afterlife revelation, the text highlights the uselessness of language in the field of desire, confirming the superiority of Tingoccio's plenitude status versus Frate Rinaldo's, which was subject to the interference of language. Eventually, the ironic makeup of Dioneo's statement contrasting supernatural and earthly world ideologies, especially in sexual relationships, emphasizes the questioning and dissenting role played by the supernatural vis-à-vis the social codification of medieval life. The world of the supernatural, then, whenever it appears in the *Decameron*, seems to serve the function of questioning and disrupting the traditional codes controlling sexuality and especially the role of woman in medieval life.

NOTE

[1] The novelle of Ser Cepparello (1.1), Ferondo (3.8), Alibech (3.10), and so forth offer interesting examples of such comic irony.

Anatomizing Boccaccio's Sexual Festivity

Raymond-Jean Frontain

How should one teach the sexual themes of the *Decameron* to students who, coming of age after the spread of AIDS, have been conditioned to speak—in the public forum of the classroom, at least—of the value of abstinence and the need for sexual restraint? Boccaccio's world of sexual play is oftentimes unsettling for them, if not outright threatening. In trying to help them overcome their resistance to Boccaccio's understanding of nature, particularly as it relates to the exercise of one's sexual nature, I have developed a unit in my sophomore-level World Literature 1 class—the texts for which are the *Norton Anthology of World Masterpieces* and the Norton Critical Edition of the *Decameron*—on "comic sexual festivity" that asks students to anatomize the operations of Boccaccio's sexual festivity with a view to understanding how sexual activity figures a larger concern.

The psychologist Robert Jay Lifton notes:

> All living beings share the struggle to remain alive. But the urge to retain and enlarge that feeling of being alive—of vitality—is specifically human, an evolutionary trait of symbolizing mentation that stands at the border of biology and culture. These basic aspirations—remaining alive and the "feeling of life"—suggest the stress in formative theory on imagery and symbolization of human continuity. (50)

The theme of my world literature course is that death, immolation, formlessness, or chaos—figure the threat as one will—must be not simply survived but survived so as to allow one to take pleasure in the act of survival and to enjoy life afterward with an enlarged or magnified capacity. Any abiding bitterness or resentment for the compromises or sacrifices entailed by survival can only diminish the quality of one's subsequent life, leaving one weary of a qualified existence and less capable of dealing with any new threat. The trick is not simply to survive but to survive happily.[1]

I ask students to consider how comedy allows both the writer and the reader to confront and overcome their worst fears by making sport of those fears. And I propose that we consider this idea in sexual terms, suggesting that talk about sex is the best way human beings have of engaging the issues of individual vitality and social continuity—of stimulating that feeling of enlargement that Lifton says is necessary to human survival.[2] Psychosexually, we conclude, what women fear most is rape, and men castration, for each act is an abrogation of the individual's creative power on the most intimate or personal level. The violated wombs of Shakespeare's Lavinia and Richardson's Clarissa are as haunting a set of symbols for destructive and overpowering circumstances as the sterility and impotence of medieval romance's Fisher King and of Lawrence's Lord

Chatterley are. The circumstances of such life are destructive, not creative; they reduce the world tragically to a wasteland, despoiling humanity's teeming, fruitful garden.

Festive comedy, by contrast, is the celebration of the individual's ability not simply to survive such threats but to do so merrily and gloriously. The symbols of such comedy are the beribboned phallus and the open, even eager, womb.[3] The phallus as proudly displayed in the large leather props worn by Aristophanes's actors, in the flagpoles and maypoles associated with festive ceremony, in the elaborate codpieces of Elizabethan clowns, or (in a more discreet manifestation that respects American bourgeois prurience but that is nonetheless subversively, festively phallic) in Harpo Marx's hip-high horn with which he slyly gooses passing girls: such a phallus is a celebration of humanity's good-natured will to survive, for in the festive world it is hard to keep a good man down. Likewise, the woman who, rather than feeling threatened by male sexual interest, happily seeks to give herself to a man or even to as many men as circumstances may permit: such comic characterization aims to seduce a sour world into sexual good humor and social tractableness. In festive comedy the life force flows madly, extravagantly onward, circumventing or overwhelming any threatened disruption.

We generally need more than one class period to establish through discussion the following, admittedly partial, anatomy of the threats that festive comedy seeks to deflect or subvert. If the festive ideal is imaged as the marriage dance, with the potent phallus verging on penetrating the willing womb (imagine Tom Jones sharing a narrative with the Wife of Bath), then the psychosexual threats that the comic work must defeat may be figured in a number of ways.

First would be as the lawless phallus that would violate the reluctant womb. In tragedy, the biblical Amnon rapes his unsuspecting half-sister Tamar, and Lovelace's unbridled lust destroys Richardson's Clarissa. But in festive comedy, Aristophanes's Lysistrata is able to redirect the phallic energy of all Greece from the destructive engagement of war to the reconciliatory act of sex; Shakespeare's "merry wives" restrain Falstaff's irresponsible and predatory urges at Windsor; Helena and Duke Vincentio are able to redirect Bertram's and Angelo's subversive sexual energies through the "bed tricks" in *All's Well That Ends Well* and *Measure for Measure*, respectively; and the old woman in Chaucer's Wife of Bath's Tale teaches the squire-rapist that the world is best organized when women have dominion over men.

A second way, the antithesis of the first, sees the reluctant or impotent phallus pursued by the willing, even overeager, womb. In tragedy, Phaedra's passion for her stepson Hippolytus results in both their deaths, while Medea's inability to accept the loss of Jason's affection destroys nearly everyone around her. In comedy, however, Rabelais's Panurge is paralyzed by his reluctance to marry; Goldsmith's Miss Hardcastle shrewdly stoops to conquer Marlowe's inhibiting shyness; and the vivacious, if nutsy, woman easily reclaims any number of absent-minded professors from sterile intellectualism in American "screwball" comedies. (Think, for example, of the characters played by Katharine Hepburn in *Bringing Up Baby*, Barbara Stanwyck in *Ball of Fire*, and Barbra Streisand in *What's Up, Doc?*) A neat variation exists in Paul Rudnick's *Jeffrey*, in which the title character is reclaimed to sexual joy after AIDS makes homosexual love suddenly "radioactive" (48).

A third way, the *vagina dentata*, which threatens men with loss of the penis and synecdochically with loss of the self, can be tragically figured as the person of Keats's "La Belle Dame sans Merci" who drains so many young knights of life or as Marlene Dietrich in *The Blue Angel* ("Men cluster to me / Like moths around a flame"), but it is comically represented by Congreve's Lady Wishfort and Fielding's Lady Booby, whose lascivious desires and social threats are thwarted or evaded by Mirabell and Joseph Andrews, respectively.

In a fourth possible category, the timid womb that fears any phallic penetration, it is the woman who feels threatened with loss of self. In tragedy Blake's Thel sinks back from her view of the world of experience, whereas in comedy Petronius's grieving widow of Ephesus finally sacrifices her husband's corpse to save her newfound lover's neck; Kate the Curst and proud Titania can be reclaimed for fruition and brought to sexual tractableness; Olivia's fear of Orsino's "bearishness" or masculine brutality is overcome by the "ganymede" Cesario; and both Shakespeare's Beatrice and Congreve's Millimant are finally convinced that they can bear the rub of a man's beard and the weight of his body in bed.

A fifth way, in which the equally willing phallus and womb are kept from uniting by some outside threat, is possibly the most common figuration, for enforced unions or separations are the most basic plot devices of both tragedy and comedy. If Romeo and Juliet are the victims of chance and of their parents' enmity, then in Shakespeare's comic retelling of their story, *A Midsummer Night's Dream*, Pyramus and Thisbe are the subject of burlesque, and Hermia and Lysander are able to avert Romeo and Juliet's fate by escaping to the green world. Likewise, whereas Webster's cardinal and duke sadistically and murderously stand in the way of their sister's happiness in *The Duchess of Malfi*, in Molière's farces there is always a Frosine or a Dorine to stage-manage the circumvention of a parent's unfair opposition to the young lovers' union. Comedy succeeds in finally reforming or in excluding from the circle of the dance those Malvolios and Rabelaisian agelasts (people of ill will who because they do not like cakes and ale want to keep others from enjoying those pleasures) and those Blifils and Frank Burnses whose envy of the sexual generosity of a Tom Jones or a Hawkeye Pierce perverts any fellow feeling and turns them into forces of illiberality and sexual repressiveness.

In short, festive comedy not only convinces its readers that happiness is possible but also suggests the stance that one must take to deflect any threat to that happiness. Operating as Bruno Bettelheim says fairy tales work for children, comedy exaggerates threats to happiness, rendering them ridiculous and thus convincing the reader or audience member that survival is possible. What is more, by arousing inexpressible good feeling, it encourages the reader or spectator to leave the world of the literary work in a festive mood and to go on living his or her own life in the festive mode. Figured sexually, the comic crisis is resolved so that every Jack has his Jill—or whatever configuration of genders the text would inscribe—and so that all Nature's vital juices flow freely, even lavishly, again. Not only is the world going to be peopled (as Shakespeare's Benedick says that it must be), but the act of peopling will be conducted with renewed gusto.[4]

In assigning the twenty-one tales of the *Decameron* reprinted in the Norton Critical Edition, I ask students to read with this anatomy at hand, grouping the novelle as best they can. I warn them that while some stories may not fall under any of these rubrics, others may fall under more than one.

The first observation generally made when we reunite for discussion is that sex is all-important in Boccaccio's world and that Boccaccio seems particularly concerned with our second and fourth categories—in which the reluctant phallus or womb is reclaimed to give sexual pleasure to others. In 1.4, the abbot, who would deny his sexual nature, is tricked by the young monk into acknowledging and accepting it. In the introduction to Day 4, the father who manipulates language to restrain his son's burgeoning sexuality discovers that nature wins out over words. In 7.10, not only is Tingoccio and Meuccio's guilt over having sex with Monna Mita assuaged, but such activity is encouraged when the one friend returns from the dead to tell the other how the souls of the departed live on the other side. And Gualtieri's reluctance to marry and share himself with a woman in 10.10 borders on the tragic until he is saved for comedy by Griselda's patience and loving self-sacrifice.

More numerous are the tales concerned with the reclamation of a woman who is unaware of the possibility of sexual pleasure or who is denied such pleasure because of marriage to an older or unsatisfying husband or because of fear of compromising her reputation. In 3.1 Masetto the gardener liberates a convent of nuns whose concern proves to be reputation, not chastity, while in 4.2 Madonna Lisetta is reclaimed from pride for sexual pleasure by Brother (Friar) Alberto. Likewise, in 3.10 Rustico turns Alibech's naive piety against her when he teaches her how to put the devil back into hell. Father Gianni exploits the gullibility of Compare Pietro in order to have his way with the beautiful—and equally gullible—Gemmata (9.10), while Peronella tricks her husband into cleaning out the barrel, permitting her to satisfy herself with her lover (7.2).[5] The abbess's hypocrisy in holding her nuns to a standard of behavior that she herself violates is exposed in 9.2, and in a series of misadventures in 2.7, Alatiel "passes through the hands of nine men in different lands in the space of four years" (Norton 48) and is not only less the worse for wear but is still believed by both father and fiancé to be a virgin. Monna Giovanna's reluctance to reciprocate Federigo degli Alberighi's love, however, borders on tragedy in 5.9, although this is a tale that my classes invariably argue over, revealing both the limitations of my categories and the complexity of Boccaccio's seemingly simple relationships.

For Boccaccio, as Robert Hastings points out, nature's law is stronger than society's:

> Whenever a hiatus occurs between social convention and natural human needs Boccaccio advocates a rejection of artificial criteria and an adherence to the natural pattern of life: nature's way is best, and it is right and proper to obey her promptings, and follow her call. It is both foolish and cruel to seek to deny our natural instincts. We should rather give way to them, indulge and satisfy them properly [. . .].   (29)

Thus Boccaccio is less concerned than other comic writers with regulating the lawless phallus and importunate womb, although instances of these behaviors do occur in the tales. Calandrino's desire (albeit nonsexual) makes him foolish in 8.3; Brother Alberto is himself tricked for tricking Madonna Lisetta in 4.2; and Frate Cipolla (Brother Onion)—whose seduction of the people is mirrored by his servant Guccio's attempted seduction of the kitchen maid in 6.10—is momentarily thwarted by local pranksters. Both Rustico (3.10) and Masetto (3.1) are exhausted sexually by the women whose religious vows they initially help violate, a reluctant or hesitant womb easily becoming an overeager one once liberated. One semester my class could not resolve the extent to which Ghismonda's desire to find a worthy lover makes her responsible for her tragedy in 4.1 or whether Federigo degli Alberighi should not initially be categorized in 5.9 as an importunate phallus whose bankruptcy is deserved.

The tales concerned with outside impediments happily lend themselves to reinforcing our initial distinction between comedy and tragedy. In 9.2 the impediment to Isabetta and her lover's fulfilling their mutual desire is comically foiled when the abbess is exposed for having committed the same sin as Isabetta (a similar situation holds in 1.4, but with the genders of the principals reversed), while in 4.5 the brothers of Lisabetta prove an impassable obstacle to her happiness with the handsome and charming Lorenzo. Likewise, the fathers in 4.1 and 5.4 respond differently when confronted with evidence of their daughters' sex drives: Tancredi's possibly incestuous reluctance to allow Ghismonda to remarry after being widowed drives her to take her own life after he kills her lover, whereas Messer Lizio da Valbona not only accepts Caterina's desire for Ricciardo but also arranges a marriage between them, after which the young couple will presumably enjoy making the nightingale sing many more times.

Student participation in these discussion analyses all too often mimes the behaviors we are categorizing. Some students are overeager, push discussion to the bawdy, and must be restrained. Others are reluctant to join the discussion except to protest having to spend two weeks on Boccaccio after just completing a three-week examination of the anthology selections by Aristophanes, Ovid, Chaucer, and Rabelais. To temper the extreme of each group, I periodically re-assert that we are considering how Boccaccio is using sex to incarnate a concern about human survival in times of trauma. And on the final day of our unit on comic sexual festivity, I quote Glending Olson to summarize how the *Decameron*'s movement "from plague to pleasure" (182)—from "a world rid-dled with pestilence to a happier, healthier environment dominated by repose and recreational enjoyment" (164)—is intended as therapy rather than for car-nal stimulation (206). As the distance between the behaviors described in the tales and that of the storytellers would suggest, sex is a way of figuring psychic well-being rather than an end in itself.[6]

Also during this final period on comic sexual festivity, I summarize the con-clusion reached by several writers on AIDS, that one needs joy—particularly sexual joy—to overcome the fear of life's volatile uncertainty. For example, writing after New York City becomes the "ground zero" of the AIDS epidemic, Andrew Holleran notes:

> The first visit I made to a friend in the hospital convinced me, as I left his room, that the only moral thing to write now was comedy—anything to amuse, to distract, to bring a laugh, an escape from this dreary, relentless, surreal reality. But when it came time to make jokes, the air in which laughter thrives seemed to have dried up. How could one write comedy when the suffering was real? (15)

One doesn't, he learns. Rather, one tries to live life as passionately as possible even when sex, which at one time seemed the only means of that vivacity and enlargement, can be deadly. His progress can be recorded in the final word of his essays, "Enjoy!" (228). Likewise, having withdrawn from all sexual contact and emotional commitment when AIDS makes life "suddenly [. . .] radioactive" (48), the title character in Paul Rudnick's *Jeffrey* is warned by the sexually ram-bunctious Father Dan that "[t]here is only one real blasphemy—the refusal of joy! Of a corsage and a kiss!" (69). Similarly, *"More life"* is the blessing that Prior Walter offers the audience at the conclusion of Tony Kushner's two-part epic drama, *Angels in America* (*Perestroika* 148), which like the *Decameron* depicts a world in the throes of a plague that assumes apocalyptic dimensions. The dan-ger, these writers insist, is to become emotionally paralyzed by trauma; one needs to find a way of celebrating the sexual festivity that allows human conti-nuity, even if only by telling stories about it.[7]

The paper assignment for the term is to compare or contrast one of Boccaccio's tales with any other text studied from the *Norton Anthology* in order to make a statement about how sex can be used to figure the comic and tragic impulses of human existence. I list below some of the more fruitful com-binations that I've received in recent semesters.

1. Panurge's humbling of the proud Parisienne and Brother Alberto's seduction of vain Madonna Lisetta (4.2)
2. The self-sacrificing love of Griselda (10.10) and Marie de France's Guilideuc (*Eliduc*) or of Federigo degli Alberighi (5.9) and Guilideuc
3. Nature versus monastic vows in Rabelais's Abbey of Theleme ("fais ce que vouldras") and any of Boccaccio's tales of the sexual hypocrisy of religious life
4. Fathers who stand in the way of a child's happiness: Tancredi (4.1) or Filippo Balducci (introduction to Day 4), and Count Garin of Beaucaire (*Aucassin and Nicolette*)
5. Tingoccio's comic (7.10) versus Enkidu's tragic description of the afterlife (*Gilgamesh*)
6. Comic stratagems to free a woman of doubts or scruples or from conventions: "handy Nicholas" (Chaucer's Miller's Tale) and Masetto (3.1)
7. Young women saddled with older, stupid, or otherwise unsatisfying husbands: Alison (Chaucer's Miller's Tale) and Madonna Lisetta (4.2)
8. Reluctant or fearful men who blame women for the woes they inflict on themselves: Gualtieri (10.10) and Chanticleer (Chaucer's Nun's Priest's Tale)
9. Containing the overeager phallus: Enkidu's counterbalancing Gilgamesh and the "good man" who exposes Brother Alberto (4.2)
10. Paradise on earth: Rabelais's Abbey of Theleme, Nicolette's bower (*Aucassin and Nicolette*), and Masetto's garden (3.1)

NOTES

[1]"Contempt for [. . .] vegetable existence is characteristic of comedy in general," notes T. G. A. Nelson. "The essence of comedy is vitality, not swinish contentment" (33). When initially presenting the nature and operations of comedy, I like to summarize the plot of Peter Shaffer's *Lettice and Lovage*, quoting the toast with which Lotte concludes the play: "Enlargement for shrunken souls—Enlivenment for dying spirits—Enlightenment for dim, prosaic eyes" (98).

[2]The connection between comedy and sex is a basic one. In the *Poetics* Aristotle locates the origins of comedy in phallic songs and fertility festivals (Nelson 38). "The same impulse that drove people, even in prehistoric times, to enact fertility rites and celebrate all phases of their biological existence, sustains their eternal interest in comedy. It is the nature of comedy to be erotic, risqué, and sensuous if not sensual, impious, and even wicked," notes Susanne K. Langer (349), for "no matter how people contrive to become reconciled to their mortality, it puts its stamp on their conception of life: since the instinctive struggle to go on living is bound to meet defeat in the end, they look for *as much life as possible* between birth and death" (333). I am indebted to Langer's discussion in chapter 18 of "the comic rhythm" as "the basic rhythm of life" (349) and "the essential comic feeling" as "the sentient aspect of organic unity, growth, and self-preservation" (35).

[3]R. Howard Bloch's discussion of episodes in medieval French fabliaux in which the body is reduced to, or transformed into, its sexual members (*Scandal* ch. 2) is a helpful parallel for such an equation, even though he is concerned not with comedy but with the body as text.

[4]Paradoxically, gestation and birth are generally outside the realm of comedy. As Nelson points out, comedy does not aim specifically at procreation; "erotic pleasure, not desire for children, predominates in the real-life sexual act" (58). His explanation can be taken further, however, by recognizing that taking responsibility for an infant demands self-denial on the part of the adult parents, whereas the basic principle of festive comedy is excess, enlargement, and joyous self-indulgence. Thus the few births that I can think of in comedy are invariably farcical, such as the Nativity parody in *The Second Shepherd's Play* and the births of Gargantua and Pantagruel in Rabelais's narrative. The latter, as outrageous and unrealistic as they are, are associated wtih eating and drinking to excess and so are well within the frame of festive comedy. In preparing students to read Boccaccio, I find it important to emphasize comedy's general lack of biological consequence to sexual intercourse.

[5]Unfortunately for my purpose, the Norton Critical Edition includes only two of the ten stories from the seventh day, all of which deal with transgression within the marriage contract—or, to adapt Edith Kern's term, with sexual "carnivalesque justice" (ch. 2). I also regret the absence of 6.7, but I do read to the class that portion of Madonna Filippa's defense in which she argues that it is disgraceful to waste the surplus of her love after her husband has had his fill.

[6]The figurative relation of plague to sexual activity is reinforced by contemporary belief that the plague damaged sex organs (Mazzotta, *World at Play* 29).

[7]Curiously, Holleran reports first looking for inspiration in the *Decameron*. He is disappointed, however, to find that Boccaccio's "plague was merely the pretext for its storytellers to entertain each other with bawdy tales about ordinary life" (14). Holleran's reading of the *Decameron* must have been cursory at best, for his description of his situation quoted above is close in spirit to Boccaccio's.

The *Decameron* and the *Canterbury Tales*

Robert W. Hanning

The task I undertake here is to discuss from a pedagogical perspective the relevance and importance of Giovanni Boccaccio's *Decameron* (*Dec.*) to the study of Geoffrey Chaucer's *Canterbury Tales* (*CT*). (I have for some years taught the two texts together, especially for graduate students.) A stranger to the field of medieval literary studies might be forgiven for thinking that the relevance of the *Decameron* to the *Canterbury Tales* is obvious and unproblematic. Each text presents tales, varied in length, genre, and tone, within a framing fiction that makes them the collective utterance of a fictive ad hoc community brought into temporary existence by particular circumstances. In addition, several of Chaucer's tales tell basically the same story as one (or in one case, two) of the *Decameron*'s novelle. (One might also add that some of the *Canterbury Tales*, like some of Chaucer's early poems, are adapted from other Boccaccian texts such as the *Filocolo*, *Filostrato*, *Teseida*, and *De casibus virorum illustrium*.)

Nonetheless, important differences between the respective framing fictions of the *Decameron* and the *Canterbury Tales*, plus Chaucer's apparent reliance, in telling or retelling tales shared with the *Decameron*, on versions other than those found there, as well as the lack of any overt mention of Bocccaccio or the *Decameron* in the *Canterbury Tales* (or elsewhere in Chaucer's works), have until recently seemed to justify the assumption by many students of late medieval narrative that Chaucer did not know, and was not influenced by, the *Decameron*; the consequent assumption is made that one need not undertake systematic comparisons of the two collections when teaching either (cf. Thompson, introd.).

In what follows, I address three issues. The first (and to me least important) is whether there is any internal evidence that Chaucer knew the *Decameron* (irrespective of whether he knew who composed it). The second is how a juxtaposition of the two texts and attention to their thematic as well as formal similarities help us understand the cultural work being done by both, thereby usefully grounding the *Canterbury Tales* in a larger context of late medieval European concerns. And the third is what some of the differences between the *Canterbury Tales* and the *Decameron*—in the way they tell what is basically the same story or create a framing environment for storytelling—reveal about the two texts' divergent interests within a larger shared cultural agenda.

Although there is no overt mention of the *Decameron* in the *Canterbury Tales*, there is, I think, a covert recognition of Chaucer's debt to the *centonovelle* embedded in the prefatory material to The Man of Law's Tale, a story of the beautiful, pious, long-suffering, and much abused Custance. After complaining that "Chaucer [. . .] hath toold of loveris, up and doun / Mo than Ovide made of mencioun / In his Episteles that been ful olde," the Lawyer adds, "I were right now of tales desolaat, / Nere that a marchant, goon is many a yeere, / Me taught a tale, which that ye shal heere (*CT* 2.47–55, 131–33).[1] Chaucer thus comically repudiates (through his surrogate, the Man of Law) his earlier dependence on classical antecedents (such as Ovid's *Metamorphoses* [also mentioned by the Man of Law, *CT* 2.93] and "Episteles that been ful olde," i.e., the *Heroides*) for his stories and signals obliquely his decision to create a tale collection radically different in form and subjects from *The Legend of Good Women*, the compendium of Ovidian and other classical adaptations on which he had recently been at work (and may well have contiued to compose in tandem with the *Canterbury Tales* over the next several years).

That the tale of Custance, although derived from earlier versions by Nicholas Trevet and John Gower, reads like a novella from the second day of the *Decameron* and is a distant analogue of its novella of Gostanza (5.2) points toward that text as a pattern for this new (to Chaucer) kind of tale-telling. In which case, the Man of Law's narrative debt to a merchant hints at what I take to be the fact that Chaucer owed his first knowledge of the *Decameron* to the "purveiaunce" of merchants who, as the Lawyer puts it, "knowen al th'estaat / of regnes [and] been fadres of tidynges / And tales, bothe of pees and of debaat" (*CT* 2.128–30). The circulation of manuscripts of the *Decameron* among Italian merchants throughout Europe is well documented (Branca, *Boccaccio medievale*), and Chaucer was undoubtedly familiar with the substantial Italian merchant communities of London and Southampton, through both his father's mercantile connections and his own career as controller of customs for the Port of London (Beardwood; Holmes).

My hypothesis is reinforced by the presence in The Man of Law's Tale of two passages that are as close to actual quotations or paraphrases of the *Decameron*'s language as anything in the *Canterbury Tales*. One describes how the "wilde see" carries Custance to the shore of Britain: "Fer in Northumberlond the wawe hire caste, / And in the sond hir ship stiked so faste / That thennes wolde it noght of al a tyde" (*CT* 2.506–10). These lines echo the *Decameron* (161–62):

> E la nave, che da impetuoso vento era sospinta, [. . .] velocissimamente correndo, in una piaggia dell'isola di Maiolica percosse. E fu tanta e sí grande la foga di quella, che quasi tutta si ficcò nella rena, vicino al lito forse una gittata di pietra; e quivi, dal mar combattuta, la notte senza poter più dal vento esser mossa si stette.

> The ship's impetus was so great that it thrust its way firmly into the sand before coming to rest a mere stone's throw from the shore, and since the wind was no longer able to move it, there it remained for the rest of the night, to be pounded by the sea.   (127)

Chaucer's choice of this particular Boccaccian material constitutes another kind of joke, since the much traveled but ever-chaste Custance is an inversion of *Decameron* 2.7's protagonist, the much traveled and much violated Alatiel.

The other Boccaccian reminiscence in The Man of Law's Tale consists of the lines, already quoted, in which the Man of Law confesses he would be "desolaat" of tales were it not for the merchant. In this case, the antecedent comes at the end of the sixth day of storytelling, when Dioneo, charged as newly elected monarch to announce a theme for the next day's novelle, confesses that, given all that has already been said,

> se donna Licisca non fosse poco avanti qui venuta, la quale con le sue parole m'ha trovata materia a' futuri ragionamenti di domane, lo dubito che io non avessi gran pezza penato a trovar tema da ragionare. (*Dec.* 575)

> If Mistress Licisca had not come here a short while ago and said something which offered me a subject for our deliberations on the morrow, I suspect I should have had a hard job to find a suitable theme.   (478)

Licisca, one of several servants whom the *brigata* of young patricians have taken with them to supply their needs and comforts during their self-imposed exile from plague-ravaged Florence, had disrupted the group's decorous routines that morning by arguing raucously with Tindaro, a male servant, about whether Florentine women are virgins when they marry. In addition to insisting that they are not, Licisca boasts, "e anche delle maritate so io ben quante e quali beffe elle fanno a' mariti" (534). ("And as for the married ones, I could tell you a thing or two about the clever tricks they play upon their husbands" [445].) This is the theme that Dioneo appropriates for the *brigata*'s "ragionamenti di domane."

Once again, the homage has a comic dimension. As Dioneo depends on Licisca for his theme, Chaucer appears to be acknowledging that he, too, owes a debt to Licisca, albeit a very different one: the idea of a person of lower estate disrupting the ordained order of storytelling by people of elevated estate. In the *Decameron*, Licisca's insistence on being heard prompts the day's monarch, Elissa, to order her to be silent on pain of a whipping; in Chaucer's hands, the squelched Licisca becomes the unsquelchable Miller, whose defiance of the Host's "monarchic" rule over the pilgrim *compaignye* transforms Harry Bailly's decorous taletelling competition for a free dinner into a discursive occasion fraught with possibilities (often realized) for rancorous social, professional, or economic rivalry among pilgrims and among the groups they represent.

If, as I suggest, Chaucer knew the *Decameron*, then the second issue I address in this essay—how a juxtaposition of the *Decameron* and the *Canterbury Tales* and attention to their thematic as well as formal similarities help us understand the cultural work being done by both—can be inflected somewhat differently, as a survey of the concerns shared by both works that illuminate late medieval cultural assumptions and tensions.

A good place to begin is Chaucer's contention, through his judicial surrogate, that the story of Custance has been transmitted, or circulated, by merchants. The Man of Law's Tale underscores this point by inserting a kind of *mise en abyme* in its opening lines, in which a company of Syrian merchants is represented not only purveying luxury goods from the East to Rome but also reciprocally conveying "tydinges" of Custance back to their patron, the sultan of Syria, who immediately falls in love with her (or the story about her). This repeated emphasis on the link between the circulation of goods and stories by means of a network of commercial intermediaries—and, in the case of stories, on the social, political, and religious connections, rivalries, and crises prompted by such brokerage—suggests a perceived nexus between the framed tale collection, as practiced by Boccaccio and Chaucer, and the complex mediated systems (commercial, but also ecclesiastical and political) that dominated their common late medieval European civilization. The *Decameron* and the *Canterbury Tales*, I would argue, derive much of their originality and energy from their meditation on, and depiction of, such systems and from their recognition that language, the most basic human instrument of mediation, can serve—especially when it transmits stories or established discourses—as both common denominator and metaphor for all other mediated systems.

The nature of, and rationale for, late medieval ecclesiastical, commercial, and political systems varied, but in each case the result was a structure of devolution that benefited both those in command and those who represented them. Each system contains at its core a binary: in Christianity, a perfect, eternal creator and fallen, mortal creatures; in commerce, buyer and seller; in government, ruler and ruled. In each case, experiential or perceptual difficulties require the generation of middle terms to make the system work, resulting in what David Wallace calls "complex networks of dependencies" (*Boccaccio* 26).

With respect to government, the increasingly centralized power of crown or commune generated ever more articulated hierarchies of officials and bureau-cratic administrators who executed the policies of, or served as surrogates for, the ultimate sources of authority and coercion. Concurrently, the institutional church deployed a system of beliefs and obligations whereby the clergy medi-ated the sacraments, which in turn mediated the grace obtained for humanity by Christ's Passion. The older cult of the saints and the newer representation of the Virgin Mary provided further levels of mediation, as did the establishment of the doctrine of purgatory. Throughout late medieval Europe, such complex mediated systems generated a variety of complaints and resistance, especially directed at the corruption (real or perceived) that resulted when the people oc-cupying the mid-level positions appropriated power and profits to themselves or took refuge behind the system to hide their own corruption or failures of re-sponsibility. Moreover, the ecclesiastical and commercial systems, although os-tensibly existing in binary opposition as to their goals—worldly wealth verses eternal salvation—were in fact, as everyone knew, thoroughly intertwined, cre-ating further problems and further resentment.

The first novella of the *Decameron* comically dramatizes the interpenetration of institutional Christianity and international commerce, while the second ex-coriates the corruption engendered at the middle levels of a commercially in-fected church. In 1.1, Cepparello/Ciappelletto, the amoral debt collector for the merchant Musciatto—he is also a notary by trade, another kind of middle-man within a complex legal system—becomes the agent of secular salvation for two Italian moneylenders by inserting himself into the mediated system of Christian grace by means of a false confession to a credulous friar. After the friar intervenes with his convent and the local populace—he in effect becomes Cepparello's agent as Cepparello was Musciatto's—the crooked notary be-comes Saint Ciappelletto, a holy intercessor ("procuratore" ["defense attor-ney"] in the nomenclature supplied by Panfilo, the novella's narrator) for the faithful who pray to him and leave generous offerings for the friars at his tomb, so that Ciappelletto becomes the convent's posthumous collection agent as well.

In 1.2, the Jewish merchant Abraam travels from Paris to Rome as a prelude to possible conversion. What Abraam sees is mediational hybridity run wild: such is the desire for gain that curial officials traffic readily in slaves, sacra-ments, and clerical benefices and do so with more commercial skill and more brokers than could even be found in the Paris cloth trade (*Dec.* 51). To cover their tracks, they have even invented a protective jargon, like merchants dis-guising usury through mediating "credit" instruments: simony becomes "pro-cureria" ("mediation") and gluttony "substentazioni" ("maintenance")—as if, Abraam says, God could, like humans, be misled by such falsely mediating ter-minology into mistaking "la 'ntenzione de' pessimi animi" (*Dec.* 51) ("the inten-tions of their wicked minds" [40]).

Chaucer's treatment of the Custance story in The Man of Law's Tale betrays, if not the influence of this Boccaccian scrutiny of mediated systems, then at least a parallel concern with them. As I have already suggested, Chaucer altered his sources for the tale to emphasize the role of merchants as purveyors of Custance (or the report of her) to the sultan, thus setting in motion an elaborate set of negotiations, which include "the popes mediacioun, / And al the chirche, and al the chivalrie" (*CT* 2.234–35). Custance is consequently dispatched to Syria against her will as a woman exchanged between groups of men (Gayle Rubin's famous formulation, applied to Custance's situation by Carolyn Dinshaw [96]), mediating with her body the sultan's agreement to convert, with his people, to Christianity. In the course of her subsequent perilous adventures, it is through Custance's own "mediacioun" (*CT* 2.684) that Alla, king of the Saxons of Northumberland is converted to Christianity; but the perils of mediated Christianity emerge in a crisis that occurs after Custance marries Alla. Separated by the king's need to go to war, the spouses must communicate by letters transmitted back and forth by a messenger—hence, a doubly mediated system—and the king's evil mother is able to corrupt the system by tampering with both the messenger (whom she inebriates) and the letters (through counterfeit substitutes). In their sincere faith, Custance and Alla, as the dependents of this mediated system, cannot imagine its violation; hence they interpret the counterfeit messages, which ultimately lead to Custance's banishment from Northumberland, as "Goddes sonde," that is, messages transparently communicating to them the providence of the Creator (*CT* 2.760, 826). The Man of Law's Tale thus dramatizes the potential for misinterpretation and victimization inherent in mediated structures and by means of the counterfeit letters equates as analogously perilous political, religious, or discursive systems.

But the presence of written texts (letters) within The Man of Law's Tale's corrupt system of mediated communication should remind us that the *Decameron* and the *Canterbury Tales*, even as they place under scrutiny the possibilities, imperfections, and dangers of late medieval mediated systems, are themselves instances of such systems. In the frame-tale collection, the author is represented by, and the authorial position is diffused and occluded among, surrogate storytellers who inhabit a fictive society, a life located between that of the writer and his or her audience, on the one hand, and that of the stories, with their imaginary or reported versions of social arrangements, on the other.

The resulting deviousness of these frame-tale collections—that is, the difficulty of assigning or assessing authorial responsibility for any particular point of view or polemical posture espoused therein—parallels the strategy of merchants who hid usurious transactions behind deflecting terminological shields or of corrupt clergy who masked their depravity and greed behind institutional authority and its sanctioned discourses. As all readers of the *Decameron* and the *Canterbury Tales* know, the two texts dramatize this very deviousness through their central narrators, raising it to the level of seriocomic self-referentiality. The subtitle of the *Decameron*, "Prencipe Galeotto," borrowed from Dante's

Commedia (*Inferno* 5), bridges two forms of mediated system: the transmission of stories through time and the arrangement of sexual couplings by a go-between. But the narrator, in his introductory comments to Day 4 of story-telling and again at the very end of the work, defends himself against charges that his stories corrupt their readers. He uses an argument that anticipates Freud's famous Jewish joke: he claims that he is only retelling stories told by others and is therefore not to be held responsible for any improprieties expressed in them; that some of the stories require such improprieties if they are to be told properly; that prudes should not read them if they will be offended by them; and that only people with corrupt minds will pay attention to, and be affected by, the words "che tanto honeste non sono" (961) ("language that is less than seemly" [799]).

Presumably responding to such Boccaccian tactics, or at least paralleling them, the Chaucerian narrator of the *Canterbury Tales* justifies the bawdy or disreputable stories he is about to relate by insisting that he is only repeating what others said and that

> Whoso shal telle a tale after a man,
> He moot reherce as ny as evere he kan
> Everich a word, if it be in his charge,
> Al speke he never so rudeliche and large,
> Or ellis he moot telle his tale untrewe [. . .].   (*CT* 1.731–35)

And a bit later, in apologizing for telling the "cherles tales" of the Miller and Reeve, he repeats his obligation to transmit all he has heard, even the most potentially offensive tales; it is up to the potentially offended audience to "turne over the leef and chese another tale; / [. . .] Blameth nat me if that ye chese amys" (*CT* 1.3169, 3177, 3181).

The effect of such passages, expressing all too obvious strategies of self-exculpation, is to comment on and enact, albeit comically, the potential for both transgression and the avoidance of responsibility, as well as the inevitable occlusion of the loci of real power and authority, inherent in mediated systems. But these moments also assimilate poet-audience relations to the tensions involved in the social dominance of such systems: we are invited to see the poet as a rather slippery middleman, using his wits, and exploiting the possibilities for avoiding responsibility, to fend off the censure of his listeners-readers as he purveys to them goods that may be morally damaged or politically dangerous or both.

Errors and slippage in transmission—a problem in any political chain of command or institutional dissemination of information and doctrine, as well as in a manuscript culture dependent on scribal reproduction of texts and documents—figure prominently in *Decameron* 7.1. A wife forgets to change a signal (an ass's skull on a stick) that welcomes or warns off her lover, so that he arrives while her husband is at home; she alerts the lover to the danger by reciting a spell against ghosts, which is actually a coded message to him to go away. Having told the tale, Emilia proceeds to offer another version of its crisis point:

> [. . .] alcuni dicono che la donna aveva ben volto il teschio dello asino verso Fiesole, ma un lavoratore per la vigna passando v'aveva entro dato d'un bastone e fattol girare intorno intorno, e era rimaso volto verso Firenze.   (591)

> Some people maintain that the lady had in fact turned the skull of the ass towards Fiesole, and that a farmhand, passing through the vineyard, had poked his stick inside it and given it a good twirl, so that it ended up facing towards Florence.   (489)

Emilia then gives another version of the comic incantation, only to suggest that both versions may be true, since, according to an ancient neighbor of hers, each happened to a different man named Gianni (cf. Marcus, *Allegory*, ch. 6; Fido, "Rhetoric").

In other words, variance stalks the transmission of stories and messages of all kinds. Faced with this fact, Emilia counsels the ladies of the *brigata*, "nella vostra elezione sta di torre qual più vi piace delle due" (592) ("I therefore leave it to you [. . .] to choose the version you prefer" [490]), although, she adds, learning both may be the better course, as either, under particular circumstances, may come in handy in fooling one's husband. Generalized, Emilia's advice suggests that the slippage—of truth, of authority, of responsibility—inherent in mediated systems cannot be avoided, but it can, when understood, be manipulated (like the ass's head?) for eloquential and competitive advantage. The gratuitous opportunity of such slippage thus functions as a kind of grace for those ready to see and exploit its advantage.

Problems of slippage in transmission, both deliberate and accidental, figure in the *Canterbury Tales* as well. In The General Prologue, the narrator, while excusing himself for presenting an unedited transcript of his pilgrim companions' words and deeds, manages to make problematic the process (neutral transmission of scandalous material) behind which he is seeking to hide; I will repeat, and extend, his apology, already quoted above:

> Whoso shal telle a tale after a man,
> He moot reherce as ny as evere he kan
> Everich a word, if it be in his charge,
> Al speke he never so rudeliche and large,
> Or ellis he moot telle his tale untrewe,
> Or feyne thyng, or fynde wordes newe.
> He may nat spare, althogh he were his brother;
> He moot as wel sey o word as another.   (*CT* 1.731–38)

It is, I think, impossible to hear or read these lines without becoming confused about the referents of the word "he" scattered through them. The result is to create the syntactic equivalent of slippage in the transmission of stories. Who is responsible for what, when?

A similar syntactic metaphor for the perils of transmission occurs in The Manciple's Tale, where we are told of the white crow trained to speak by his master, the god Phebus Apollo, that "countrefete the speche of every man / he koude whan he wolde tell a tale" (*CT* 9.134–35). Does the second "he" refer to the crow or the "man" he is imitating? (cf. Axton 34). If it refers to the man, the implication is that there is a particular tale-telling voice, which would in effect be the voice of the representative of a mediated system—literary, religious, commercial, political—the ideological voice and, by extension, the official message it relays.

But as we have seen, official voices and their messages can be counterfeited, and the problem of transmission receives its starkest exposition, already considered here, in the episode of counterfeit letters in The Man of Law's Tale, where deliberate slippage introduced into the mediated chain of communication between Alla and Custance leads to her separation from her husband, near ravishment, and several more years of exile at sea.

One interesting and important consequence of the *Decameron* and the *Canterbury Tales* being tale collections encased in, and mediated by, the framing fiction of a congeries of tale tellers is the displacement away from an authorial point of origin, and into the mouths of the dramatis personae, of satiric and polemical discourses borrowed from the circumambient culture. Such recourse to fictive intermediaries emphasizes what I call the sitedness of these discourses, that is, their status as expressions of particular personal or class interests, rather than statements of fact; they constitute what I have just referred to, in considering Phebus's talking crow, as the tale-telling voice. In the *Decameron*, the *brigata* of tale tellers share youth, gentle status, wealth, and an attachment to ideals of personal and social decorum, and this commonality of rank, outlook, and class relations establishes a collective sitedness and a distinctive tale-telling voice, with respect to the world outside.

For example, if Chaucer had indeed read the *Decameron*, he would have found in several novelle and in the prefatory remarks of their tellers attacks on the mendicant orders reflecting a widespread lay anticlericalism (see 3.3, 4.2). On another front, Neifile's novella (7.8) (in which Monna Sismonda cuckolds her husband, Arriguccio, and then cleverly turns against him his accusation of her to her kinfolk) depicts Arriguccio as a nouveau riche merchant, recently arrived in Florence from its *contado*, who has "married up" to the daughter of an established patrician family, and for that reason is ridiculed by Neifile. The representation of sited discourses in the *Canterbury Tales* goes even further than in the *Decameron*, as a function of two linked choices made by Chaucer in constructing his framing fiction: to make his surrogate tale tellers a diverse company and, as I have already mentioned, to dramatize the rivalries—of profession, rank, or gender—among them.

Within the *Decameron's* socially homogeneous *brigata*, rivalry is primarily constituted as a genteel, stylized battle of the sexes, its discursive weapons being euphemism and double entendre. Although rivalries between professions, classes, communes, and kings abound in the novelle, they lose some of their power to move or shock as instances of discourse—political, satirical, or erotic—sited within the *brigata's* refined existence, where they function as elements of a recreational, therapeutic regime (Olson).

The *Canterbury Tales* embodies the same distancing effect, but in a less comfortable version than the *Decameron's*. Because the pilgrim *compaignye* embraces a fairly wide range of social stations, drawn primarily from the ranks of the gentry, middling professions, and lesser crafts, it offers more sites for the production of interested discourses. And as Chaucer constructs his unfinished framing fiction, he opposes to the model of social decorum and harmony I believe he knew in the *Decameron* a contrary paradigm, one of pilgrims who bring professional rivalries and class animosities with them on the road to Canterbury. This decision allows Chaucer to cast several of his tales as instances par excellence of pilgrim sitedness: agonic exercises that transform the Host's holiday competition into an occasion for expressing personal or group resentments and settling old scores. To this end, pilgrims press into service preexistent satirical and polemical discourses, fabliaux, and moral exempla and in the process demonstrate what I take to be one of Chaucer's main points: many, if not all, combative indictments or negative characterizations must be understood in the context of the particular interests and agendas they promote.

The major example of such sitedness of description is the narrator of the *Canterbury Tales*, who, if he shares with his *Decameron* counterpart a penchant for playing the role of the innocent mediator of others' stories, differs from that worthy in his attempt to describe for his audience subjectively, "so as it semed me" (*CT* 1.39), the nine and twenty in whose company he has recently spent several days on pilgrimage to the shrine of Saint Thomas the martyr. Faced with such a task of re-creation, the narrator brings to it both the lens of "estates theory" and "estates satire" (see Mann)—by-products respectively of traditional, conservative social analysis and penitential taxonomizing—and what I call the erotics of memory: recollections, often acute, of particular pilgrims' bodily or behavioral features that attracted or repelled him. One can hardly read the portraits of the Knight, Prioress, or Pardoner attentively without becoming aware of the extent to which they are exercises in subjective, sited description.

Other famous instances of discursive sitedness in the *Canterbury Tales* include The Reeve's Tale of a thieving miller and The Summoner's Tale, an antifraternal satire told in response to The Friar's Tale about a summoner carried off to hell for seeking to extort money from an old woman. Compared with instances of antifraternal discourse by members of the *Decameron brigata*,

Chaucer's use of it in the context of a feud between pilgrims at once endows it with topical and strategic intensity and demonstrates beyond cavil its availability as a discursive weapon, rather than a dispassionate analysis of facts, by those who, like the extortionate Summoner or like the parish clergy of late medieval England, are caught up in economic competition with the mendicant orders.

Understanding the *Decameron* and the *Canterbury Tales* as, in part, collections of sited discourses—stories that, in the former work, express generally shared, status-based outlooks within a setting of relaxed, therapeutic escape from social crisis and, in the latter, bring contrasting or inimical outlooks into rather more anxious juxtaposition—can be reformulated as an appreciation of the two texts as analogous exercises in social eloquence and as fictive models of social construction.

By social eloquence I mean the use of established discourses and narratives for persuasive, not just communicative or recreational, purposes. In creating communities or polities the chief activity of which is storytelling, the *Decameron* and the *Canterbury Tales* suggest that social and political existence are defined and propelled through time by the ongoing construction of useful fictions: fictions of self and others, of private desires and public activities, of individual and group trajectories; fictions that solidify personal and group conscience, construct or stigmatize other individuals and groups, and suggest proper or improper ways for individuals, families, and polities to pursue goals, fulfill desires, deal with associates, allies, or rivals.

But as a prelude to depicting the process of constructing society by constructing (or, more precisely, by self-interestedly transmitting or reconstructing) fictions, what kind of polities do the *Decameron* and the *Canterbury Tales* construct by means of their framing fictions? In fact, the introductions to both texts illustrate in some detail processes by which a community takes shape—processes that, while fictional, resonate with actual, contemporaneous social practices and issues and thus constitute a major dimension of the cultural work done by the *Decameron* and the *Canterbury Tales*.

The *Decameron* locates the origin of its ad hoc polity in prudential decision making—in this case, the decision to leave Florence—by similar, and likeminded, people who form an alliance against the deleterious effects of a sociopolitical calamity. The *Decameron*'s representation of the *brigata*'s self-construction thus stresses a hegemony that is as fragile and contingent as it is self-involved and all-controlling. Repeatedly stressed in the novelle is the crucial importance of eloquence in the functioning of the social order, as well as in the pursuit of personal happiness. At one extreme, elaborate speeches, illustrating quite precisely one or more of classical rhetoric's basic categories—forensic, deliberative, and epideictic orations—abound. At the other extreme, a few well-chosen words—an aphorism, a metaphor, a joke; what the *brigata* call a *motto* or "pronta risposta" ("a quick comeback")—uttered at precisely the right moment, can completely transform the speaker's situation from negative to positive, hopeless to triumphant.

Comparison and contrast of the *Decameron's brigata* with the society constructed in The General Prologue of the *Canterbury Tales* and carried out
through the unfinished interstitial exchanges of its framing fiction, provide a
range of useful insights both social and poetic. In the *Canterbury Tales*, the pilgrim community takes its origin from an inextricably mixed natural and spiritual
impulse to celebrate new life, snatched from the jaws of winter's dark and sickness's ravages, "whan that Aprill, with his shoures soote, / The droghte of March
hath perced to the roote" (*CT* 1.1–2). This impulse—different, yet not entirely
different, from the *brigata's* desire to escape the plague—played out along the
network of well-worn pilgrimage roads "from every shires ende / of Engelond"
to the shrine of Becket the martyr, eventually brings together at the Tabard in
Southwark "wel nyne and twenty in a compaignye / of sondry folk, by aventure
yfalle / in felaweshipe" (*CT* 1.15–16, 24–26). Out of this coincidence comes a
functioning community, in which language plays a more than merely communi-
cational role. First the narrator talks himself into the nascent community: "so
hadde I spoken with hem everichon / That I was of hir felaweship anon" (*CT*
1.31–32). Then its members begin to negotiate agreements out of mutual interest: they "made forward erly for to ryse / to take our weye" to Canterbury (*CT*
1.33–34). Only at this point, with something like a parliamentary system in
place for making laws among varying social strata, does Harry Bailly, Host of
the Tabard, intervene to impose his own rules on the pilgrimage, with the
somewhat grudging acquiescence of the newly governed (cf. *CT* 1.784–87).

Harry proposes a social model in which competition, under his supervision
and control, will increase general satisfaction, or "mirthe." In fact, his eloquence introduces a new element of verbal legerdemain into the process of
community formation: a discourse of common profit that occludes the personal
profit he will derive from having the pilgrim company return to his inn for a
farewell dinner and an embrace of competitive storytelling that masks the real
competition involved, namely, Harry's with other Southwark innkeepers. (The
only specific information about the Tabard's location is that it is "faste by the
Belle" [*CT* 1.719], that is, another inn with which Harry must compete for
the pilgrim and other trade.)

Harry Bailly's installation of himself as absolute and unique monarch over an
already established polity constitutes an interesting and perhaps transgressive
commentary on the often tense relations between king and Parliament (especially the Commons) at the time Chaucer was writing. The progression from
multistatus "felaweship" to monarchy also mimics and inverts the Ciceronian
myth of social origins at the beginning of the widely known rhetorical manual,
De inventione, where a single eloquent man is able to turn a previously savage
humanity into a law-abiding polity with differentiated occupations analogous to
those of the Chaucerian *compaignye*. But notwithstanding Harry's rule, and in
obvious (and I believe deliberate) contrast to the *Decameron's* socially exclusive
brigata, the inclusive pilgrim company soon (indeed, after the Knight's opening
tale) abandons social harmony, and some of its members, from the Miller on-

ward, prefer to commandeer sited discourses and preexistent stories as instruments of social agon. Such appropriative verbal strategies are analogous to, yet instructively different from, the Ciceronian set speeches given to characters in the *Decameron's novelle* (and occasionally, in the framing fiction, to members of the *brigata*, as when Pampinea deploys her rhetorical skills to convince her women friends to leave Florence before they too become the plague's victims [20–23]). And—a final touch of Chaucerian resistance to Boccaccian social construction—where the *brigata* agrees its pleasure would be hindered by the arrival of outsiders, Chaucer scripts the arrival of a canon and his yeoman amidst the pilgrims en route and makes it the occasion for a reconception of the principles of *descriptio* operative in The General Prologue.

By admitting into its framing fiction professional rivalries and institutionally grounded (as opposed to conversationally inflected) gender tensions (The Wife of Bath's attack on clerical misogyny prompts rejoinders by the Friar, the Clerk of Oxenford, and the Nun's Priest), *Canterbury Tales* defines its constructed society as, at times, a rough-and-tumble interplay of interests and quest for mastery. That Chaucer displaces criticism away from institutions and onto individuals, avoids imprudent attacks on powerful figures, and hides his own opinions, whatever they may be, behind the pilgrims' mediating voices (while pretending, through his narrator, to be only the innocent mediator of *their* opinions) does not change the fact that the *Canterbury Tales* as a whole, like the *Decameron* with its different strategies, offers a simulacrum—however distanced and comically sanitized—of many of the controversies, polemics, and cultural anxieties of its time and place. For example, comparison of the two collections with respect to issues of confession and penance—component parts of the only centrally rhetorical Christian sacrament and foci of continuing ecclesiastical and lay anxiety—offers extremely interesting insights into their strategies of indirect cultural observation and critique.

I turn, finally, to a consideration of tales shared by the *Decameron* and the *Canterbury Tales*. That five of the twenty-four tales in Chaucer's text have obvious analogues in the *Decameron* (the Reeve's [9.6], the Clerk's [10.10], the Merchant's [7.9], Franklin's [10.5], Shipman's [8.1, 8.2]) while two others (the Man of Law's [5.2], the Miller's [3.4]) are more distantly related has seemed to some a clear indication of Chaucer's knowledge of the *Canterbury Tale's* Italian forerunner. Some explanation must be offered for the fact that in almost all these instances, Chaucer's version is closer to other antecedent versions than to the *Decameron's*. (In the case of The Clerk's Tale, Petrarch's Latin translation of the *Decameron* 10.10 is the immediate antecedent; The Franklin's Tale is closer to Boccaccio's earlier version of that tale in book 4 of *Il filocolo* than to the *Decameron* 10.5.)

The comparison of the *Decameron* and the *Canterbury Tales* versions of the same story is a fairly straightforward and quite rewarding classroom exercise, of which I offer but one example. For *Decameron* 9.6 and The Reeve's Tale, the common antecedent is a French fabliau much like the extant "Le meunier et les

II. clers" ("The Miller and the Two Clerks"). At the core of the story, the head of a family comprising husband, wife, and two children—a nubile daughter and an infant—invites two young men to share their single bedroom. During the night, one visitor has sex with the daughter (an encounter premeditated by at least one member of that couple), the other with the wife (a more impromptu encounter, brought about by the infant's cradle being moved, by design or inadvertence, from beside its mother's bed to the young man's while the wife is temporarily out of the room). The displaced cradle also brings the first young man mistakenly into the husband's bed instead of his own when he returns from his time with the daughter. His boast (supposedly to his friend) awakens the husband and leads to a crisis that is differently resolved in all three versions.

In the French version, the young men are poor clerics who propose to make a living as bakers during a time of famine; they bring wheat to the mill, where the miller cheats them by stealing both their grain and their horse, although they do not realize this. The miller offers the bewildered and impoverished clerics hospitality, and the subsequent sexual escapades in the dark constitute attempts by the young clerics to make the most of a bad situation. Physical violence results after the miller's accidental discovery that his daughter has had sex with one of the strangers, and during the altercation the wife reveals inadvertently that the miller has stolen the clerics' grain and horse. Having beaten the miller, the clerics retrieve their property.

Boccaccio's adaptation of this tale secularizes the young men, making them wealthy young Florentine patricians, Pinuccio and Adriano. Pinuccio loves Niccolosa, daughter of a humble innkeeper in a village just outside Florence, and she, pleased to have a noble admirer, reciprocates his passion. Her father, decriminalized by Boccaccio, becomes the dupe of Pinnuccio's plot to consummate his desires. (The story sanitizes the situation of young Florentine patricians who, required to marry on grounds of family advantage rather than personal desire, often satisfied their sexual needs before and during marriage by forced or consensual liaisons with women of lower status.) After Pinuccio and Adriano have, by a ruse, convinced the innkeeper to let them spend the night at the inn, Pinuccio and Niccolosa mingle consensually. The cradle, moved deliberately in the fabliau, is here moved accidentally, so Adriano's sexual pleasure with the wife is an unexpected, but quickly seized occasion when she mistakenly enters his bed. And when Pinuccio, similarly confused, tells the innkeeper instead of Adriano how fine sex with Niccolosa has been, the potentially disastrous situation is defused by the quick thinking of the wife, who with the connivance of Adriano convinces her husband that Pinuccio has been dreaming of lovemaking and has been walking in his sleep. The wife's eloquence, a kind of extended *pronta risposta*, saves the day; the innkeeper is mollified, Pinuccio and Niccolosa satisfied, and the wife, persuaded by Niccolosa's insistent avowals of chastity, convinced that only she has tasted the pleasure of sex with a handsome stranger.

As David Wallace suggests (*Polity*), this novella of Boccaccio's is one of many in which canny Florentines make fools of country folk. But it is also a story of how eloquence can prevent violence and facilitate the attainment of personal desires. The wife's quick-witted response to an explosive situation is held up to admiration as a lubricant for social relations between disparate classes that threaten to turn sour. Although the wife has in effect conspired to let Pinuccio have her daughter, her main aim is clearly to save the daughter's reputation (for future marriage to one of her own rank) and to prevent a nasty encounter, which her husband, outranked by Pinuccio, can hardly expect to win in the long run. The message can be read as a recommendation of eloquence over violence, of negotiation rather than confrontation as a principle of postplague Florentine multiclass politics. That Pinuccio, representing the patriciate, is the clear winner reminds us of the sitedness of this novella's discourse of negotiation: it is told, as are all the novelle of the *Decameron*, by someone allied in rank to Pinuccio rather than to the humble innkeeper.

By contrast, The Reeve's Tale compounds the violence of the French fabliau. The reason is easy to seek: the Reeve appropriates a fabliau of violence against a Miller as a sited discourse expressing his anger at the pilgrim Miller, Robin, for (in the Reeve's view) having insulted him by telling a tale in which a carpenter (the Reeve's other occupation) is cuckolded. The rivalry between the Reeve and the Miller, emblematic of the difference between the harmonious world of the *Decameron's brigata* and the more agonic "sondry folk" of the *Canterbury Tale's* framing fiction, is in fact overdetermined (reeves and millers were often manorial enemies, while the physical contrast between the robust Robin and the spindly Oswald is near absolute). The Reeve's resentment fuels an adaptation of the fabliau that loses no occasion to attack Robin through his literary surrogate. (That the Reeve can mount no physical attack only gives him further impetus to sharpen his fictional one.) Thus the Miller in this version is not only a thief but a bully and a ridiculous snob with an absurdly presumptuous plan to marry his daughter genteelly because his wife is the village parson's illegitimate offspring. His antagonists are two Cambridge students who speak with Northern accents (sure signs to Chaucer's audience of their stereotypical dim-wittedness), yet these yokels not only rape the Miller's wife and daughter—thus sullying his lineage and marital fantasies—but also beat the Miller to a pulp himself and get their stolen grain back with the assistance of the daughter.

In short, at every turn where he adapts the French fabliau, Chaucer does so in a direction opposite to Boccaccio's. If Chaucer did indeed know the *Decameron*, we may, I believe, assume that he recognized the changes wrought by the Italian master on the French fabliau and, in keeping with his very different, rivalrous conception of the framing fiction—a construction of society as agonic rather than harmonious—decided to modify the fabliau to create a tale the sitedness of which, in the Reeve's mouth, was as appropriate to the competitive world of the Canterbury-bound *compaignye* as the *Decameron* 9.6 is to the world of the elegant young Florentines.

Mutatis mutandis, a pedagogical approach to the shared tales of the

Decameron and the *Canterbury Tales* will be most fruitful if it recognizes Boccaccio's and Chaucer's common interest in mediated systems yet remains attentive to how diversely the two writers responded to the same challenge: constructing an ad hoc society whose fiction making stands in complex but suggestive relation to the mediated structures of their respective worlds.

NOTE

[1]Citations of the *Decameron* in English are from G. H. McWilliam's translation. Citations of the *Canterbury Tales* are from *The Riverside Chaucer*.

The Novella Tradition in Italy after Boccaccio

James H. McGregor

The novella is an important, interesting, and generally pleasurable genre, but it is difficult to teach. Approaching it in Italian, the instructor is confounded by the enormity of the field. The series of anthologies published by Garzanti help to limit the choices while they include a rich sampling of the tradition (*Novelle italiane: Il Trecento*, ed. Lucia Battaglia Ricci; *Il Quattrocento*, ed. Gioachino Chiarini; *Il Cinquecento*, ed. Marcello Ciccuto). The instructor who attempts to teach the tradition in English faces the opposite problem. Despite the importance and appeal of the novella, access to it in English translation is severely limited. Two anthologies have appeared within recent years. *Italian Renaissance Tales*, edited and translated by Janet Smarr, is unique in that it includes selections not only from the novelle of individual writers but materials from the frame sequences as well. The translations are very readable, and there are abundant notes and a detailed bibliography. The collection is out of print, but I have used it twice in courses after obtaining permission to photocopy it from the publisher at a nominal cost. Valerie Martone and Robert L. Martone have produced a more limited anthology, *Renaissance Comic Tales of Love, Treachery, and Revenge*.

Smarr's translation begins with nine tales from *Il novellino*, written in the late thirteenth century, and ends with selections from Giambattista Basile's *Il Pentameron*, published posthumously between 1634 and 1636. Between these two poles Smarr includes selections from the most celebrated authors including Franco Sacchetti (d. 1400) and his near contemporary Ser Giovanni Fiorentino; Giovanni Sercambi (d. 1428); Masuccio Salernitano (d. 1475); Antonio Manetti (d. 1497), who is famous for the extended, unframed *Il grasso legnaiuolo*, translated by Smarr as "Fatso the Carpenter." Luigi da Porto (d. 1529), author of the *Giulietta*, another unframed, single novella and the source of Shakespeare's *Romeo and Juliet*, bridges the fifteenth and sixteenth centuries. Giovan Francesco Straparola, author of the *Piacevoli notti* (d. 1558?); Matteo Bandello (d. c. 1561), who wrote unframed novelle with introductory letters; and Basile complete the collection.

Like Smarr's, the Martone anthology includes selections from Bandello and Masuccio, but there are no duplications. In addition the Martone anthology includes novelle from the unframed collection of Gentile Sermini (active first half of fifteenth century). Two novelle from *Il paradiso degli Alberti*, by Giovanni Gherardi da Prato (d. 1446?), and one by Lorenzo de' Medici (d. 1492) complete the fifteenth century. Two novelle from *Le cene*, by Anton Francesco Grazzini (d. 1584), are the only representatives of the sixteenth century in this collection. Given the thematic bias of the collection, the relatively small number of texts it includes and its focus on the novella writers of the fifteenth century, it seems too slim to stand by itself, but it makes a useful supplement to the Smarr collection.

When I teach the novella tradition in translation, I begin with selections from the *Decameron* (which, wisely, is excluded from Smarr's anthology). These usually include the proem, the introduction to Day 1, and all the stories from that day. In addition I add all of Day 4 and the Bruno and Buffalmacco stories (8.3, 8.6, 8.9, 9.3, 9.5). I include all the novelle in Smarr's anthology, paying special attention to the stories focused on women, as most of Boccaccio's Day 4 stories are, and on *Il grasso legnaiuolo*, which carries out many of the themes of the Bruno and Buffalmacco stories. The two stories by Grazzini in the Martone anthology are also related to these novelle. I include two texts that are not novella collections but that have clear links to the tradition, Giorgio Vasari's *Le vite de' più eccellenti pittori, scultori e architettori* (*Lives of the Artists*) and Baldassare Castiglione's *Il cortegiano* (*Courtier*). In Castiglione we read books 2 and 3. Book 2 is concerned with humor, and it offers a guide to the courtier's effective use of anecdotes and bon mots, or *motti*. Book 3 of the *Cortegiano* focuses on the woman courtier. Novelle are extensively used there as well, not as techniques of social interaction as they are for men, but as a source of anecdotes and exempla, which are argued to be better suited for reaching women. All the participants in the dialogue, male and female, agree that the inferiority of women's education and their widespread illiteracy make the novella a more effective tool in reaching them than the logical arguments in which men have been trained.

In the final weeks of the course, I usually move to the tradition outside Italy. Marguerite de Navarre's *Heptaméron* is directly linked to the *Decameron*, but it brings elements into the tradition that are distinct and that students find exciting. Marguerite's work is discussed in this volume in Aldo Scaglione's essay on the novella tradition outside Italy. The course ends with some reference to the dramatic works that are rooted in the novella tradition. These are the subject of the essay by Angelo Mazzocco and Elizabeth Mazzocco.

My aim in the course is to present students with the broadest possible exposure to the range of novella types. I hope the course will lead them to arrive at their own definition of the genre's range and concerns. I also want them to understand one of the strong popular currents that feeds into the reorganization and redefinition of literature in the Italian Renaissance. Students who approach the Italian Renaissance without such a background in popular literature are prone to overestimate the role classical models play in literary debate and in texts like the *Cortegiano* or Vasari's *Vite*. Much of the dynamism of the Italian Renaissance comes from the continual dialogue between classical and popular forms, but in many Renaissance texts only one half of that dialogue is explicitly identified. Classicism dominates the language of debate so completely that popular forms and ideas must be repackaged in classical terms in order to be heard.

Numerous texts have focused on the difficult issue of what defines the novella as a genre (see "Materials," "The Novella Tradition," in this volume).

One approach is offered by Erich Auerbach. In his celebrated essay on Boccaccio's novella about Frate Alberto, Auerbach considers the origins and development of the genre to which the *Decameron* belongs. As a literary movement, he argues, the novella collection grew out of, and reflected important transformations in, the social and psychological realm:

> Inner and outer perception broadened, threw off the fetters of class restriction, even invaded the realm of learning, thitherto the prerogative of clerical specialists, and gradually gave it the pleasant and winning form of personal culture in the service of social intercourse. (219)

It is easy to see in this blanket description a number of features that tie the novella as a genre to broad currents in social and literary history. The broadening of inner and outer perception, to which Auerbach first refers, reflects Jakob Burckhardt's notions of the new consciousness of self and the sharpening of all forms of perception that distinguished men and women of the Renaissance from those of the Middle Ages. These changes lead to an ascendancy within and ultimate domination over cultural and economic life by the bourgeoisie—a domination, as Auerbach points out, that extends into the field of learning, where it challenges a traditional clerical monopoly. Yet, Auerbach suggests, this movement toward self-consciousness and cultural hegemony by the bourgeoisie is "pleasant and winning." Such personal culture is not to be understood as self-centered or as antagonistic toward others. It has an aesthetic dimension both in actuality and in its presentation in the novella, and it is implicitly or explicitly "in the service of social intercourse."

One could easily quarrel with Auerbach's assertions, and many scholars have taken issue with the theories he embraces. Students of the Renaissance who follow Stephen Greenblatt rather than Burckhardt would certainly counter the uncomplex and optimistic picture of Renaissance individualism Auerbach offers. Many Boccaccio scholars, most prominent among them Vittore Branca, would argue that Boccaccio himself (although not the novella tradition) represents a peculiarly medieval rather than Renaissance or proto-Renaissance development. A Marxist historian would recognize the progressive nature of the first phase of bourgeois culture, but such an untroubled picture of bourgeois cultural hegemony as Auerbach paints would not appeal to Marxist sensibilities. While giving these objections their due, I would like to return to a principal feature of Auerbach's description, the notion that in the novella tradition we have the "pleasant and winning form of personal culture in the service of social intercourse." This statement certainly captures a lot of what is richest in the novella tradition: the portrayal of individuals who are interesting precisely in their unique abilities and characteristics and a new kind of didacticism that establishes such individuals—often humorously presented—as models for social formation.

As Franco Sachetti points out in his introduction to the *Trecentonovelle*, "la gente è vaga di udire cose nuove, e spezialmente di quelle letture che sono agevoli a intendere" (3) ("people are eager to hear new things and especially for readings that are easy to understand" [my trans.]). In this he combines two of the essential features of Auerbach's description, the appeal of the new and the importance of a pleasant, accessible style. A more direct appeal to this new didacticism is made in the introduction of the *Novellino*: "let us here recall some flowers of speech, of handsome courtesies, witty replies, fine worthy deeds, handsome gifts and noble loves enacted in times past" (Smarr, *Tales* 2). But these are differences of emphasis, not of opinion, and both the *Novellino* and the *Trecentonovelle*, and with them the bulk of the novella tradition, refer their collection to the larger ends of "recreation" (Clements and Gibaldi 8–12).

The novella collection, then, gives us a portrait of what there is to be enjoyed about the new ways of living that were developing in the Italian city-states as the Middle Ages waned, and it chronicles new attitudes toward this life. The genre itself might be considered exemplary of these new developments in culture. It is not a learned form, and as Armando Balduino has shown, serious men of letters shied away from it (161). Freed from the claims of high purpose, it was available to chronicle the ephemeral aspects of popular culture and to reflect viewpoints beyond the range of serious literature. Both in subject matter and in audience it breaks new ground. The vicissitudes of the merchant's life, for example, are hardly represented in serious literature, but they are a major preoccupation of the novelle. The incessant traveling, the animosity of strangers, the shrewd deals, the losses, and the missed opportunities are all recurrent themes (Clements and Gibaldi 127–39). An excellent example of the celebration of mercantile ingenuity is found in story 175 of Sacchetti. Antonio Pucci is the owner of a walled garden of which he is inordinately proud, and one night some friends find a way to introduce three destructive animals into it. Sacchetti's story is interested less in this practical joke, however, than in the cleverness Antonio demonstrates in uncovering the guilty parties. A more romanticized version of the merchant's life is found in Ser Giovanni Fiorentino's story 4, "A merchant's son making three voyages nearly ruins his adoptive father in order to win a wealthy lady who then saves the old man's life" (Smarr, *Tales* vi). This story, from the collection called *Il Pecorone* ("The Big Sheep"), is the source for Shakespeare's *Merchant of Venice*.

Illicit love affairs are the most common subject in the novella tradition. Sexual misconduct is interesting in itself, of course, but there is also an important historical dimension to this theme in the novella. Since social transformation of any kind is likely to be accompanied by changes in the relationship between men and women, the subject, despite its evident antiquity and ubiquity, also reflects new social realities. As life patterns change, new opportunities for love affairs are created. Novelle can reflect, applaud, or deplore these opportunities themselves and the activities they lead to, and in the process this genre reaffirms established moral positions or paves the way for new ideals. As many have contended, novelle can chronicle and articulate new mores for men and women to supplement the morality of the confessional. The official condemnation of such sexual activity hides the fact that love affairs can be carried on in ways that are arguably better or worse. Both fornication and rape are morally wrong, but as the novella evolves, one is clearly portrayed as worse than the other. Distancing itself from the way religion and ethics portray the world, the novella tradition describes action in a realm of pragmatic values.

If we accept the calculations of Dominic P. Rotunda, in "A Tabulation of Early Italian Tales," on average one in every five stories is focused on this theme. The stories are most often told from the male point of view, and women in the novella tradition are commonly portrayed as objects of desire. Despite this objectification, the roles women play in the novelle often break with tradition. In a significant number of stories women are portrayed as ingenious and courageous protagonists in the pursuit of love. Individual authors vary in their assessment of these characteristics. Boccaccio appears to applaud them and defends them explicitly in such novelle as 4.1; Masuccio portrays such women as monsters, especially in a story like 24 under the rubric, "A youth loves a lady but is not loved in return; he hides in her house; a blackamoor has carnal knowledge of the lady where the youth is hidden [; . . .] he rebukes the lady's wickedness and his love is changed to hatred" (Smarr, *Tales* vii).

Frequently the novella collections show the oppressive conditions under which women, especially women of the upper classes, were forced to live (Clements and Gibaldi 165–83). Probably the most famous novella on the theme of illicit love is the *Giulietta* of Luigi da Porto. The lesser-known *Bianchabella (Piacevoli notti* 3.3), by Straparola, a distant ancestor of Snow White, displays in fantastic terms the oppressive conditions of women's lives and the near impossibility of a realistic remedy.

While the focus of the collections is frequently on the activities of the bourgeoisie, the lives of the rich and famous are a constant interest (Clements and Gibaldi 98–124). Emperors, kings, and noblemen are especially prominent in the *Novellino*. While Sachetti sees the nobility as a resource that the wise bourgeois can exploit, in the tradition generally nobles are most often seen through a sentimental haze or from a melodramatic point of view. They appear at a distance from the world of the novella and its audience. Bandello reflects this dual viewpoint in 1.26 (Smarr, *Tales* 205–14), the story of Antonio Bologna and the duchess of Amalfi.

Although nobles are viewed from a distance, the omnipresent clergy are viewed up close. By Rotunda's measure, roughly one in ten of the novelle focus on clerics of various sorts, and the bulk of these are satirical. To read the novelle is to discover the medieval and Renaissance obsession with the men and women of the cloth, not primarily in their performance of the sacred offices but in their abundant shortcomings. The novelle repeatedly describe clerical greed, hypocrisy, pettiness, and lechery, and of course the enormous power clerics wield. As with illicit love affairs, the novella spurns the official viewpoint and offers the pragmatic experience of those who must deal daily with clerics who struggle often unsuccessfully with the restraints imposed and temptations offered by the life they lead. The grotesque parody of clerical villainy in Masuccio of Salerno's story about Fra Diego (Smarr, *Tales* 71–74) is an extreme example of this approach. While attempting to seduce a married woman, Fra Diego is murdered by her husband, who returns the friar's body to the monastery and sets it upright on a privy. The monk is "killed" again when another friar in anger knocks him from his seat, and his twice-dead body is tied to a horse. The dead friar then pursues the living one on horseback. The muddle is too much for monastic authorities to sort out, and it is turned over to Don Ferrando of Aragon. The virulence of the satire here is similar to that of Marguerite de Navarre, whose religious leanings are, of course, Protestant. Clerics are not always viewed satirically. Some stories describe their cleverness, and in others they act like powerful magicians or wizards. These mythical powers of the clergy are well represented by Straparola's story of Scarpacifico: "Father Scarpacifico, duped only once by three rogues, dupes them three times; and finally victorious, lives happily everafter with his Nina" (Smarr, *Tales* vii).

While these various kinds of stories illustrate the preoccupation with new social roles that Auerbach outlines, the novella type that most concretely exemplifies the aesthetic dimension of the genre is the great abundance of stories that center on so-called *motti*, sometimes called *detti arguti*. A *motto* is a prompt and witty reply to a challenging statement or situation: a bon mot; *detti arguti* are simply pointed remarks, in the sense both of sharp and acute. The *motto* is a simultaneous manifestation of inventive capacity and social adroitness, and in this way it is a model of the process by which "the pleasant and winning form of personal culture" passes into "the service of social intercourse." It is for just this reason that Castiglione explores them at length in the second book of the *Courtier*. Stories about *motti* do not offer lessons in manners—a *motto* is generally too pointed to be the polite thing to say. These tales are more a training in social tactics. The *motto* is often a form of indirect social aggression useful in many contexts but perhaps especially suitable for less powerful people to use in confrontations with their superiors. The novelle centering on the *motto* offer a model of how to defuse a difficult situation or redirect its energy in a beneficial direction.

Boccaccio's story of Chichibio (6.4) is a good example of the *motto*'s use and power. Chichibio eats one leg of a crane that is to be served to his master, Currado Gianfigliazzi. When Currado challenges him, Chichibio replies that cranes have only one leg. The court sets out to view cranes in the wild, where, sure enough, since the cranes are standing on one leg asleep, Chichibio's view is apparently proved. Currado, however, suddenly cries "hu hu" and the sleeping cranes unfold their legs and fly away. Unfazed Chichibio promptly replies that Currado had not yelled "hu hu" to the crane on his dinner table, and so wins the argument and escapes punishment.

Beffe and *burle* are also favorite subjects in the novella tradition (Rochon).

Both are practical jokes, often very clever, but sometimes exceedingly crude and violent. The late Middle Ages and Renaissance seemed inordinately fond of these jokes, and considerable ingenuity went into their making. A successful joke could make a reputation. Sacchetti records with obvious pride a *beffa* carried out by his own father that involves stealing a cow's stomach from the cooking pot and replacing it with an old felt hat (254–60; Novella 98).

The most famous of all Renaissance *beffe* is narrated in the novella by Antonio Manetti called *Il grasso legnaiuolo*. In this story from the Smarr collection, the architect Filippo Brunelleschi and his allies contrive to convince a woodworker everyone calls "il Grasso" (Fatso) that the woodworker has exchanged identities with a character named Matteo. As the novella progresses, however, the focus moves away from the process of victimization toward a collaborative reassembly of all the elements of the joke including the victim's own thoughts and feelings at each turn of the plot. The joke stops being a mere trick and becomes an art object, something to share, appreciate, and enjoy. It is a climax in the Renaissance celebration of "personal culture" and a demonstration of that culture's transformation into the aesthetic realm.

Artists generally have a special place in the novella collections. Vasari's use of novelle about artists and our own continuing curiosity about men like Leonardo and Michelangelo make this genre especially important and appealing. Novelle about artists also offer the opportunity for the *novellieri* to reflect on their own art especially when they look at painters. Generally such novelle emphasize two characteristics that writers and painters share: an interest in narrative and an interest in, for lack of a better word, psychology. The tradition begins with Boccaccio's Giotto story (6.5) and is defined by the series of novelle focused on the painters Bruno, Buffalmacco and Calandrino. Sacchetti continues the tradition with two Giotto stories and a handful of others about various painters including Buffalmacco. In addition to *Il grasso legnaiuolo*, there are three linked stories by Grazzini, two of which are included in the Martone anthology. I am currently working on a translation of the complete series.

The aestheticizing of the novella, which is implicit in some of the themes of individual stories, is given its most concrete embodiment in the variety of devices by which writers frame their collections. The history and theory of the frame is described in the essay by Bonnie D. Irwin in this volume. Teaching the frame sequences is difficult because most anthologies, whether in Italian or English, present novelle in isolation even though they might include brief summaries of a frame tale. Smarr's anthology is the exception. She describes the framing devices for all the authors she includes and gives illustrative samples from the frames. Neither the author of the *Novellino* nor Sacchetti frames his collection. The frame of the *Pecorone* of Ser Giovanni Fiorentino involves a monk and a nun who meet for twenty-five days and exchange stories. As Smarr points out, the day structure and the ending of each day with a song echo the *Decameron*. While the narrators exchange a handshake or a kiss at the conclusion of each day, there is no romantic or climactic resolution to the sequence.

The frame story of Sercambi's *Novelle* describes the peregrinations around Italy of a group of men and women intent on avoiding the plague of 1374, a clear echo of Boccaccio. The pilgrims themselves do not tell stories, however; they are the work of a single designated narrator. Masuccio's book is organized into days, but each story is separately framed and there is no overarching story. Similarly, Bandello pairs each story with a dedicatory letter that sets it in context, but the various novelle have no obvious link to one another. Straparola's frame is the most complex of all: it has historical and liturgical resonances, a large cast of characters, and a complex method for choosing or rejecting storytellers on each of its thirteen *Piacevoli notti*, or "Entertaining Nights." By contrast the *Pentameron* focuses the task of storytelling on a single goal, that of making an unhappy girl laugh.

Despite the difficulty of bringing the novella tradition into the classroom, the effort is well rewarded. Students take to the stories with the same genuine delight they find in the *Decameron* itself. In the process they learn a lot about daily life in the Renaissance, the dimensions of popular literature, and the transformation of social novelty into art.

From the *Decameron* to the *Heptaméron*

Aldo Scaglione

Even for their imitators beyond Italy, Dante's *Vita nuova*, Petrarch's *Canzoniere*, and Boccaccio's *Decameron* introduced a novelty in their respective genres: the idea and habit of collecting singular compositions—lyrical poems or short stories—into some sort of unitary, systematic sequence. The collection would give the impression of a planned whole making a story with a beginning, a middle, and an end: perhaps a life story, if lyrical, or a human comedy, if narrative and objective.

In Italy the impact of the *Decameron* was immediate and widespread, starting with the structure and material content of the single stories and extending to the practice of tying the stories together with a frame, or *cornice* (see the preceding essay by James McGregor). This impact was also felt in the theater genres and the epic, classical or romance, like the *Orlando innamorato* and the *Furioso*. With regard to the technique of the *cornice*, in Italy just about every single novella collection except the one by Francesco Molza used it. As to the imitation of single stories, Masuccio Salernitano, for one, borrowed at least fifteen *novelle* from Boccaccio for his *Novellino*, Matteo Bandello at least thirty, and Giraldi Cintio about ten.

Outside Italy, we find Boccaccian stories in some plays of Lope de Rueda, Lope de Vega, and Molière; in the collections of stories by the poet Christine de Pisan (c. 1400); in the fifteenth-century Spanish poet Juan de Mena; in the sixteenth century, in the Portuguese playwright Gil Vicente, the English writer Stephen Hawes, the German poet and playwright Hans Sachs; and, in the seventeenth century, in the contes of La Fontaine, among others.

Both in and out of Italy the habit of encasing *novelle* within a frame story is a major aspect of Boccaccio's influence, even though he did not invent the device but only gave it the weight of his authority. The device was already found in collections that had reached Europe from the Orient, including the Italian versions of the *Libro dei sette savi*, the *Panchatantra* (which first landed in Spain), and the Arabic *Kalilah and Dimnah*. The best-known case of a frame story is that of Shahrazad within the story of Shahrayar's and Shahzaman's search for a faithful woman (the story of Giocondo in *Orlando furioso* 28), which became the frame story for the *Thousand and One Nights* (or *Arabian Nights*). But this complex and extremely fluid set of narratives, of Oriental origin, particularly Indian and Persian, did not find an organic form before the end of the fourteenth century, in Egypt, and the fuller form that eventually became the well-known collection only started to take shape between the fifteenth and the sixteenth centuries. Although isolated tales appeared in Europe, the fuller form did not reach the Continent until the early eighteenth century when it was translated into French, very liberally and with arbitrary additions, by Antoine

Galland. Even in its Arabic version it did not find a canonic form before the beginning of the nineteenth century.

A polemic began at the end of the nineteenth century concerning the originality of the French novella genre vis-à-vis the Italian models (chiefly the *Decameron*). A sensible conclusion today would appear to be that, even though the French had a rich native tradition of storytelling behind them, the main impulse toward writing *novelle* in whatever new forms they took in the fifteenth century came primarily from the circulation of the *Decameron*, in the original or in translation. The same conclusion applies to the use of the frame. As in Italy, Oriental and Arabic frames had been available in France at very early dates (e.g., in the *Dolopathos*, 1210), but after 1400 the main impulse came from the *Decameron*. The first major example of (very partial) derivation from Boccaccio was the anonymous *Les cent nouvelles nouvelles* (1456–62), followed by another collection with the same title by a learned writer, Philippe de Vigneulle (1505–15). Laurent de Premierfait's French translation of the *Decameron* was published at least nine times between 1485 and 1541. It was then superseded by the new one which Antoine le Maçon began in 1531 at the instigation of Marguerite de Navarre. As Marguerite tells us at the beginning of her *Heptaméron*, that translation was much appreciated at the court of Marguerite's brother, Francis I. It was first printed in Paris in 1545 and then some twenty more times in the remainder of the century.

Marguerite de Valois and d'Angoulême, duchess of Alençon and queen of Navarre (1492–1549), wrote her *Heptaméron* around 1540; it was published by Pierre Boaistuau in 1558 in a much corrupted form and by Claude Gruget in a somewhat restored form in 1559. The story of the text shows hasty composition and sloppy handling of the manuscript tradition by editors who rearranged it, added to it, and edited it extensively. This itinerary was very different from the Italian way of scrupulously preserving the authors' transmitted texts. To date, Michel François's edition is still considered the best, followed by another one by Yves Le Hir, and one more by S. de Reyff, but Slatkine's reprint of the 1853–54, three-volume edition by A. J. V. Le Roux de Lincy and Anatole de Montaiglon is still current. There is a full English translation by Walter K. Kelly, another by John S. Chartres, and one more unexpurgated version by W. M. Thompson. A good partial translation is in Patricia F. Cholakian and Rouben C. Cholakian's *The Early French Novella*, and we now have a competent complete one by Paul A. Chilton. For the sake of simplification I proceed by assuming Marguerite's authorship, but it has been challenged: an informed presentation of the problem is in Chilton's introduction to the Penguin translation.

Marguerite had clearly read at least Boccaccio, Gian Francesco Poggio Bracciolini (for his successful *Facetiae*, in Latin), and the French *Cent nouvelles nouvelles* (printed only in 1486), but she owes them little more than the idea of the frame and of the novella as a generic form. Her themes were largely derived from courtly love, since the practice, or rather the idea, of the type of love that now goes under that name had been nurtured in the Middle Ages in a social milieu that was close to the one in which the author operated. In that milieu, to love according to the conventions of courtly love was the chief hobby and the chief form of entertainment in action and especially in conversation, that is, the art of the salon, which was then being born and would become a hallmark of classical French literature. Marguerite's stories of love at court took many different forms, from the coarsest to the most refined, morally elevated, and even spiritual level of perfect friendship. The psychological curiosity of the French literary public made it delight in investigating all the nuances of love and in raising all the questions that pertained to it. Yet, even though Marguerite operates on the basis of courtly love, it is more a point of departure than one of arrival, since she goes beyond it in her moralism, which makes her strive to save marriage, honest behavior, and the sort of perfection that had become associated with the new Platonism, in a serious vein of reformed Christianity. Honesty applies especially to the woman, even while Marguerite keeps wondering about this difference in standards and keeps pointing out that it is really a form of playacting, ready to be left behind when real desire and passion are involved. All this emphasis on morality is tempered by a basic realism that makes the author and her characters realize the difficulty of living up to abstract standards. The realism that one notices in the *Heptaméron* is common to the French novella of the Renaissance, and it was demanded by the rising middle class with its bourgeois tastes, in contrast to the tastes of the medieval aristocracy. This propensity of the middle class made it natural to accept the *Decameron* as a model, since, with all its incomparable richness, Boccaccio's collection was eminently a bourgeois text for an audience of merchants. It was, in Vittore Branca's words, a "mercantile epic" (*Boccaccio medievale*).

It seems fair to conclude that the *Heptaméron* has not yet received a satisfactory critical assessment, and the critics who have worked on it have vainly attempted to identify a central or guiding principle for it. Marcel Tetel in his book (*Marguerite*) and succinctly in "Ambiguité chez Boccacce et Marguerite de Navarre," in Carlo Pellegrini's *Il Boccaccio nella cultura francese*, is wrong in interpreting Lisabetta da Messina (4.5) as being at fault for loving too passionately (563). (This interpretation is contrary to Branca, whose *Boccaccio medievale* Tetel does not mention.) A love that is too passionate is ostensibly the negative part of Marguerite's twofold theme—too passionate love being condemned as lacking in regard for society's and the family's rights and as opposed to perfect, spiritual love or ideal friendship. It appears rather unconvincing to set the central theme of the *Heptaméron* in the privileged presentation of perfect love as against sensual love, as some critics have done. Marguerite, and her characters in their articulate comments after the telling of the stories, present all aspects of passion, in all their contradictions, and even if Parlemente appears to have the role of the author's spokeswoman, her voice is only one in the richly enfolding storytelling and ensuing comments. Consider, for example, the end of the twelfth story. Saffredent concludes: "[t]o me it seems much better to love a woman as a woman, than to make her one's idol, as many do" (1: 94).[1] ("C'est beaucoup mieulx faict d'aymer une femme comme femme que d'en idolatrer plusieurs comme on fait d'une imaige" [2: 26].) Protesting her husband's neglect and her own chaste reaction to it, without having taken the radical revenge that Boccaccio's wives had regularly sought with impunity, the unnamed wife of the fifteenth story makes the liberated statement that "though the laws of men condemn to infamy women who love any others than their husbands, the law of God, [. . .] condemns men who love any other women than their own wives" (1: 117) ("Combien que la loy des hommes donne si grand deshonneur aux femmes qui ayment autres que leurs maris, si est ce que la loy de Dieu n'exempte point les mariz qui ayment autres que leur femmes" (2: 73).

But the husband counters that "a man's honor and a woman's were different things" (1: 18.) ("L'honneur d'un homme et d'une femme n'estoient pas semblables" (2: 75.) We can compare this with the story of Madonna Filippa in *Decameron* 6.7, among others, for a more radical issue than just words. One of the most Boccaccian among the novellas of the *Heptaméron* is the fourteenth, that of the seigneur de Bonnivet, the Milanese lady, and her Italian gentleman lover. It includes the trick of replacing the lover in bed unbeknownst to the lady, who first refused Bonnivet and preferred the Italian gentleman. However, like a renewed Donna Lucrezia of the *Mandragola*, she easily makes her peace with it after the fact and vows to privilege henceforth the French over Italian lovers, in recognition of Bonnivet's shrewdness and determination.

The reader notices the different quality of the *Heptaméron* narrative right away. As Marguerite says in her introduction, her stories are based "on the truth" and refer to the courtly world of her own acquaintance (on all its social levels). Her world is in contrast to the mercantile world of Boccaccio, even though she says the book was occasioned by the success at court of Boccaccio's recent translation into French. Indeed she was planning to write one hundred stories (only seventy-two are extant, and the title "Seven Days" came from the second editor, since the eighth day remained incomplete). More important, in addition to concentrating on the Christian contrast between mundane and sacred or the Platonic between passionate or carnal and perfect or spiritual love, the stories have a very different complexion from those of Boccaccio. They look more like Bandello's stories (also mostly based on hearsay about recent happenings), seemingly distrusting the fictional or creative narrative with a logical (artistic) beginning, middle, and end, and making a critical point, with a problem that demands a solution (see Scaglione, "Giovanni Boccaccio"). Noticeable also is the greater space given to direct moral comments by the storytellers—comments that are rather sparse in the *Decameron*.

This emphasis on realism is an important rhetorical twist, which consciously places the novella on a plane different from the novel or romance and alongside the chronicle or history—but only for the rhetorical purpose of inviting the reader's suspension of disbelief.[2] The most conspicuous infraction of the principle of chronicle-like truthfulness, or verisimilitude, is probably the thirtieth novella, in itself a unique case of intertextual connection with a very rich vein of

exemplary religious preaching.[3] The story is found, with variations and often in
independent versions, especially in France, but it is also in Masuccio Salernitano's *Novellino* (novella 24), in the second part of Bandello's *Novelle* (1554),
in Martin Luther's *Colloquia mensalia* or *Tischreden* (where, under the rubric
"auricular confessions," the incident is said to have occurred in Erfurt [24–25]),
and in other later, English and Spanish writers. The story concerns an extreme
case of double incest, mother with son and then son with sister/daughter, or father with daughter and then son with mother/sister. What is most interesting is
that in Marguerite the tale is meant, as we learn from the prolonged commentary of the storytellers, to stress the principle of inescapable sinfulness after the
Edenic lapse. Hence it is necessary to rely not on our moral strength, which, in
the Lutheran message, is pride—the worst of sins—but on a humble determination to avoid the occasion for sin. Boccaccio's basic message, that nature cannot be suppressed and will prevail if given a chance, is thus repeated but in a
novel spirit:

> There, ladies, is what happens to those of our sex who think to vanquish,
> by their own strength, love and nature with all the faculties which God
> has given them. Better were it to own their weakness, avoid exposure to
> temptation, and say to God, like David: "Lord I suffer force: answer for
> me."   (2: 40)

> Voylà, mes Dames, comme il en prend à celles qui cuydent par leurs forces
> et vertu vaincre Amour et Nature avecq toutes les puissances que Dieu y a
> mises. Mais le meilleur seroit, congnoissant sa faiblesse, ne jouster point
> contre tel ennemy, et se retirer au vray ami et luy dire avecq le Psalmiste:
> «Seigneur, je souffre force, respondez pour moy.»   (2: 282)

Critics have underlined the poverty of the *Heptaméron*'s style, a feature that
clearly contrasts with the unparalleled formal excellence of the *Decameron*.
One tradition has it that Marguerite dictated her stories to a lady-in-waiting
while traveling. Her style has been called flat, unpolished, colorless, and lax. Yet
she offers a first glimpse at what would become the most admired feature of
French classical prose, the elegant conversation of the salon, which derived
from the court society that was already at the center of the *Heptaméron*.

Other French collections of novelle contemporaneous with or slightly later
than the *Heptaméron* are Nicolas de Troyes's *Grand parangon des nouvelles
nouvelles* (1537); the jurist Noël de Fail's (1520?–91) *Propos rustiques* (1547),
Baliverneries (1548), and *Contes et discours d'Eutrapel* (1585); Bonaventure
des Périers's (1510?–44?) *Nouvelles récréations et joyeux devis* (1558, posthumous); and the widely circulating *Histoires tragiques*, by Pierre Boaistuau and
François de Belleforest (1559–82).[4]

The *Heptaméron* is a telling example of the inspirational impact of Boccaccio's masterpiece even when its imitators were moved by different literary or

moral motives. Marguerite de Navarre never lost sight of her model even when she drew on independent sources. In teaching the *Decameron* in a comparative context, we can profitably keep in mind this aspect of its wide and deep influence by stressing Marguerite's example. This particular rapprochement illustrates the Italian work's exemplary quality in one of its many international reverberations. The marked differences between the two texts are also clear witness to the variations within the novella genre, and teachers can use these two outstanding cases to develop theoretical concerns about possible definitions of the novella's various kinds. Tzvetan Todorov and Cesare Segre, among others, have suggested structuralist analyses of the genre, but the field is now wide open for other, perhaps more promising, possibilities.

NOTES

[1]All French quotations from *Heptaméron* in this essay are taken from the 1969 version in three volumes, edited by A. J. V. Le Roux de Lincy and Anatole de Montaiglon. All English translations are by Walter K. Kelly from the 1855 edition published by Henry G. Bohn.

[2]See Gisèle Mathieu-Castellani's *La conversation conteuse: Les nouvelles de Marguerite de Navarre*, especially pages 7–22 and 33–34, citing Lionello Sozzi's *La nouvelle française de la Renaissance* and Marcel Raymond's "Histoire et poétique de la nouvelle," in his *Vérité et poésie*. Mathieu-Castellani observes that, in a parodic inversion of courtly love, a lady is called *courtoise* by virtue of her *puterie*! (34). This echoes the semantic shift the word was then undergoing, whereby *cortegiana* or courtesan meant other than the simple feminine of *cortegiano*, so that Castiglione avoids it in favor of *donna di palazzo* when speaking of the lady of court.

[3]See a summary of the manifold cross-references in the Kelly translation (2: 39–40, 40n) and the Cazauran edition (36–37) of the *Heptaméron*, as well as in the appendix to Scaglione's *Knights at Court*, which deals with the similar parables of Saint Alban (Albrecht von Eyb, fifteenth century), and Saint Gregory (Hartmann von Aue, twelfth century), down to Thomas Mann.

[4]Despite numerous studies and various attempts to map out the novella's progress through time and space, the genre still needs more spadework for a satisfactory and fully comprehensive survey. One such attempt is Robert J. Clements and Joseph Gibaldi's, *Anatomy of the Novella: The European Tale Collection from Boccaccio and Chaucer to Cervantes*. See also Michelangelo Picone, Giuseppe Di Stefano, and Pamela D. Stewart's *Formation, codification et rayonnement d'un genre médiéval: La nouvelle*. Patricia F. Cholakian's *Rape and Writing in the* Heptaméron *of Marguerite de Navarre* suggests a feminist reading of the *Heptaméron*.

APPENDIX
SUPPLEMENTAL STUDIES ON MARGUERITE DE NAVARRE

Bernard, John D. "Realism and Closure in the *Heptaméron*: Marguerite de Navarre and Boccaccio." *MLR* 84 (1989): 305–18.

Cazauran, Nicole. *L'Heptaméron de Marguerite de Navarre*. Paris: Société d'enseignement supérieur, 1976.

Cholakian, Patricia F. *Rape and Writing in the* Heptaméron *of Marguerite de Navarre*. Carbondale: Southern Illinois UP, 1991.

Clive, H. P. *Marguerite de Navarre: An Annotated Bibliography*. London: Grant, 1986.

Cottrell, Robert D. *The Grammar of Silence: A Reading of Marguerite de Navarre's Poetry*. Washington: Catholic U of America P, 1986.

Gelernt, Jules. *World of Many Loves: The* Heptaméron *of Marguerite de Navarre*. Chapel Hill: U of North Carolina P, 1966.

Kinney, Arthur F. *Continental Humanist Poetics: Studies in Erasmus, Castiglione, Marguerite de Navarre, Rabelais, and Cervantes*. Amherst: U of Massachusetts P, 1989.

Lyons, John D., and Mary B. McKinley, eds. *Critical Tales: New Studies of the* Heptaméron *and Early Modern Culture*. Philadelphia: U of Pennsylvania P, 1993.

Pollachek, Dora E., ed. *Heroic Virtue, Comic Infidelity: Reassessing Marguerite de Navarre's* Heptaméron. Amherst: Hestia, 1993.

Reynolds, Régine. *Les devisants de l'*Heptaméron: *Dix personnages en quête d'audience*. Washington: UP of America, 1977.

Tetel, Marcel. *Marguerite de Navarre's* Heptaméron: *Themes, Language, and Structure*. Durham: Duke UP, 1973.

Wright, Elizabeth C. "Marguerite Reads Giovanni: Gender and Narration in the *Heptaméron* and the *Decameron*." *Renaissance and Reformation* 27 (1991): 21–36.

The *Decameron* in Spain

Robert E. Bayliss

A casual knowledge of the literature produced in Spain in the Renaissance and baroque eras might lead one to believe that assessing Boccaccio's influence on Iberian literature is a simple matter of examining the collections of *novelas cortas* that appeared in no small number in Spain during the three centuries following the *Decameron*. Such a focus, however, is too limited in scope and to a great extent inaccurate: these collections are perhaps more accurately attributed to the influence of those who followed Boccaccio in the Italian novella tradition, especially Matteo Bandello. More to the point, they are seldom the focus of modern attention—with the important exception of María de Zayas y Sotomayor. Meanwhile, it is difficult to imagine what would have become of Golden Age Spain's great literary traditions, especially the picaresque novel and the comedia, and its great prose masterpiece, *Don Quixote*, had the *Decameron* never been known in Spain.

Regardless of which work one might choose to present in the classroom, the Spanish Golden Age represents a period that is both heavily indebted to Boccaccio and demonstrative of how his more influential admirers went beyond a formal imitation of his work to offer their own original contributions to Spanish literature. This overview focuses on some major figures of the Golden Age whose debt to Boccaccio is clear and pedagogically useful. Zayas retains the format of framed *novelas*, but within this format she treats issues which may be useful as a counterpoint to presenting the *Heptaméron*. Lope de Vega and his followers drastically alter the generic traits of Boccaccio's novelle in their adaptation of his plots and topoi to the sixteenth-century Spanish stage. The picaresque novel is heavily indebted to Boccaccio's treatment of human behavior from a nonidealized perspective, especially in his use of trickery and roguery as the subject for several of the *Decameron*'s stories. Cervantes's *Novelas ejemplares* are a marked departure from the *Decameron* but demonstrate a similar concern for the artistic presentation of the short narrative; *Don Quixote* demonstrates this same concern in its interpolated stories but also involves an examination of Boccaccio's protorealism in its own realistic tendencies considered pivotal to the foundation of the modern novel. But this most important point of Boccaccian impact on the *Quixote* has much to do with Cervantes's response to the *novela* tradition in Spain—a tradition that may not appear in the classroom today (except for Zayas) but is nonetheless the clearest evidence of Boccaccio's reception in the Golden Age.

In the centuries following Boccaccio's death, the *Decameron* was translated into Castilian and Catalan (the earliest surviving manuscripts have been roughly dated to the first half of the fifteenth century) and eventually printed in Seville. This translation enjoyed enough popular success to merit four editions before being placed on the Index of the Inquisition in 1559. The strict moral standards of the Inquisition were, of course, the same faced by Spain's own *novela* authors. It is difficult to tell, then, whether the often morally didactic Spanish *novela* collections reflected a cultural orthodoxy at odds with the *Decameron* or whether they simply avoided a dangerous conflict with the Inquisition.

By 1566 the first successful collection of *novelas* written in Spain was printed in Valencia: Juan de Timoneda's *El patrañuelo*. Cathy Bourland's important study "Boccaccio and the *Decameron* in Castilian and Catalan Literature" offers an extensive listing of *novela* collections written in Spanish in the two hundred years following the *Decameron*. As with the *Patrañuelo*, though, the distinction between translation or appropriation and imitation is not always clear. What is clear is that the novella tradition was appreciated by the Spanish audience—and that it is not until the early seventeenth century that any significant attempt is made at a more original contribution to the *novela corta* in Spain. Until Cervantes's *Novelas ejemplares* was published in 1613, the influence of Boccaccio on the *novela corta* is obvious, but the Spanish tradition offered little in terms of an original contribution to the genre. Several collections published after the *Novelas ejemplares* are likewise clear imitations of the *Decameron*. Alonso Jerónimo de Salas Barbadillo's *Casa del placer honesto* (1620), Alonso de Castillo Solórzano's *Tardes entretenidas* (1625) and *Noches de placer* (1631), and Juan Pérez de Montalbán's *Sucesos y prodigios de amor en ocho novelas ejemplares* (1624) all contribute to a tradition of *novelas cortas* that attempt to balance the artistic concerns of the Italian model without incurring church censorship.

Modern translations of such works into English are virtually nonexistent—a fact that reflects modern critical attitudes toward this pseudotradition. While the Spanish imitations may not merit extensive attention for undergraduate classes (they are rarely treated within university Spanish departments), their existence indicates that Spanish writers and readers found the Italian tradition compelling and worthy of imitation. Of course, the significance of these imitations pales in comparison to that of the great dramatists (especially Lope de Vega, Tirso de Molina, and Calderón de la Barca) and the more appropriately called Spanish literary traditions (the picaresque, pastoral romance, and eventually the longer prose *novelas* of Cervantes). Much more needs to be said regarding Boccaccio's influence on these monuments of the national literature of Spain—an influence that is useful in presenting major works of the Spanish Golden Age to American undergraduates.

The prolific comedia tradition, roughly contemporary to Cervantes (more than twenty thousand comedies are believed to have been written and performed), offers rich possibilities for comparison to the *Decameron*. Figures such as Lope de Rueda are important to the tradition's evolution from a medieval drama (*autos de fe* 'acts of faith'), best described as religious and often allegorical, to a secular and popular tradition in the sixteenth century. But the ultimate popular success of the comedia depended on Lope de Vega, whose "New Art of Making Comedies" (*Arte nuevo de hacer comedias en este tiempo*) offered the first formal written codification of the tradition's conventions. This treatise was actually written by request of the *Real Academia* in an effort to make the immense popular success of the drama better understood by the intellectual elite. The comedia's universal success suggests that the effort succeeded: the most successful dramas were performed for both royal, or courtly, and *vulgo*, or popular, audiences. Lope's treatise argues that his new art is justified by its popular success ("because the vulgar pay"), but later important figures such as Tirso de Molina (*El burlador de Sevilla*, the classic dramatization of the Don Juan myth) and Calderón de la Barca (*La vida es sueño*) are, because of their religious affiliation, more concerned with reconciling mass appeal with morally instructive dramas. (Lope himself was ordained late in life after a famously hedonistic lifestyle in his younger days.) Thus the same concern with balancing pleasure and moral instruction, which led to the censure of the *Decameron* and to the more conservative nature of its Spanish imitations, is more successfully negotiated by the comedia dramatists.

Nancy L. D'Antuono's *Boccaccio's 'Novelle' in the Theater of Lope de Vega* offers an excellent contemporary study of the eight plays of the Spanish comedia's leading figure that are more or less direct adaptations of novelle from the *Decameron*. This use of the Italian tradition as a source for the plot and action of Lope's comedies indicates the novella's presence in Spanish Golden Age theater as a whole. Bourland's study mentioned above charts the vast number of plots borrowed by various Spanish dramatists including Tirso de Molina, Pedro Navarro, and Juan Pérez de Montalbán. Clearly these dramatists found the novelle to be easily adapted to their tradition—which suggests a deeper affinity between the two traditions that D'Antuono discusses at length. The necessary transformation from short novella to three-act dramatic spectacle is accompanied, she argues, by the psychological amplification so important to Lope's plays. In other words, the dramatists built on the foundations given in the often tersely accounted plots of the *Decameron*, and the result is a unique and truly national dramatic tradition—the most popular of the Golden Age arts. Here we can see the importance of Boccaccio as a model for Spanish literature, but the departure from that model—how that model is transformed into something unique to Spain—makes his contribution here more valuable than in the *novela corta*.

Thematic concerns and conventional topoi are perhaps the clearest levels on which one might present the comedia as an extension of Boccaccian thought and narrative art. Standard motifs such as the *villano-noble* paradox (the villager, whose rural status shares the same term as villain, behaves with true nobility, while the noble demonstrates true villainy) and nobility of heart (or nobility of soul) are undoubtedly at the heart of the tradition's appeal to a popular audience, while the correlation between chastity and honor for the typical heroine of the comedia reflects the Christian orthodoxy of the tradition. They also clearly echo themes treated in the *Decameron*. Two of the more internationally famous dramas of the tradition, *La vida es sueño* (*Life Is a Dream*) and

Fuenteovejuna (named after the town in which the action takes place), are both easily found translated into modern English and exemplary of such conventions. These plays are sure to be included in any Spanish course devoted to the comedia, but the critical attention paid to them is not restricted to this field. Hymen Alpern's *Three Classic Spanish Plays* contains his translation of both plays (along with Rojas Zorilla's *None beneath the King*) in a modern English translation, and *Lope de Vega: Five Plays* offers Jill Booty's translations of classic works by Lope (including *Fuenteovejuna*).

It is typical of the tradition to find a plot based on the restoration of the heroine's honor after it has been taken, either by seduction (as in *El burlador de Sevilla* and *La vida es sueño*) or force (*Fuenteovejuna*). The restoration of violated honor, in turn, tends to follow two paths—usually (as in *La vida es sueño*) through marriage but occasionally through violent revenge (as in *Fuenteovejuna*). Within this framework, dramatists such as Lope de Vega were able to appeal to the masses (by invoking their interior nobility) while carefully avoiding an overt criticism of church or royal authority. Boccaccian plots are translated to a Spanish setting involving the Spanish political atmosphere of the day (far more stable than Boccaccio's); therefore an easy point of departure for presenting Spanish Renaissance culture through the comedia is to consider how it manipulates plots and themes from the *Decameron*. For example, the theme of nobility of the soul, present in the Italian novella, is transformed (one might say from the nobility of the Italian soul to that of the Spanish soul). The Spanish comedia therefore offers the college teacher a rich dramatic tradition heavily indebted to its Italian prose model, and this shift alone (from written text to dramatic spectacle) suggests fruitful pedagogical possibilities.

The specific comedies mentioned above, and virtually all the comedies available in English translation, consist of plots that are more or less original to their Spanish dramatists. There is also a tradition of comedias whose plots are directly borrowed from the *Decameron*, and again Lope is the central figure of this dramatic strain. Both D'Antuono and Bourland note eight of his works with direct and clear analogues in the *Decameron*. Of the *capa y espada* ("cloak and dagger") comedies, in which multiple plotlines are tied into a seemingly insoluble knot until the final scene, *La discreta enamorada* is perhaps the most famous. (Its *Decameron* analogue is 3.3.) Another noteworthy example of a Boccaccian novella appropriated by Lope de Vega is *El halcón de Federigo* (see *Decameron* 5.9). While such comedies are inaccessible in English, they would be of great use in a Spanish course both as examples of the Spanish comedia and as clear points of departure in delineating Boccaccio's reception in Spain.

Of course, one cannot discuss Spanish literary traditions at any length without considering the picaresque novel. The contribution made by Boccaccio in paving the way for this genre is tremendous. Fifteen fifty-four was the year of publication for *Lazarillo de Tormes* (available in English in Michael Alpert's *Two Spanish Picaresque Novels*), the founding work of the tradition. The other great picaresque novel whose fame has endured into the current century,

Mateo Alemán's *Guzmán de Alfarache* (1599), continues the tradition's auto-biographical format of portraying an antihero's career of social and moral transgression while offering a protagonist who, in the wake of the Counter-Reformation, undergoes a moral conversion at the end of his career. The realism recognized in the picaresque is unimaginable without Boccaccio's own naturalism preceding it. The emphasis on psychological motivations and the view of the world offered—a total departure from that of romance—can easily be discussed as an amplification of these same traits in Boccaccian short fiction. What *Lazarillo* and *Guzmán* offer is, like Boccaccio, an alternative to romance rather than a parody or satire of it. For Joseph V. Ricapito ("Boccaccio and the Picaresque Tradition"), the debt to Boccaccio is greater still: his study offers a detailed analysis of *Decameron* stories in comparison with elements of the Spanish picaresque, especially those involving trickery (the *pícaro*'s professional skill). Among the many stories cited by Ricapito as demonstrative of the *Decameron*'s protopicaresque elements, 1.1 is discussed in terms of Ser Ciappelletto as a trickster; 2.3 as a precursor to a similar episode in *Guzmán*; and 2.5 as similar to *Lazarillo* in depicting a young and naive protagonist who is faced with misfortune after misfortune (his being duped by a girl is again echoed in the *Guzmán*) before learning to turn his circumstances to his own advantage.

One of Cervantes's *Novelas ejemplares*, *Rinconete and Cortadillo*, begins as a picaresque enterprise, only to have that premise ultimately undermined (see El Saffar); in this *novela* as well as in parts of *Don Quixote* (especially 1.22) Cervantes makes clear his distaste for the tradition. But this is not to suggest that one cannot discuss the *Novelas ejemplares* as influenced by the same Boccaccio so important to the picaresque; as with *Lazarillo de Tormes*, the influence is not to be found in formal or structural characteristics. None of the plots of these *novelas* can be considered an appropriation from any Italian novella; this collection, in fact, is best considered a response to the imitative Spanish works that precede it. Cervantes makes this response explicit in his prologue (91):

> To this my genius applied itself, toward which my inclination carries me, which leads me to understand, as it is so, that I am the first who has written *novelas* in the Spanish tongue, that the many *novelas* which continue to be produced here are all translated from foreign tongues, and these are my own, neither imitated nor stolen; my genius created them, my pen gave them birth, and they grow in the arms of the print.   (my trans.)

Clearly Cervantes wants the reader to recognize that his "genius" is original, defined above as different from those more faithful to the Italian model. His "inclinations" have been demonstrated (see El Saffar; Riley) to tend more toward romance than does the Italian tradition. This view suggests not that the established romance traditions (pastoral, chivalric) are imitated instead but that the reality recognized in the realism (Scaglione's "medieval naturalism" [*Nature and Love* 2]) that characterizes Boccaccio's prose is replaced by what Ruth El Saffar calls a "transcendent reality" (14) in *novelas* such as *La fuerza de la sangre*, *Las dos doncellas*, and *La española inglesa*. This might also be considered a reconciliation of the two generic extremes of romance and novella.

If such a difference from Boccaccio is accepted, Tirso de Molina's consideration of Cervantes as "nuestro Boccaccio español" (*Cigarrales*, prologue) may seem puzzling. In fact later on in the same work Tirso finds fault with the *Novelas ejemplares* for failing to follow the trend in adapting the framing technique that unifies the *Decameron*. Whatever Tirso's reasons may have been in coining this epithet, the connection he makes between Boccaccio and Cervantes does seem accurate in terms of each author's role in establishing a new literary tradition distinct from his literary sources. Just as Boccaccio forged a new tradition of short fiction from medieval exempla and fabliaux, Cervantes, through his *novelas*, forges a new direction for short fiction from the novella. Both, in this sense, are pioneers. Salvador Fajardo ("The Frame as Formal Contrast: Boccaccio and Cervantes") sees Cervantes's role in this relationship as a shift from Boccaccio's concern for the spoken word to an unprecedented concern for the enterprise of the written word. Both writers share a strong aesthetic concern for the narrative as an art form, in contrast to the focus on moral didacticism in several of the Italian authors who continue the novella tradition after Boccaccio and their Spanish imitators of the fifteenth and sixteenth centuries. This aesthetic concern is even the subject matter of the exemplary *Coloquio de los perros* ("The Dialogue of the Dogs"), a dialogue between two dogs regarding, basically, the best way to narrate a story (but Fajardo points out that the *novela* is framed around its narrator's written account of this dialogue).

Regardless of how productive it might be to treat the *Novelas ejemplares* in terms of the *Decameron*'s influence, however, it is invariably *Don Quixote* that is presented to the American undergraduate, either in a Spanish class or as part of a comparative literature course. This work is, of course, generally offered in terms of its pioneering role in the genesis of the modern novel—not in terms of its roots in medieval and early Renaissance prose fiction. By discussing Boccaccio's influence on the novel, the teacher is open to fresh possibilities for new approaches to a work about which so much has been said. Much of the novel's complexity stems from the fact that so many varied traditions (pastoral and chivalric romance, comedia, Byzantine novel, and Italian novella are the most apparent) are treated and responded to through the work. Chivalric romance is, of course, the tradition under the most critical scrutiny, but the relation between *Don Quixote* and the *Decameron* is also important if one is to understand the realism for which the novel is so often recognized. Cervantes's attitude toward the Boccaccian tradition is to treat it, like romance, as a fictional world brought into contact with reality, where its fictiveness is laid bare. Thus in part 2 when Don Quixote narrates his adventure in the Cave of Montesinos to Sancho, the Boccaccian tale of presenting a lady with her lover's heart after his death is accompanied by comments that point to realistic concerns not treated in the *Decameron*: the organ must be salted to prevent its decay and the odor that accompanies it. The humor of such details points to the very reason why *Don Quixote* may appear more modern to students than the *Decameron*: much of the novel's humor is generated by pointing to the incompatibility of the fiction of earlier traditions with the concerns of reality—the incompatibility of art and life.

One difficulty of discussing pedagogical approaches to *Don Quixote* is that it is rarely taught in its full length. Literary anthologies tend to condense the thousand-plus-page work into a selection of less than two hundred pages, and the easiest way to accomplish this condensation is by removing virtually all the interpolated stories and keeping intact only those parts of the novel directly involving the knight and his squire, Sancho Panza. These interpolations, though, and the conversations that frame them are important to understanding Cervantes's attitude toward the novella. They also demonstrate the extent to which Cervantes has departed from the project of the *Decameron*: the short narratives contribute to the design of the main narrative that frames them (rather than the frame functioning as a pretext for the *novelle*).

To this point Zayas has been conspicuously absent from the discussion. While similar to Timoneda (*El patrañuelo*) in imitating Boccaccio's frame, her *Novelas exemplares y amorosas* (in two volumes published in 1637 and 1649) and *Desengaños amorosos* (*The Disenchantments of Love*) (1647), like the works of Lope and Cervantes, build constructively on the foundation that Boccaccio offers. The concerns of the author regarding a woman's place in Spanish society are the most obvious departure from the *Decameron*: such concerns, explicitly voiced in her prologue and implicit in the stories that follow, are of primary importance to any understanding of her work. A discussion of any length about the work of Doña María must also consider its reconciliation to the rigid moralism of her day—the same moralism demonstrated in the Inquisition's censorship of the *Decameron*. The presentation of Zayas's *novelas* may be especially provocative if compared with the *Heptaméron*: Marguerite de Navarre's treatment of the tension between Protestants and Catholics is replaced by a concern for reconciling feminist progressivism to a Catholic hegemony.

Such issues suggest that Zayas would be a more provocative writer to present than her male peers in the Spanish *novela* tradition. Her work does more than imitate the Italian model: it adapts its framework to treat issues with which Boccaccio is less concerned. Within that framework, tales of seduction and amorous intrigue are told from a protofeminist perspective that makes the work of this novelist attractive to modern readers. Modern critics find her work inviting to commentary, while little attention is paid to any other *novelista* other than Cervantes. This critical attention has also precipitated a new translation of Zayas's *novelas* in this decade by H. Patsy Boyer: *The Enchantments of Love: Amorous and Exemplary Novels* and *The Disenchantments of Love*. Tirso de Molina may have considered Cervantes "nuestro Boccaccio español," but a modern Spanish edition of *Novelas ejemplares y amorosas*, edited by Eduardo Rincón, bears the subtitle "*Decameron* español." While such an epithet may be as simplistic as to call the *Heptaméron* the "French *Decameron*," it does suggest that Zayas may be read as a unique example of Boccaccian influence in Spanish literature.

Of course, we have seen that while the specific way in which Zayas departs from the Boccaccian model may be unique, the actual use of the *Decameron* as a model (whether formally or otherwise) places her at the end of a long tradition of Spanish admirers. While several directions have been suggested for presenting the extensive Boccaccian influence on Spanish literature, there are no doubt other works that also reveal a debt to the *Decameron*. The purpose here is to point to the most important works (and therefore those most accessible in English translation) whose use in the classroom can be twofold: to demonstrate the debt to Boccaccio while at the same time presenting Spanish classics that have thrived on their own intrinsic literary merit. The fiction of Spain's Golden Age as a whole demonstrates an appreciation for Boccaccio that is fundamental to its important place in Western literature.

The *Decameron* and Italian Renaissance Comedy

Angelo Mazzocco and Elizabeth H. D. Mazzocco

Giovanni Boccaccio's *Decameron* exercised a significant influence on Italian literature of the Renaissance, particularly on the development of the narrative and the birth and evolution of the comedy. Consequently, a course on Italian Renaissance comedy, whether taught in Italian or in English, is not complete without the students' discovering the tremendous debt that both comedic themes and characters owe to Boccaccio.

The first task of organizing such a course is to select comedies to be studied; depending on the scope and language of the course, the possibilities loom large. In Italian, individual plays and anthology volumes are available through most major textbook importers. In English, the number of translations multiplies every year, giving teachers a good choice among the major plays and playwrights. The final selection should consist of no more than ten plays and possibly as few as seven. The plays we usually cover include Ludovico Ariosto's *I suppositi* and *La Lena*; Bernardo Dovizi's (Bibbiena's) *La Calandria*; Niccolò Machiavelli's *La mandragola*; Pietro Aretino's *La cortigiana* and *Gl'ingannati*, by the Accademici Intronati di Siena; and Angelo Beolco's (Ruzzante's) *I due dialoghi*. Additional plays that bear consideration are Ariosto's *La cassaria* and *Il negromante*, Machiavelli's *La Clizia*, Aretino's *Il marescalco*, and Ruzzante's *La moscheta*. Reading order of the plays may be determined by chronology, locale, or author. We have discovered that each method of study has its selling points. Whatever the choice and the order of plays, the influence of Boccaccio on the playwrights shines through. If the students are all Italian majors and have had a solid grounding in Boccaccio, one can spend a few days discussing the comedic art of the ancient playwrights Plautus and Terence, the other important sources, besides Boccaccio, of Italian Renaissance comedy. If they are less familiar with theatrical sources and the history of the Renaissance, more time should be devoted to preparing them to be sophisticated readers of Renaissance texts. Before students can appreciate the intricacies of Renaissance comedy, they must be able to understand the plays in their original cultural context.

In all our courses, we begin with a study of source material. Renaissance comedy, especially in its early stages (Ariosto, Bibbiena, Machiavelli), is a hybrid entity consisting of two important strains: the classical comic tradition, that is, the comedies of Plautus and Terence, and the Boccaccian novelistic element. The classical strain contributes to the scheme of the play: type of character, Aristotelian unities, mistaken identity, comic irony, double plot, dual character, and so forth. The Boccaccian strain provides the sociohistorical mold and comic techniques such as farce, slapstick, and linguistic jests. For a study of cinquecento comedy to be effective, one needs to consider both of these strains rather closely. In the classical tradition, one needs to explore some key comedies of

Plautus and Terence. We have found most useful Plautus's *Casina,* the *Brothers Menaechmus*, and the *Prisoners* and Terence's *Fair Andrian*, the *Self-Tormentor* and the *Eunuch.* As to Boccaccio, one needs to read those novelle that best lend themselves to cinquecento comedy and whose echoes recur throughout many of the plays. We consider the following novelle the most pertinent: Day 1, tales 1, 2, and 3; Day 2, tales 5 and 9; Day 3, tales 1, 3, 5, 6, and 10; Day 4, introduction, tales 1, 2, and 10; Day 5, tales 4 and 10; Day 6, tales 7 and 10; Day 7, tales 1, 2, 4, 5, 7, and 9; Day 8, tales 3, 4, 6, 7, and 9; Day 9, tales 2, 3, 5, 6, and 10.

In considering Boccaccio's contribution to Italian Renaissance comedy, one should emphasize the realistic and sometimes grotesque qualities of the characters and the way that Boccaccio cleverly coordinates each character's role and language, a language that is chock-full of popular imagery and colloquialisms. Attention should be given to the stylistic and linguistic strategies of the *Decameron*, to their concise and lively exposition of the comedic action and to their shrewd verbal jabs and rapid-fire verbal exchanges. One should note how the stylistic and verbal virtuosity is coupled with pantomime and slapstick. Indeed, it is the way Boccaccio combines linguistic jests with farcical movements that makes the *Decameron* so humorous and why it lends itself so easily to incorporation into stage comedy. One should also consider the sociohistorical meaning of the *Decameron* with its emphasis on sexual pleasure and its disregard (at least in the novelle we have chosen) for moral consideration.

Viewing portions of Pier Paolo Pasolini's film *The Decameron* can enrich students' understanding of the Boccaccian component of cinquecento comedy and provide a visual point of reference. Students might also transform the more mimetic Boccaccian novelle into miniplays, an exercise that not only broadens their understanding of the comedic inventiveness of Boccaccio but also demonstrates to them why the *Decameron* was so influential in the formulation of Renaissance comedy. Having reviewed the source material, one is ready to make the transition from the worlds of Plautus, Terence, and Boccaccio to the comedy of the cinquecento. The study of the comedy involves a detailed analysis of the two strains noted above as well as such issues as social criticism, gender roles, political theory, historical veracity, the *questione della lingua*, and so forth, most of which are directly connected to and fueled by the *Decameron*. The impact of the *Decameron* was especially strong on the character formulation, the language, the style, the pantomime, the plotline, and the spiritual and cultural orientation of the comedy.

In character formulation, the most imitated character is, undoubtedly, Calandrino. Appearing in four of Boccaccio's tales, Calandrino first surfaces in *Decameron* 8.3 when he, with the assistance of his tormentor-friends Bruno and Buffalmacco, goes heliotrope hunting along the banks of the Mugnone River, becomes "invisible," returns home, and encounters his wife, whom he beats after she unwittingly breaks the nonexistent spell by speaking to him. The tale was so well received that its protagonist makes an unprecedented encore in

8.6, the story of the disappearing pig, a disappearance perpetrated by Bruno and Buffalmacco but blamed on Calandrino, who fails the "ginger sweets" (dog stools seasoned with aloes) test administered by the gleeful perpetrators. In 9.3, Calandrino is convinced by another recurring *Decameron* figure, Maestro Simone, that he is pregnant. A few hundred lire and capons are a small price to pay for obtaining the magic potion needed to abort the pregnancy. Finally in 9.5, Calandrino falls giddily in love with a prostitute who, prodded by Bruno, Buffalmacco, and Nello, leads him on. After extracting as many meals and material goods as they can out of Calandrino, his friends create a magic scroll through which Calandrino is to seduce the girl. He has just got himself in a position to do so when Nello arrives with Tessa, Calandrino's wife, who pays him back for the beating he gave her in 8.3. Calandrino returns home ripped to shreds and unsatisfied in love.

The influence of Calandrino is pervasive throughout Renaissance comedy, but it plays a pivotal role in Bibbiena's *Calandria* through the Calandro character, in Machiavelli's *La mandragola* through Nicia, and in Ariosto's *La Lena* through Pacifico. Bibbiena transforms Calandrino into Calandro, the hapless husband, forever a loser in love. The Calandro character is an older man, married to a sexually unsatisfied woman named Fulvia; nonetheless, he, like Boccaccio's Calandrino in 9.5, imagines himself a great lover and is, in this instance, attracted to a character he believes to be a young female but who is, in reality, Fulvia's male lover, Lidio, dressed as a woman in order to facilitate their trysts. Act 1, scene 3, is typically Boccaccian in its language, its intent, and its echo as Fessenio (Lidio's servant, who is doing double duty as Calandro's servant) explains Calandro's lust to Lidio.

What is emphasized in Bibbiena's *Calandria*, as in the tales of Calandrino, is the simplicity and foolishness of the intended dupe and the perpetrators' desire to have a good laugh at his expense. Calandro's gullibility and credulous nature make him the perfect object for the practical jokes of others. Just as Calandrino willingly believes Maso del Saggio's story of the invisibility-inducing heliotrope, so too does his counterpart Calandro accept the notion that a magical spell will render his body in pieces to facilitate its fitting in a trunk (*Calandria* 2.7). Both protagonists find that they cannot rely on their senses—neither their common sense of which they have little nor their sense of sight, which consistently betrays them.

Calandrino's simplistic features are apparent also in Machiavelli's Messer Nicia, the credulous old husband who is easily manipulated by the whole cast. Yet another rendering of Calandrino is Messer Maco, of Aretino's *La cortigiana*. In Nicia and Messer Maco, the comedic qualities of Calandrino are supplemented by those of the gullible pedant Maestro Simone, another important figure of the *Decameron* (8.9) who has numerous echoes in sixteenth-century Italian comedy. The characters of Ricciardo Minutolo and Catella (3.6) are also influential in Machiavelli's *La mandragola*. In fact, the calculating and opportunistic Ricciardo has his parallel in Callimaco, though Ricciardo is more resourceful and decisive than Callimaco. Likewise Catella, the woman seduced by Ricciardo, has her counterpart in Lucrezia, the woman pursued by Callimaco, but whereas Catella is driven by jealousy and sexual motives, Lucrezia, at least before her erotic encounter with Callimaco, is motivated by ethical reasons.

Old men, like Boccaccio's Ricciardo di Chinzica (2.10), who are in love with young women and who think they are viral enough to satisfy them, are common on the Renaissance stage. Messer Nicia and Calandro have been discussed above but they are not alone; Cleandro in *I suppositi* wants to marry the young Polinesta, and Nicomaco in Machiavelli's *La Clizia* is after the title character. Other characters of the *Decameron* who have relevance in cinquecento comedy are the go-between friar of 3.3 and the procuress of 5.10, who have their counterparts respectively in Timoteo of *La mandragola* and Aloigia of *La cortigiana*. The parasite Ciacco of *Decameron* 9.8 anticipates the conniving and resourceful Ligurio in *La mandragola*.

The *Decameron*'s language with its witticisms, malapropisms, obscene metaphors, evocative imagery, popular lingo, and equivocal terminology becomes an integral part of cinquecento comedy, providing much of its vigor and gaiety. Boccaccio's influence on language is both direct and indirect, that is to say, the playwrights of the cinquecento borrowed directly from the *Decameron*, or they used a comedic jargon that is analogous to Boccaccio's. Boccaccio's evocative term "ventura," meaning erect penis (8.2 [313]); his sexually charged imagery of the knight arriving fresh for battle (3.6 [368]); his colloquial term "millanta," which stands for thousands (8.3 [321]); and his proverb stating that it is better to do something and to regret it than to regret not having done anything at all (3.5 [365]) find direct appropriation in *La Calandria* (1.2, 3.12, 2.9, 3.5).[1] Likewise the sexual metaphor of "la coda," meaning penis (*Dec.* 9.10 [518]), recurs in *La Lena* (prologue) where the character Lena suggests that all women would like to have a "coda" attached to them; the suggestive term "segno," which stands for a urine sample, and the sexually evocative expression "ben coperto" ("well-covered") (*Dec.* 9.3 [464]) appear in *La mandragola* (2.2), where Lucrezia's infertile state is discussed. *La mandragola* (5.2) also echoes the obscene expression "unto bisunto" ("overly lubricated") in the *Decameron* (7.1 [207]). The double entendre "io mi dimeno quanto io posso" ("I'm shaking as much as I can" in *Decameron* 3.4 (355) gives impetus to a lively, humorous scene in *La Calandria* (3.10) filled with much punning, in which lovemaking is described as fitting a key into the keyhole. The numerous malapropisms of Boccaccio such as "Porcograsso and Vannacena" for "Ipocrasso and Avicenna" (Hippocrates and Avicenna) (8.9 [405]) and the many plays on words such as Messer "Nonmiblasmete Sevoipiace" ("Mr. Besokindas Tocursemenot") of *Decameron* 6.10 (182) find analogous usages in the comedy of the cinquecento. For example, in *La Calandria*, the magician Ruffo mangles "ermafrodito" ("hermaphrodite") into "merdafiorito" ("flowering excrement") (3.17) and Fessenio's magic-inducing word "ambracullac" is variously mispronounced by Calandro as "anculabrac," "alabracuc," and "alucambrac" (2.6).

The sparkling and concise style of the *Decameron*, with its ever-present consideration for the linguistic and behavioral decorum of the characters, is imitated by the Italian Renaissance playwrights. Thus the priestlike mannerisms and language of Ser Ciappelletto (1.1), a first-rate criminal who masterfully and convincingly acquires the behavior and language of a man of the cloth, are paralleled by the saintly decorum of Frate Timoteo, an amoral clergyman, who manipulates patristic doctrines in his effort to lead Lucrezia into an adulterous relationship (*Mandragola* 3.7). The rapid-fire, verbal exchanges in some of Boccaccio's tales, such as 6.4 and 7.2, become an important model for the exposition of some of the livelier scenes of cinquecento comedy (*Calandria* 1.7, 2.6, 3.10, for example).

The rich pantomime, the common caricaturing, and the inventiveness (*ingegno*) of some of the more successful comedic tales of the *Decameron* (2.1, 2.5, 3.5, 4.2, 6.10, 7.9, 8.3, 8.9, 9.2) find their way into the comedy of the cinquecento, giving it a vitality that it might otherwise have lacked. However, of the many comedic techniques peculiar to the *Decameron*, the slapstick episodes and various farcical stratagems have the greatest recurrence in the comedy of the cinquecento. The gesticulations of Bruno and Buffalmacco as they force "ginger-sweets" on Calandrino (*Dec.* 8.6) are repeated in *La mandragola* by Ligurio, who does the same to Nicia (4.9). The jealous husband in *Decameron* 7.5 puts pebbles in his mouth to disguise his voice so that he will be unrecognizable to his wife; Timoteo does the same to fool Messer Nicia in *La mandragola* (4.9). Indeed the shovings, beating, beratings, and wild gesticulations prevalent in many of the *Decameron* tales, such as 2.5, 7.4, 7.7, and 9.8, become almost a topos in Renaissance comedy.

The farcical stratagems of the *Decameron* also make their way into sixteenth-century comedy. *Decameron* 4.10 finds a young lover accidentally drinking a sleeping potion and passing out at an inopportune moment; his mistress hides him in a chest, and he is carried away during the night. An abbess conceals her priest-lover in a chest to get him into her room in *Decameron* 9.2, while in 7.2 a wife quickly thrusts her lover in a barrel to hide him when her husband unexpectedly returns home. Ariosto took full advantage of these stratagems; hence, in *Il negromante*, Camillo Pocosale convinces himself that if he hides in a chest, he will be spirited away to Emilia's house, while in *La Lena*, Flavio uses a barrel for a hiding place and is serendipitously transported into the home of his beloved Licinia.

Other stratagems that cinquecento comedy appropriates from the *Decameron* are cross-dressing and the substitution of one person for another. *Decameron* 2.3 finds the daughter of the king of England going to Rome disguised as an abbot, and *Decameron* 2.9 portrays Zinevra's escaping the wrath of her husband by dressing as a man and entering the service of a sultan. These situations are echoed in *La Calandria*, when Santilla is forced to take her brother's identity to avoid capture and when Fulvia has to dress as a man in order to leave her house in search of her lover. In *Decameron* 7.8 and 8.4 maids are substituted for their mistresses. These substitutions are echoed in *La cortigiana*, when a prostitute is substituted for Parabolano's beloved and in *La Clizia*, when Nicomaco ends up in bed with his manservant instead of the desired Clizia. At times Renaissance comedy borrows entire comedic situations from the *Decameron*. Gianni Lotteringhi's wife's incantation to rid herself of a sexually charged werewolf (*Dec.* 7.1) is repeated in its entirety in *Gl'ingannati* (4.6). Similarly Fessenio's description of his master in *La Calandria* (1.3) is a verbatim rendition of Frate Cipolla's description of his servant Guccio (*Dec.* 6.10).

As a portrait of contemporary society in its many facets, the *Decameron* provides much of the impetus for the idiosyncrasies and the social realism of the comedy of the cinquecento. The influence of the *Decameron* in the comedy's ideology is pervasive and varied, but it is especially strong in its hedonistic fervor and in its perception of the woman. Deduced from the classical maxim "Omnia vincit amor" and its corollary "Carpe diem" and pursued (at least in the novelle most imitated by sixteenth-century drama) at the expense of any ethical objective, the *Decameron's* hedonism becomes the elixir vitae of much of the comedy of the cinquecento. Thus Boccaccio's description of love in *Decameron* 7.4 (225–26) as an irresistible force that engenders ingenuity and resolve as it is carried out to its logical conclusion is appropriated verbatim by *La Calandria* (3.13) and is transformed into a literary maxim that affects the entire evolution of the play.

In the *Decameron*, the right to sexual gratification applies to women as well as men, thereby endowing the women of the *Decameron* with resilience, resourcefulness, and independence uncommon in the literature of the trecento. Most women are in charge of their husbands, lovers, and lives. Some, such as Madonna Filippa (6.7), even get popular opinion on their side. The self-assertiveness of the women of the *Decameron* translates into the comedies of the cinquecento. In *La Calandria* Fulvia cavorts with a young lover with impunity while her husband Calandro is chastised for trying to do the same. Likewise in *La mandragola*, men try to manipulate Lucrezia, but she outfoxes them by taking charge and arranging not only to meet with her lover whenever she wants but to have him actually live in her home.

Many of the comedic elements noted above are also part of the dramatic art of Ruzzante; however, in Ruzzante, the characters are no longer seen as strictly instruments of caricature and buffoonery (as is Calandro, for example) but are imbued with a certain sentimentalism and empathy. Thus the beating that the character Ruzzante receives in *Il parlamento* and in *I due dialoghi* engenders empathy more than laughter. Similarly, when his wife abandons him for another man, which she does for the sake of sustenance rather than sex, the usual objective in cinquecento comedies, she evokes sympathy instead of derisive scorn. To the extent that the Italian comedy of the cinquecento played an important role in the development of European comedy in general, the *Decameron* plays at least an indirect role in the works of such distinguished playwrights as

Molière, Lope de Vega, and Shakespeare. However, in their plays the Boccaccian element is tempered by indigenous circumstances and modes of thinking.

Italian Renaissance comedy owes a significant debt to Boccaccio's *Decameron*, both generally and particularly. It gave the plays of the cinquecento a certain constancy and unity. It is therefore somewhat ironic that Boccaccio, who was concerned about the constant changing and instability of the world ("I will grant you, however, that the things of this world have no stability, but are subject to constant change [. . .]" [author's conclusion, trans. McWilliam 833 (1981)]), provided the substance that gave a sense of stability to sixteenth-century Italian comedy.

NOTE

[1]Italian terms and expressions are taken from Giovanni Boccaccio, *Decameron*, ed. Vittore Branca (Florence: Le Monnier, 1960), 2 vols. The English rendition of the terms is ours.

Early Portraits of Boccaccio:
A Doorway to the *Decameron*

Victoria Kirkham

No other Western author has enjoyed a visual afterlife as luxuriant as Boccaccio's. A poet who loved to draw, he would doubtless have twinkled with delight to know that during the first three centuries after his death, his voluminous writings in Italian, Latin, and in their European vernacular translations generated for posterity a corpus of nearly eight thousand illustrations—not counting those made in printed books. Most appear in the more than thirteen hundred surviving manuscripts of his works, but a good number have also been documented in other Renaissance media. Boccaccio's own pen-and-ink drawings initiated the tradition, carried on internationally by the most famous miniaturists of their day, among them Jean Fouquet, the Master of the *Cité des dames*, the Boucicaut Master, and Taddeo Crivelli. They worked at the behest of patrons ranging from the burghers of Florence to the rulers of France, producing images unique for the sweep of their geographic and social origins (Branca, "Bocc. vis. I: Interpretazioni" 87–119; *Bocc. vis.* 1: 20–34; Rossi 153–87; Griseri 155–211). From Italy, over a hundred Boccaccian subjects are known in panels, frescoes, marriage chests, salvers, and *spalliere* by such painters as Apollonio di Giovanni, Pesellino, Vittore Carpaccio, Palma il Vecchio, Piero di Cosimo, Sandro Botticelli, Andrea del Castagno, Raphael, and Giorgio Vasari (Watson, "List"; Callmann; Rossi 189–231). In this worldwide virtual museum, hung mainly with scenes and characters inspired by the master's histories and fictions, a subgroup of images serves conveniently as a point of entry into the larger collection. They are Giovanni Boccaccio's portraits. Mostly idealized stereotypes of a generic author, these likenesses depict a poet, often smiling

and always plump in his physical proportions, who has come to be characterized over time by his defining book, the *Decameron* (Kirkham, "Renaissance
Portraits"; "L'immagine").

Boccaccio's portraits as author, a family of pictures that has continued to
flourish into our day in *Decameron* frontispieces, florid book jackets, and a
voyeuristic poster for the Broadway musical flop *Boccaccio* (reproduced in
Kirkham, "John Badmouth") make a good subject for an introductory lecture
on his writings. Unlike Dante and Petrarch, Boccaccio has not survived in any
monumental early public image, but he did leave us two self-portraits in manuscript drawings. All the later images, when surveyed chronologically, have much
to tell us about the man in his legendary constructions. What matters more than
what he really looked like is what sort of person his public thinks he was; the
artists' ever-shifting views capture in visual nutshells historical trends in reader
response. With passing eras, the canon lawyer so respected for his skills in ora-
tory that he was sent on ambassadorial missions by the *comune* of Florence,
even to the pope in Avignon, was transformed by the collective imagination
from a venerated Christian scholar to an iconoclastic, licentious raconteur. Our
earliest witnesses, fourteenth-century manuscripts, portray him as a learned
cleric and distinguished citizen. By the sixteenth century, that identity begins
shifting from sober humanist to another persona, someone whose appearance
complements the humorous, amorous voice that we hear as the *Decameron's*
vernacular narrator. Our contemporary popular culture has made his name synonymous with sensual pleasure in such sites as Boccaccio restaurants, a Boccaccio disco club for frenzied New Beat dancing in Belgium, and a Boccacio
[sic] massage parlor for men in San Francisco (Kirkham, "John Badmouth").

We know from letters Boccaccio and Petrarch exchanged, as well as a sequence of the Certaldan's late sonnets, that he was obese. Never married,
Boccaccio must have taken priestly vows because his will mentions vestments
and instruments for saying the Mass (Branca, *Bocc.: The Man* 187). Thus it is a
plump cleric who lectures from a stall chair to a circle of seated monks in his
oldest-known author portrait, the rather crudely painted frontispiece for a
manuscript of his *Bucolicum carmen* (Biblioteca Medicea-Laurenziana, ms.
34.49; reproduced in color, Muscetta 320; Kirkham, "L'immagine" 87; Ciardi
DuPré, "L'iconografia," fig. 50, 73).[1] Maria Grazia Ciardi DuPré has recently
proposed a dating of circa 1350 for this image and suggested that it could be an
early self-portrait designed to announce Boccaccio's intention of composing a
pastoral anthology. A muse wings her way down from top right to inform us in
a Latin couplet that here is a poet worthy of a laurel crown, while a vernacular
motto beneath him teaches that whoever sows virtue reaps fame. Boccaccio,
identified as a renowned authority on morality, is shown explicating the allegorical Christian meanings of his pastoral poetry (Kirkham, "Renaissance
Portraits"). A second portrait old enough to have a claim to authenticity appears in a manuscript of the *Filostrato* copied in 1397 (Florence, Biblioteca
Nazionale Centrale, ms. II.II.38, f. 3v; reproduced in color, *Decameron*, ed.

Branca, 1966, 1: x; black and white in Kirkham, "L'immagine" 97). Standing in three-quarter view on a dentate socle, Boccaccio is a corpulent figure hooded in *cappuccio* (the clerical cowl) who holds a large unidentified book. Its model was probably a fresco in the monumental cycle *Famous Men* designed by Coluccio Salutati, chancellor of Florence, around 1390. These twenty-two worthies, frescoed in Palazzo Vecchio, were unfortunately destroyed before the end of the fifteenth century (Degenhart and Schmitt 195–96). Salutati's program included Boccaccio as one of the five founding poets of Florence, a canon established by Filippo Villani in the 1380s with his *Liber de origine civitatis Florentiae et eiusdem famosis civibus* ("Book on the Origin of the City of Florence and Her Famous Citizens"; translated into Italian as *Le vite d'uomini illustri fiorentini*). They were Claudian, Dante, Zanobi da Strada, Boccaccio, and Petrarch (see Donato). Of those Palazzo Vecchio tributes, the *tituli*, or legends, alone survive. Boccaccio's label recalled his encyclopedic Latin works, not his *Decameron*, and it proclaimed that Florence has painted him here for his merits: "Dominus Iohannes Boccaccius [. . .] ex meritis, hic te Florentia pinxit" (Hankey).

The title "Dominus," referring to Boccaccio's respected professional status in the city as a canon lawyer (Ricci), returns in Domenico Castagno's *Uomini famosi* of 1450–52, now at the Uffizi (reproduced in color in *Decameron*, 1966, 1: xv; Horster, pl. 75, 84; Kirkham, "L'immagine" 97). His selection of three warriors, three women, and three poets marks the first time the Three Crowns of Florence—Dante, Petrarch, and Boccaccio—unite as a trio in the visual arts. These three are the new canon, which has prevailed into modern times. Villani's trecento family of Florentine poets, outdated by Castagno's time, has lost Claudian, an Egyptian interloper, and Zanobi, merely an ephemeral courtier in Angevin Naples. Castagno's Boccaccio again carries a book, sign of his status as an author, but it bears no name. Not until the sixteenth century will the *Decameron* supplant his Latin histories and encyclopedias as the poet's defining book (Branca, *Linee*).

Phases in Boccaccio's transition from scholar to *novelliere* are attested in the marble bust sculpted in 1503 by Gian Francesco Rustici as a cenotaph in his parish church, Santi Michele and Jacopo, in Certaldo. Rustici envisions Boccaccio wrapped in a *cappuccio*, jovial of mood, round of face, with a double chin and the hint of a dimple (reproduced in Kirkham, "L'immagine" 88). The book he clasps to his breast was originally untitled. Probably in connection with a church renovation about two hundred years later, the uneven letters "Decameron" were clumsily incised on it. By then, people in Italy had largely forgotten the serious author who, together with his friend Petrarch, had forged a new Latin humanism, and they preferred to read his more accessible humor in the mother tongue. As for the pocket in the subject's chin, that was doubtless suggested by Filippo Villani, whose biography of Boccaccio—the earliest of the Certaldan's lives—reports that he was a cordial man who had a dimple when he smiled ("Life" 191). The smile that makes Rustici's Boccaccio simpatico, so much so that in the eighteenth century English tourists were said to have climbed the wall to hug the bust, may also be a visual echo of Villani's vita. As likely as not, though, it was prompted more immediately by Boccaccio's associations with the *Decameron*, already ascendant by the turn of the sixteenth century. When a later hand chiseled the word *Decameron* on the book Rustici's Boccaccio holds, the effect was to make explicit what was already implicit in the bust's amiable facial expression: "He is the good-natured narrator of amusing short stories."

Rustici's high relief achieved authority because it adorns the poet's burial site. Moreover, the bust enjoyed prestige conferred by proximity to a portrait of Boccaccio made during his lifetime, in 1366. Although now lost, we have an idea of what it looked like thanks to the committee of churchmen headed by Vincenzo Borghini, the so-called deputies, who prepared the expurgated edition that saved the *Decameron* from the Index of Prohibited Books. Among Borghini's papers are three surviving drawings by the artist whom he dispatched to Certaldo to copy Boccaccio's image in Santi Michele and Jacopo (reproduced in Williams; Kirkham, "L'immagine" 91). They show a composition with the Madonna and child at center. Flanking her are San Miniato and Boccaccio kneeling as donor at left; at right Saint Catherine with a child, perhaps the Blessed Giulia, patron of Certaldo. The detailed drawing that would have shown Boccaccio's face up close is missing (it was used to cut the frontispiece), but we can perceive the outlines of his figure, dimly sketched. With hands pressed together in a prayerful gesture, he is a man of heavy proportions whose head is wrapped in a hood with a long liripipe hanging down his back. Boccaccio's profile as the deputies transmit it is not particularly flattering (reproduced in Boccaccio, *Decameron*, 1573, frontispiece; Kirkham, "John Badmouth" and "L'immagine" 90). Features that show within the window of an encroaching *cappuccio* suggest a man whose cheek is not round but sunken beneath the bone, implying that the teeth under it are gone. The nose is almost bulbous and slightly retroussé. The mouth is fleshy, and a shadow under the lower lip indicates a pocket in the chin, knoblike in its shape.

Artists and public alike have for the most part rejected this unprepossessing image, although it resembles the oldest manuscript portrait—now ascribed to Boccaccio himself—the mid-fourteenth-century frontispiece of his *Bucolicum carmen*. Although Rustici had it to hand as a model and did keep the *cappuccio*, he clearly reworked his subject's features to sculpture an idealized mask. Raphael, for his *Parnassus* of circa 1510 in the Vatican Stanza della Segnatura, preferred Rustici's revised Boccaccio to the donor portrait unmediated. What is more, he stripped Boccaccio of the very feature that the deputies believed best characterized him historically, his medieval clerical *cappuccio*. In this, he followed the Boccaccian type that had already emerged in a series of Florentine astrological woodcuts (c. 1460), in which the Three Crowns sit at their desks as representatives of poetic activity in the family under the influence of the planet Jupiter (reproduced in Hind 2, pl. 116, 117; Kirkham "L'immagine" 97). Now crowned with laurel like all the other poets assembled on Mount Parnassus, Raphael's Boccaccio stands far from the epic authors Dante, Homer, Vergil, and Statius, congregated at top left, and he is positioned diagonally opposite the lyric poets Sappho and Petrarch on the lower left. His place is high at the right rear, where he gazes into the distance with contemplative contentment. (He stands just to the left of the second laurel tree from the right, and he faces right in three-quarter view. His body is blocked from us by an imposing bearded full-length male figure—Tebaldeo? Ariosto?—who stands in front of him and looks out over his shoulder toward the viewer.) Near Boccaccio one identifiable figure is Sannazaro. Assuming that Raphael grouped his poets according to literary genres in which they excelled, as Paul F. Watson ("Window") has proposed, the papal painter must commemorate Boccaccio the pastoral author of Latin eclogues (*Bucolicum carmen*) and vernacular nymphals (*Comedia delle ninfe fiorentine, Ninfale fiesolano*). It is tempting to think that Raphael also had in mind the *Decameron*, which relates the story of a Utopian retreat with rustic, pastoral resonance (Gibaldi).

Raphael's laureate in turn provided the close visual source for Boccaccio's head in Giorgio Vasari's *Portrait of Six Tuscan Poets* of 1544, now at the Minneapolis Institute of Arts (reproduced in Bowron; Kirkham, "Renaissance Portraits"; Franklin; Parker; and in color in Kirkham, "L'immagine" 86). Vasari's panel honors primarily Dante, who dominates the picture space as the foremost Italian poet. He holds up a copy of "Virgil" and explains it to a handsome young man behind his shoulder, Guido Cavalcanti. The gesture must allude to Dante's conversation with Cavalcanti senior among the heretics of *Inferno* 10, in which commentators such as Boccaccio and Cristoforo Landino detected a veiled reproach of his son, Guido, for having failed to write an epic. Close to Dante on the other side stands Petrarch, identified by the book in his hand, a copy of his *Rime* for Madonna Laura. Boccaccio brings up the rear between them. All we see is his head, both tonsured and crowned with laurel. There is no identifying book. This Boccaccio joins his fellow classic poets at the center of the composition, third-ranked of the Three Crowns of Florence, after Dante and Petrarch. Like Cavalcanti, he is in the second row of figures, whose other members are Landino and Marsilio Ficino. What these second-tier *litterati* of the fifteenth century have in common is their activity as Dante scholars: Landino was his commentator; Ficino translated his *De monarchia* into Italian. Boccaccio can well stand beside them since he was both Dante's biographer (*Trattatello in laude di Dante*) and his expositor (*Esposizioni sopra la* Comedìa *di Dante*).

The type originating with Raphael and closely reproduced by Vasari, whose panel of six poets was often copied, seems to have given rise indirectly to the so-called Titian Boccaccio. It appears as the frontispiece of the English *Decameron* of 1684. This apocryphal engraving spawned many successors in the Anglo-Saxon world, eventually producing a mustachioed dandy who traveled throughout Europe in the nineteenth century and reached America in the twentieth (reproduced in Kirkham, "John Badmouth"). With features that have taken on an oriental cast, he can still be seen on the cover of a South Korean *Decameron*, published at Seoul in 1963 (Esposito 27).

How Titian's name came to be associated with Boccaccio's portrait is a mystery, but it illustrates two patterns in the legends and images that evolve from poets' lives. First, there is a universal, anecdotal tendency to assimilate great minds, the sort of impulse that dictated Walter Savage Landor's *Imaginary Conversations* among famous persons of all ages. Hence, just as it was popularly believed that Giotto painted Dante because the two of them were "good friends," so it would have seemed natural for a grand master and portraitist like Titian, famous for such sensuous female figures as *Flora* and *Venus*, to put his hand to reproducing the features of a fellow Italian and kindred female admirer. Second, the portraits that become most authoritative are not necessarily the oldest—hence presumably closest to life. Instead, they seem to be either the most attractive and anodyne likenesses or those attributed to the most famous artists, regardless of physiognomic authenticity. Thus when a Finnish scholar, Tauno Nurmela, contributed two articles to the question of Boccaccio's appearance in the late 1950s and early 1960s, he decided that our best evidence was a different picture altogether (reproduced in Nurmela, "Physionomie"; Watson, *Garden*, pl. 85; and in Kirkham, "L'immagine" 102). A lovely full-folio drawing by a mid-quattrocento Florentine master, it decorates the colophon of a *Corbaccio* at the Marciana Library in Venice (ms. It. X, 127). The only historically accurate detail in Nurmela's Boccaccio is the liripipe; for the rest, it is sheer invention. From the wrappings of the liripipe emerges a face highly idealized, so smooth and regular that it looks like the reconstruction of a plastic surgeon. We see a subject neither fat nor thin. Wrinkles ever so slight and neatly parallel across the brow could delicately refer to any man over forty who has aged well. His nose is Roman, not retroussé; he has no jowls or any distinctive topography of the chin. Clearly, this image has been accepted as true because of its fine artistic quality and because it depicts a man of classic features.

Still often cited today is Castagno's Boccaccio, a different fellow altogether, but no less ideal and so generic as to be nearly faceless. Reproduced on postcards and frontispieces of Italian *Decamerons*, its popularity is due more to Andrea del Castagno, a well-remembered Renaissance painter, than to any intrinsic verisimilitude. The artist—not the subject—validates the image. In much the same way, Raphael's Boccaccio was authoritative for Vasari, who was himself often copied, and Elizabethan England legitimized the "Titian" Boccaccio. Context also doubtless helped ensure the survival and diffusion of Castagno's "Dominus Iohannes Boccaccius." Unlike the early manuscript images, miniatures in books that did not circulate widely, this picture belongs to a monumental cycle of worthies that in its various locations has been accessible to generations of viewers (most recently at the Uffizi). Our poet further benefits from being enshrined with his classic companions, Dante and Petrarch. He rides, so to speak, on their coattails. Although all three have comparable height and weight in Castagno's mural lineup, they are not exactly equal. Boccaccio stands at the periphery, at the far outside right of nine figures. Castagno thus marginalizes him, and so about a century later would Vasari, whose arrangement of the Three Crowns makes clear their ranked order: first Dante, second Petrarch, and only third, bringing up the rear, Boccaccio. As far back as Filippo Villani, Boccaccio had followed the leaders, Dante and Petrarch, coming with Zanobi da Strada in a second wave of moderns. A half century later, Leonardo Bruni reinforces this marching order in history—minus Zanobi—with his *Lives of Dante and Petrarch* (1436). To maintain the Plutarchan parallel, Bruni must delegate Boccaccio to a role that is peripheral to his two *vite* subjects, but Bruni (60) does not let the Third Crown fade from memory:

> [W]hen Petrarch died, the Florentine Muses, as if by hereditary succession, were left to Boccaccio, and in him fame resided for the above-mentioned studies, and it was a succession in time, too, because when Dante died, Petrarch was seventeen years of age, and when Petrarch died, Boccaccio was younger than he by nine years, and so by succession went the Muses.   (my trans.)

Actually, Boccaccio's place as third of the Three Crowns was sealed even before his death, and it is not just dependent on chronology. The person responsible was none other than his dearest friend, Petrarch. When word reached Petrarch that Boccaccio had burned all his vernacular poetry, Petrarch was quick to send a letter reassuring his friend of his worth as a writer (*Letters* 5.3). Praise for his correspondent, however, does not prevent Petrarch from going on to assert his own superiority. He would, he claims, much rather be ranked lower than his friend, or simply aspire to be as good, and yet— "Suppose for the moment that I surpass you, I who would so gladly be your equal; suppose that you are surpassed by the great master of our mother tongue [. . .]?" (Robinson 203). Granting to Dante, "master of our mother tongue," the first place, Petrarch appropriates second, and goes on to argue with eloquent force that Boccaccio should take pride in occupying the third place in such an illustrious triad.

In summary, what emerges most strikingly from a historical survey of Boccaccio's portraits is the instability of his image. Unlike Dante, whose physiognomy we still can instantly recognize, Boccaccio is a poet of many faces. Dante's profile was constant from the trecento (whether true or not is another matter), transmitted by early monumental archetypes visible for all to see in the great public buildings of Florence. Petrarch, too, had early authoritative images (Trapp). For Boccaccio no such public, official image survived. The oldest portraits are in manuscripts, where for all practical purposes they remained buried. The donor portrait of him in the panel of the Madonna that he commissioned for his parish church in Certaldo has disappeared, leaving as visual echoes two adaptations, so different that they are almost impossible to reconcile—Rustici's smiling bust of 1503 and Borghini's somber profile of 1573.

Boccaccio's kaleidoscopic iconography over the centuries illustrates the most fundamental rule of legend formation in the lives of the poets: authors write books, but as time passes, the book makes the author. The phenomenon can be verified from as far back as ancient times and continues still (Lefkowitz; Foucault). In the absence of an archetype, the field is open to artistic fantasy. Boccaccio became what people imagined he was, which is to say, his appearance has mirrored their assumptions as readers. Gian Francesco Rustici, a character whom Vasari reports kept a snake pit in his house and regaled his friends at costly banquets, doubtless enjoyed the *Decameron* as an anthology of amusing, spicy tales. So did his contemporaries, still privileged to know the book before the Council of Trent (1547–63) and its long shadows of censorship. By the time Borghini and his zealous Committee of Church Deputies carried out their assignment, saving the *Decameron* meant excising all the escapades of nuns and clergy to meet the standards of Catholic Reformation morality deployed in full sobriety. Hence their return to the medieval image of the poet as cleric, unsmiling and deeply cocooned in his *cappuccio*. As for the Elizabethans and later generations of English readers, what could make a better frontispiece to their *Decameron* than a Boccaccio engraved after a "Titian," especially when the poet, perhaps not by coincidence, resembles their traditional portrait of Shakespeare?

We can find as many Boccaccios as there are generations and nations of his readers. The Florentine historian Filippo Villani, writing in the late fourteenth century, left our earliest description:

> Tall and of rather stout build, Boccaccio had a round face with the nose slightly flat above the nostrils; rather large, but nonetheless attractive and well-defined lips: and a dimpled chin that was charming when he laughed. He was pleasant and considerate in conversation and he greatly enjoyed talking. He was engaging and acquired many friends [. . .].
> ("Life" 191)

The earliest visual record is Boccaccio's self-portrait, inserted as the frontispiece to his *Bucolicum carmen*, and there follow the corpulent hooded figure of the 1397 *Filostrato* who during the early Renaissance must have marched in a frescoed frieze inside the city hall of Florence among twenty-two of the city's most famous sons; Rustici's dimpled bust, a smiling soul in marble carved to decorate the church of the Certaldan's tomb site; Raphael's happy contemplative, who rightly takes his place in a universal gathering of the greatest poets of all time; Vasari's pensive scholar, a tonsured laureate who was the first Dantista; the deputies' austere cleric, resuscitated for Counter-Reformation Europe; and that pseudo-Titianesque reincarnation so dear to the Anglo-Saxons. Allowance made for iconographic drift and ideological tilt, they are all the same person. With no surviving public portrait from life to authenticate his appearance historically, he has over the passing centuries gradually settled into another, fictional identity. Although this protean author wrote narrative and nonfiction, in

Italian and Latin, verse and prose, and tried his quill at virtually every poetic genre known to the medieval repertory, his fame has come to focus on one single title, the masterwork honored in this pedagogical anthology. The great book he created has come to characterize both his reputation and his appearance. The man has merged with his *Decameron*.

If no reproduction is available in a published source, photographs can be obtained by writing directly to the museums or libraries where a given monument is housed. Addresses can be found in *The World of Learning 1999*. The Alinari archive rents photos through Art Resource (65 Bleeker Street, 9th fl.; New York, NY 10012; tel. 212 505-8700; fax 212 429-9286). Alinari also has published a serviceable set of microfiche reproductions of its photo archive, available in reference libraries. In Italy, two economical sources for purchasing photos are Soprintendenza per i Beni Artistici e Storici di Firenze (Piazzale degli Uffizi, 50122 Firenze; http://www.sbas.firenze.it/fotografico/index.HTML); Gabinetto Fotografico Nazionale (Istituto Centrale per il Catalogo e Documentazione, Ministero per i Beni Culturali e Ambientali, Via San Michele 18, Rome). They both charge a minimal fee for making a black-and-white print from a negative.

I find that a slide presentation with an overview of Boccaccio's portraits makes an appealing introduction to a course in which we discuss his literature. This may be a monographic seminar or a class on the *Decameron* and the Italian novella, on Boccaccio and Petrarch, or on the Three Crowns of Florence. When I first started incorporating visual material into my classes, I borrowed slides from our art history department library or had them made by that library's reproduction facility from photographs in books. Since then, I have assembled a personal slide collection, using my own camera with a lens ground for close-up photography. I distribute to the students a sheet listing all the photographs we see. A sample entry might read:

> *Boccaccio Lectures to the Monks*. Florence, Biblioteca Medicea-Laurenziana, ms. 34.49, frontispiece. Giovanni Boccaccio, *Bucolicum carmen* ("Pastoral Poetry"), c. 1350 (reproduced in Muscetta [320]; Ciardi DuPré, fig. 48; Kirkham, "L'immagine 87).

In addition, the students have a course bibliography that includes references to visual material. The single most useful resource has been the beautifully illustrated three-volume *Decameron* edited by Branca in 1966, unfortunately out of print. Branca's *Boccaccio visualizzato* now updates it as an invaluable treasury of images. These can be computer-scanned for projection on a large classroom screen or for printout and distribution.

Depending on the material to be covered in class, I like to include depictions of Boccaccio with his fellow poets (e.g., Domenico Castagno's Three Crowns in his *Uomini famosi*, Vasari's *Portrait of Six Tuscan Poets*, Raphael's *Parnassus*).

These group portraits situate the author in a conceptual framework that prompts considerations on Boccaccio's place in the Italian tradition and invites a general discussion of canon formation. Sometimes, instead of joining a peer group, Boccaccio makes an appearance with his lady, Fiammetta. For example, a sixteenth-century engraving, entirely imaginary, by Enea Vico links the pair in a typology probably inspired by a more frequently represented couple, Petrarch and Madonna Laura (Hirth 2, nos. 957, 958). The 1573 *Decameron* frontispiece also shows Boccaccio beside a lady. Crowned and unnamed, she has sometimes been called Queen Giovanna of Naples, sometimes Fiammetta.

Another category of images is the apocryphal—as opposed to imaginary— portraits of Boccaccio. The most famous is in the Spanish Chapel at Santa Maria Novella in Florence in a fresco of the *Way to Salvation*, by Andrea Bonaiuti da Firenze (1366–68). Since this "Boccaccio" is said to be accompanied by "Fiammetta," the identification is doubly fanciful. As Watson has compellingly argued ("Chapel"), it was romantic English travelers of the last century who were responsible for imagining the poet and his mistress into Andrea's Dominican mural. Although wrong about the attributions, they were correctly remembering their *Decameron*, which opens in the Gothic setting of Santa Maria Novella. Notwithstanding Watson's debunking, this likeness still floats about, persisting as Boccaccio's. It decorates the front cover of Anna Vaglio's recent manual *Invito alla lettura di Boccaccio*.

Boccaccio can also be presented from a wide variety of his works other than the *Decameron*, including the late Latin encyclopedias—author portraits in incipit initials, dedication-of-the-book scenes, the author as visionary narrator, and so forth. His *De casibus virorum illustrium* and *De mulieribus claris*, which circulated in both the original language and in all the major European vernaculars, survive in magnificent exemplars made for the French and Burgundian courts. They are texts that generated between them more illuminations than those in all Boccaccio's other works combined. For that reason, I have also included in this bibliography recent published work on these princely manuscripts.

Some of these illustrations were made for women of the aristocracy, which opens possibilities for comparison with the *Decameron* and its symbolic dedication to women. The miniature that best complements Boccaccio's preface to the "idle ladies in love" is in the Giovanni d'Agnolo Capponi *Decameron* (Paris, Bibliothèque Nationale, ms. It. 482, f. 5; reproduced in *Decameron*, ed. Branca, 1966, 1: 2; Ciardi DuPré, fig. 33). Ciardi DuPré now attributes to Boccaccio himself the illustrations in this manuscript, the first to provide programmatically an illustration at the beginning of each day of storytelling. Beneath a pen-and-ink drawing of two couples on horseback (identified by Daniela Delcorno Branca as an Arthurian allusion to Lancelot and the *Decameron* subtitle, "Prince Gallehault"), the incipit initial "H" of "Humana cosa è" represents the author in cathedra lecturing to a class of ladies with smiling, upturned faces, while overhead Cupid flutters with a bow and arrow.

In our visually enhanced study of the *Decameron*, my students and I have sometimes looked at the manuscript illustrations of several stories and discussed how the scene or scenes chosen by an artist as visual epitomes correlate with the narrative structure of the tale and the interpretative emphasis we would give it. Best for this method are those codices that contain a complete cycle of one hundred illustrations, one for each of the novelle. The first was made in the French translation of Laurent de Premierfait for Jean sans Peur before 1420 (Vatican City, Biblioteca Apostolica Vaticana, ms. Pal. Lat., 1989).

The most provocative approach I have found is to compare illustrations made across time and in differing media of a single tale. In my Boccaccio Visualized course we focused on Ghismonda (4.1), one of the two novelle most frequently anthologized in the manuscript tradition (the other is the Griselda story, 10.10). We began with the Capponi *Decameron*, closest to the written text in its details, and then continued with several Franco-Burgundian *Decameron*s of the fifteenth and sixteenth centuries. Our point of arrival was the sensuous, grieving *Ghismonda* painted in the seventeenth century by the Sienese artist Bernardino Mei (Branca, *"Lusus"* and "Ostensione"; reproduced in color in Branca, *Bocc. vis.* 1: 60). A splendid personification of anger and lust, she holds her lover's heart in the first illustration of the tale with the distinction of representing that organ in an anatomically correct version. Tracking three centuries of images, we can read the evolution of the heart from courtly metaphor to scientific object. From this chronological and cross-cultural perspective, it is also fruitful to consider such issues as the socioeconomic origins of the various manuscripts, from mercantile to courtly; art as ornament versus art as commentary; and the relation of the *cornice* to the novelle (visual versus narrative framing).

Until recently it was believed that Boccaccio inaugurated the tradition of illustrating his works around 1373 with his own thirteen surviving catchword drawings for the *Decameron* autograph, a transcription of his youthful masterpiece lovingly revised late in life (Berlin, Staatsbibliothek, ms. Hamilton 90; reproduced in color in *Decameron*, ed. Singleton, 1974, 1982; Branca, *Bocc. vis.* 1: 15–18). We now are discovering that his activity as an illuminator was far more extensive than previously recognized and that it began early in his career. Scholars have identified his hand not only in the text or glosses of manuscripts once in his possession but also in artistic commentary. Graceful curlicues and ink flourishes embellish the red and blue capital letters that typically articulate paragraph and chapter divisions. Elsewhere tiny marginal sketches of humans or animals allow him to visualize passages in the written text. Ciardi DuPré ("L'iconografia") attributes to him the very faded *Presentation of the Book* that heads his autograph of the *Teseida delle nozze d'Emilia*, the epic that was Chaucer's source for The Knight's Tale, dated to 1340–41. Boccaccio, she proposes, may also have done circa 1350 the pen and color wash author portrait that serves as frontispiece to his anthology of pastoral poetry (Florence, Biblioteca Medicea-Laurenziana, ms. 34.49). She has now assembled a preliminary list of his known drawings (with photographs), including some in manuscripts that belonged to Petrarch, and a copy of the *Divine Comedy*. This newly emerging evidence, which Branca reckons at 150 images ("Boccaccio II"), produced a corpus that could in itself organize a discussion on the author as illustrator and visual commentator of his own writings. Further studies on Boccaccio's whimsical decorations in his manuscripts (e.g., Morello) appear in the anthology edited by Claude Cazalé-Bérard and Michelangelo Picone.

Finally, illustrations provide a point of entry for study of the medieval book as a material object. Boccaccio's catchword illustrations for ms. Hamilton 90 demonstrate how a codex was formed of gatherings—as well as the author's sense of humor: his bust of Alatiel (2.7), the most promiscuous of all *Decameron* heroines, decorates the word "vivere," whose letters march across her low-cut dress on a prominent bosom. Watson ("Gatherings") has shown how the different gatherings of the Ceffini *Decameron* of 1427 were made in a workshop as stints by different artists. It bespeaks the popularity of Boccaccio's stories and the demand for accelerated production of manuscript copies.

NOTE

[1]Some material in this essay is drawn from my chapter entitled "L'immagine del Boccaccio nella memoria tardo-gotica e rinascimentale" ("The Lost Image: Boccaccio's Likeness in Renaissance Memory"), in Branca's *Boccaccio visualizzato*. Here, for convenience, I include references to reproductions of illustrations in bibliographic sources.

APPENDIX
ICONOGRAPHIC BIBLIOGRAPHY

Boccaccio, Giovanni. *Il* Decameron *di Messer Giovanni Boccacci, Cittadino Fiorentino.* Ricorretto in Roma et Emendato secondo l'ordine del Sacro Concilio di Trento. Et riscontrato in Firenze con Testi Antichi et alla sua vera lezione ridotto da' Deputati di loro Alt. Ser. Florence: Giunti, 1573. (With woodcut frontispiece based on Boccaccio's portrait as donor in a lost panel of 1366).

———. *Decameron.* Ed. Vittore Branca. 3 vols. Florence: Sadea, 1966. (Hundreds of color reproductions from manuscripts and scenes of medieval life).

———. Decameron. *Edizione diplomatico-interpretativa dell'autografo Hamilton 90.* Ed. Charles S. Singleton. Baltimore: Johns Hopkins UP, 1974. (With color reproductions of the catchwords in ms. Hamilton 90).

———. *Decameron.* Trans. with commentary by Charles S. Singleton. 3 vols. Berkeley: U of California P, 1982. (With color reproductions in vol. 3 of the catchwords in ms. Hamilton 90).

Bowron, E. P. "Giorgio Vasari's *Portrait of Six Tuscan Poets.*" *Minneapolis Institute of Arts Bulletin* 60 (1971–73): 43–54. (Vasari's Boccaccio).

Branca, Vittore. "Ancora manoscritti figurati: Boccaccio 'visualizzato' IV." *Studi sul Boccaccio* 18 (1989): 167.

———, ed. *Boccaccio visualizzato.* 3 vols. Turin: Einaudi, 1999.

————. "Boccaccio visualizzato I: 1. Interpretazioni visuali del *Decameron*; 2. Un primo elenco di codici illustrati di opere di Boccaccio." *Studi sul Boccaccio* 15 (1985–86): 85–148.

————. "Boccaccio 'visualizzato' dal Boccaccio II: Possibile identificazione nel Parigino It. 482 di una redazione del *Decameron* anteriore all'autografo degli anni Settanta." *Studi sul Boccaccio* 22 (1994): 225–34.

————. "Un *lusus* del Bruni cancelliere: Il rifacimento di una novella del *Decameron* (IV,1) e la sua irradiazione europea." *Leonardo Bruni cancelliere della Repubblica di Firenze: Convegno di studi (Firenze 27–29 ottobre 1987).* Ed. P. Viti. Florence: Olschki, 1990. 207–26. (Visual iconography of the Ghismonda novella).

————. "Nuove segnalazioni di manoscritti e dipinti: Boccaccio 'visualizzato' III." *Studi sul Boccaccio* 17 (1988): 99–100.

————. "Ostensione del cuore e «Amore e Morte»." *Forma e parola: Studi in onore di Fredi Chiappelli.* Ed. Dennis J. Dutschke et al. Rome: Bulzoni, 1992. 155–73. (Same material as in Branca's "Un *lusus*," but with inferior reproductions).

Brownlee, Kevin, and Victoria Kirkham, eds. *Boccaccio 1990: The Poet and His Renaissance Reception.* Spec. issue of *Studi sul Boccaccio* 20 (1991–92): 167–397.

Buettner, Brigitte. "Les affinités sélectives: Image et texte dans les premiers manuscrits des «Clères femmes»." *Studi sul Boccaccio* 18 (1989): 281–300.

————. *Boccaccio's Des clères et nobles femmes: Systems of Signification in an Illuminated Manuscript.* Seattle: College Art Assn. in association with U of Washington P, 1996.

Callmann, Ellen. "Subjects from Boccaccio in Italian Painting, 1375–1525." *Studi sul Boccaccio* 23 (1995): 19–78.

Cazalé-Bérard, Claude, and Michelangelo Picone, eds. *Atti del Convegno "Gli Zibaldoni di Boccaccio: Memoria, scrittura, riscrittura."* Firenze, 26–28 aprile 1996. Florence: Cesati, 1998. (Includes essays on Boccaccio's own activity as illustrator).

Ciardi DuPré dal Poggetto, Maria Grazia. "Boccaccio 'visualizzato' dal Boccaccio I: 'Corpus' dei disegni e cod. Parigino It. 482." *Studi sul Boccaccio* 22 (1994): 197–225. (Abundantly illustrated).

————. "L'iconografia nei codici miniati boccacciani dell'Italia centrale e meridionale." Branca, *Boccaccio visualizzato* 2: 3–152. (Corpus of Boccaccio's own drawings and a number of manuscripts with author portraits).

Degenhart, Bernhard, and Annegrit Schmitt. *Corpus der italienischen Zeichnungen 1300–1450.* Vol. 1, pt. 1. Berlin: Mann, 1968. (Includes reproductions of early portraits of Boccaccio).

Delcorno Brancą, Daniela. " 'Cognominato Prencipe Galeotto.' Il sottotitolo illustrato del Parigino It. 482." *Studi sul Boccaccio* 23 (1995): 79–88. (On the first narrative illustration in this manuscript).

Donato, Maria Monica. "Per la fortuna monumentale di Giovanni Boccaccio fra i grandi Fiorentini: Notizie e problemi." *Studi sul Boccaccio* 17 (1988): 287–342. (With reproductions of paintings inspired by Villani's canon of poets).

Franklin, Margaret. "A Note on Boccaccio in Hiding." *Source* 14.1 (1994): 1–5. (On Vasari's debt to Raphael's *Parnassus* for his iconography of Boccaccio).

Gilbert, Creighton. *Poets Seeing Artists at Work: Instances in the Italian Renaissance.* Florence: Olschki, 1991. (Includes discussion of Castagno's Boccaccio).

Griseri, Andreina. "Di fronte al «*Decameron*» : L'età moderna." Branca, *Boccaccio visualizzato* 1: 155–211. (Illustrations from the sixteenth century to the Pre-Raphaelites and Chagall).

Hankey, Teresa. "Salutati's Epigrams for the Palazzo Vecchio at Florence." *Journal of the Warburg and Courtauld Institutes* 22 (1959): 363–65. (Discussion of lost fresco cycle that included Boccaccio).

Hind, A. M. *Early Italian Engraving: A Critical Catalogue with Complete Reproduction of All the Prints Described.* 1938. Lichtenstein: Nendeln, 1970.

Hirth, Georg, ed. *Kulturgeschichtliches Bilderbuch aus drei Jahrhunderten: Picture Book of the Graphic Arts, 1500–1800.* 1882–90. New York: Blom, 1972.

Horster, Marita. *Andrea del Castagno: Complete Edition with a Critical Catalogue.* Ithaca: Cornell UP, 1980. (Reproduces Castagno's Boccaccio).

Kirkham, Victoria. "L'immagine del Boccaccio nella memoria tardo-gotica e rinascimentale." Branca, *Boccaccio visualizzato* 1: 85–144.

———. "John Badmouth: Fortunes of the Poet's Image." *Boccaccio 1990: The Poet and His Renaissance Reception.* Brownlee and Kirkham 355–76.

———. "Portraits of Boccaccio. First Addenda and Corrigenda to a Preliminary List of Boccaccio Portraits." *Studi sul Boccaccio* 16 (1987): 275–83.

———. "A Preliminary List of Boccaccio Portraits from the Fourteenth to the Mid-Sixteenth Centuries." *Studi sul Boccaccio* 15 (1985-86): 167–88.

———. "Renaissance Portraits of Boccaccio. A Look into the Kaleidoscope." *Studi sul Boccaccio* 16 (1987): 284–305.

Marcon, Susy. "I codici di Verona. Boccaccio visualizzato III." *Studi sul Boccaccio* 17 (1988): 101–11.

Morello, Giovanni. "Disegni marginali nei manoscritti di Giovanni Boccaccio." Cazalé-Bérard and Picone 161–77.

Musa, Mark, and Peter Bondanella, eds. *The Decameron.* By Giovanni Boccaccio. Norton Critical Edition. Norton: New York, 1977.

Muscetta, Carlo. "Giovanni Boccaccio e i novellieri." *Il Trecento.* Vol. 2 of *Storia della letteratura italiana.* Ed. Emilio Cecchi and Natalino Sapegno. Milan: Garzanti, 1965. 316–558. (Reproduces in color frontispiece of Florence, Bib. Med.-Laur. ms. Plut. 34.49).

Nurmela, Tauno. "Contribution à l'iconographie de Dante et de Boccace." *Neuphilologische Mitteilungen* 66 (1965): 508–11.

———. "Physionomie de Boccace." *Neuphilologische Mitteilungen* 60 (1959): 321–34.

Parker, Deborah. "Vasari's *Portrait of Six Tuscan Poets*: A Visible Literary History." *Visibile Parlare: Dante and the Art of the Italian Renaissance.* Ed. Parker. Spec. issue of *Lectura Dantis* 22–23 (1998): 45–62. (Reproduces Vasari's Boccaccio).

Reynolds, Catherine. "Illustrated Boccaccio Manuscripts in the British Library (London). Boccaccio visualizzato III." *Studi sul Boccaccio* 17 (1988): 113–81.

———. "Illustrated Boccaccio Manuscripts in the British Library (London). Additional List. Boccaccio visualizzato IV." *Studi sul Boccaccio* 18 (1989): 169–74.

Rossi, Massimiliano. "I dipiniti—Introduzione: La novella di Sandro e Nastagio."

Branca, *Boccaccio visualizzato* 2: 153–231. (Many panel paintings, including *cassoni* and Botticelli's *spalliere*).

Tesnière, Marie-Hélène. "'Lecture illustrées' di Boccace, en France, au XVe siècle. Boccaccio visualizzato IV." *Studi sul Boccaccio* 18 (1989): 175–280.

Trapp, J. B. "The Iconography of Petrarch in the Age of Humanism." *Quaderni Petrarcheschi* 9–10 (1992–93): 11–73. (Copiously illustrated study of Petrarch's portraits).

Villani, Filippo. "The Life of Giovanni Boccaccio." Musa and Bondanella 188–91.

Watson, Paul F. "Boccaccio's *Ninfale fiesolano* in Early Florentine Cassone Painting." *Journal of the Warburg and Courtauld Institutes* 34 (1971): 331–33.

———. "The Cement of Fiction: Giovanni Boccaccio and the Painters of Florence." *MLN* 99 (1984): 43–64.

———. *The Garden of Love in Tuscan Art of the Early Renaissance*. Philadelphia: Art Alliance, 1979. (Reproduces portrait of Boccaccio in Venice, Bibl. Marciana., ms. It. X,127).

———. "Gatherings of Artists: The Illustrators of a *Decameron* of 1427." *TEXT: Transactions of the Society for Textual Scholarship* 1 (1981 for 1984): 147–56. (Reproductions of Ceffini *Decameron*).

———. "In a Court of Love: Giovanni Toscani and Giovanni Boccaccio at the Elvehjem." *Elvehjem Museum of Art Annual Report*, Univ. of Wisconsin-Madison Bulletin 1985–86: 4–16. (On a *cassone* illustrating the "Questioni' d'amore" in the *Filocolo*).

———. "On a Window in Parnassus." *Artibus et historiae* 16 (1987): 127–48. (Reproduces Raphael's *Parnassus*).

———. "A Preliminary List of Subjects from Boccaccio in Italian Painting, 1400–1500." *Studi sul Boccaccio* 15 (1985–86): 149–66.

———. "The Spanish Chapel: Portraits of Poets or a Portrait of Christian Order?" *Memorie domenicane* ns 11 (1980): 471–87. (Reproduces apocryphal "Boccaccio and Fiammetta").

Watson, Paul F., and Victoria Kirkham. "*Amore e virtù*: Two Salvers Depicting Boccaccio's *Comedia delle ninfe fiorentine* in the Metropolitan Museum." *Metropolitan Museum Journal* 10 (1975): 35–50.

Williams, Robert. "Boccaccio's Altarpiece." *Studi sul Boccaccio* 19 (1990): 229–40. (Reproduces drawings by artist whom Vincenzo Borghini sent to Certaldo to obtain an image for the frontispiece of the 1573 *Decameron*).

The *Decameron* on Film

Kevin J. Harty

[P]erché realizzare un'opera, quando è così bello sognarla
soltanto?

—Pier Paolo Pasolini

Why make a work of art, when it is enough to dream
about it?

The great Swedish film director Ingmar Bergman argued that film and literature had nothing to do with each other: "the character and substance of the art
forms are usually in conflict" (Ross 1). D. W. Griffith had thought otherwise.
"When someone said novel writing was different from filmmaking, Griffith responded that movies are 'picture stories; not so different' " (Ross 1). Students
today have their own views on the relation between film and literature. For
many students, the cinematic text is primary; the printed text, secondary. They
often see the film before they read the book—if they even read the book.

The *Decameron* has come to the screen more than three dozen times. The
three film versions of Boccaccio's work most readily available because they
are on videotape—Hugo Fregonese's Decameron *Nights* (1953), Pier Paolo
Pasolini's *Decameron* (1971), and Mino Guerrini's Decameron *N°. 2: Le altre
novelle del Boccaccio* (1972)[1]—suggest a great deal about the views proffered
by Bergman, Griffith, and students on the sometimes uneasy relation between
film and literature.

Fregonese's Decameron *Nights* was one of a series of films made in the 1950s
in both England and the United States using medieval settings and plots. Other
directors brought the stories of Quentin Durward, Ivanhoe, and several figures
from the court of King Arthur to the screen, but Fregonese's project was a bit
more daring than those of these other directors because of Boccaccio's reputation as a teller of bawdy tales and because of the general tendency at that time to
apply rigorous standards of censorship to anything that was sexually suggestive.

The introductory screen text announces the plot of Fregonese's film: "Giovanni Boccaccio, teller of bawdy tales, was convinced by the lady he loves that
virtue triumphs over evil." The framing cinematic narrative finds fourteenth-
century Florence under siege, its inhabitants fleeing for the countryside.
Boccaccio (Louis Jourdan), knowing no fear, enters the city in search of his
beloved, the recently widowed Fiametta (Fiammetta in Boccaccio), played by
Joan Fontaine. She in turn has fled to an isolated villa where Boccaccio joins
her and a company of noble women and their ladies in waiting. The poet
promises to seduce none of them and to entertain them with a series of tales.

The screenplay, by George Oppenheimer, adds to this narrative frame three tales from the *Decameron*. In all three, Jourdan and Fontaine play roles along with Godfrey Tearle, always the older husband; Binnie Barnes, alternately an aging countess or serving maid; and Joan Collins, a coquettish serving girl or maiden. The first and third tales are told by Boccaccio; the second, by a disapproving Fiametta, who labels Boccaccio's efforts lewd, bawdy, and immoral. In the end, Fiametta succumbs to Boccaccio's charms, and the two kiss, sealing their relationship as the final screen credits roll.

The versions of the three tales told in the film differ from their sources in Boccaccio in incidental and major details. The first tale (2.10) is that of Ricciardo di Chinzica. The pirate Paganino da Majorca (in Boccaccio he is from Monaco) kidnaps and eventually marries Ricciardo's wife. Fiametta thinks the tale scandalous, and she chastises Boccaccio for telling this tale and twenty-nine others that only ridicule virtue. To counter these thirty bawdy tales, Fiametta tells the tale of Bernabò da Genoa (2.9), whom Guilio (Boccaccio's Ambrogiuolo, Ambruogiulo in the film) deceives into believing his wife, Ginevra, has been unfaithful. Bernabò orders Ginevra murdered, but she escapes her would-be assassins, becomes a cabin boy on a ship bound for Morocco, enters the sultan's service, revenges herself on Guilio (whom the film spares the torture Boccaccio has the sultan mete out to him), and upbraids her doubting husband before gladly reuniting with him. Boccaccio in turn questions the moral of Fiametta's tale, wondering why a wife would remain faithful to a man who doubted her and who attempted to have her murdered.

Fiametta's retort to Boccaccio, that he is incapable of telling a tale about a faithful wife, introduces the film's third rendering of a tale from the *Decameron*. The physician Isabella da Marco (Boccaccio's Giletta di Nerbona) cures the king (3.9), thereby saving his life. As reward for her medical services, she asks for the hand of Don Bertrando (Boccaccio's Beltramo di Rossiglione) in marriage. Don Bertrando agrees to the marriage, but he abandons his bride on their wedding night, vowing not to return until Isabella has possession of his ring and bears him a son. An elaborate ruse allows her to achieve both tasks, and Isabella is reunited with her husband. Boccaccio clearly believes he has met Fiametta's challenge, but she dismisses the story as indecent, a view students may find they do not share.

What Decameron *Nights* offers students is a lavish costume piece. Boccaccio is the obvious source for the tales told, but there is hardly a hint of anything in the film that students will find controversial. Reviews of the film on both sides of the Atlantic were, on the whole, positive. Those critics who praised the film saw it as a solid draw in Britain and as an art house success in the United States. Only one critic, Robert Kass, writing in *Catholic World*, believed that the film came close to challenging the limits of decorum: "This may be adulterated Boccaccio but it is, I hope, as far as the movies will venture into his work" (224). While Kass's view may have much in common with Fiametta's responses to the tales told by the Boccaccio character in the film, students are likely to find such criticism of the film puzzling.[2]

If Fregonese's Decameron *Nights* is simply a costume period piece based on a bowdlerized text intent only on entertaining a 1950s' film audience already used to medieval settings and plots, Pasolini's *Decameron*, the first film in the controversial director's *Trilogia della vita*,[3] offers an entirely different cinematic reading of Boccaccio. An accomplished poet and writer himself, Pasolini provides nothing less than a complete cinematic deconstruction of Boccaccio's text, "in its own way, as important as the many scholarly commentaries on Boccaccio's masterpiece" (Lawton, "Boccaccio" 306).[4]

Pasolini's film falls into two parts, each retelling or presenting a series of tales from Boccaccio. Part 1 begins with the tale of the three misadventures of Andreuccio da Perguia (2.5), who, coming to Naples to buy horses, dupes those who would dupe him and returns home with a ruby of great value. A Neapolitan storyteller then steps forward to summarize the tale of the abbess (9.2) who is caught in bed with a priest after she has threatened to expel a nun from her convent for a similar offense.

Part 1 continues with the tale of Masetto, who pretends to be a deaf mute, becomes the gardener for a convent, and sleeps with all the nuns (3.1); the tale of Peronella, who hides her lover from her husband in a barrel and then tricks her husband into believing that she is a shrewd businesswoman by telling him that the lover has come to buy the barrel (7.2); and the tale of the villain Ser Cepparello (1.1), whom the church canonizes and venerates as Saint Ciappelletto thanks to his false deathbed confession.

Part 2 of Pasolini's film presents five additional tales from Boccaccio: the comic exchange between Messer Forese and the painter Giotto about each other's shabby appearance (6.5); the tale of Riccardo Manardi and the daughter of Messer Lizio da Valbona, who agree to marry once her parents discover them in bed together (5.4); the tale of Lisabetta, who, when her brothers kill her lover, digs up his head and preserves it in a pot of basil (4.5); the prank that Father Gianni plays on Compare Pietro and his wife, whom the priest attempts to bed by convincing the couple he can turn the wife into a mare (9.10); and the tale of the two Sienese men who are in love with the same woman that culminates in the return from the grave of one man who tells the other how the souls fare in the hereafter (7.10).

While it is easy enough to trace Pasolini's reworking of Boccaccio—and Ben Lawton's careful chart of the relation between the film and its source remains the most detailed comparison between the two ("Boccaccio" 319–22)—more important to the film, and to the director's interpretation of the *Decameron*, are Pasolini's additions to and deletions from his sources.

Pasolini strips the framing narrative device away from his source. No group of plague-weary Florentines gather to pass the time by telling tales. Instead, Pasolini provides separate, but related, framing narratives for each of the film's two parts. In part 1, the story of Ser Cepparello is central. He appears in the opening scene committing a murder and in the final scene as a saint of the Catholic Church. In scenes interwoven into the film by Pasolini to link the tales he has taken from Boccaccio, Cepparello appears as a thief, a pederast, a scoundrel, and ultimately an unrepentant sinner who, thanks to his false deathbed confession, becomes a saint of the Catholic Church. Pasolini introduces the final tale from Boccaccio that concludes the first part of the film with two tableaux vivants, one depicting Brueghel's *The Combat of Carnival and Lent* and the second the painter's *The Triumph of Death*. We may at first see irony in Cepparello's holy end, but the many facets of his personality that Pasolini presents, when juxtaposed with the scenes depicting Brueghel's two paintings, suggest that more than irony is at work in Pasolini's film.

Pasolini's film is an attack on all that is bourgeois, and nothing seems more bourgeois to Pasolini than the Catholic Church. Cepparello begins the film by murdering an unidentified man. His victim's last scream is, "You have understood nothing." The Catholic Church, in Pasolini's view, is party to a larger murder, a murder of the hopes and trust of the poor whom it continues to dupe. Cepparello is the appropriate spokesperson for a church, medieval and modern, that Pasolini regards with nothing but disdain.

The different scenes that involve Cepparello present a mural of the life of the thief turned saint, and the image of the mural is essential to the second half of Pasolini's film. Here the frame involves a disciple of the painter Giotto—played by Pasolini himself[5]—and his attempt to paint a great mural in the chapel of the Convent of Santa Chiara. The mural, now lost, becomes a model for the film itself. Just as the painter must collaborate with many other artisans to affix the mural to the wall, Pasolini—like all filmmakers—works in a medium that requires collaboration among many. Pasolini as Giotto's disciple appears in the links between the tales that make up the film's second half, and as in the first half, Pasolini presents a tableau vivant—this time Giotto's *Last Judgment* with the Madonna replacing Christ—where compassion and forgiveness replace justice. The tableau vivant leads into the tale of Tingoccio and Meuccio, the Sienese twins, in which the former returns from the grave to tell his brother that sex "is not a sin" (subtitle translation). The film then cuts to the completion of the mural, and, in the final scene, the ensuing celebration as the filmmaker/painter muses about the relation between art and reality ("why make a work of art, when it is enough to dream about it?") (Pasolini 68; my trans.).

Initially, Pasolini's film received mixed reviews. As Peter Bondanella (291) points out, Boccaccio scholars were wary, and the response among film critics was various, although the film was awarded a Silver Bear in the 1971 Berlin Film Festival. Since Pasolini's murder in 1975, his films have received a continuing series of new analyses from which the *Decameron* has especially benefited—Maurizio Viano calls these new analyses "hagiographic" (xix). Millicent Marcus argues that the film is an important piece in the ongoing dialogue that Pasolini had with his audiences about the role of art as a means of reclaiming a mythic past (*Filmmaking* 136–55). Patrick Rumble, the film's most recent critic, takes Marcus's argument a step further, opining that the film presents Boccaccio's message in a new guise. Pasolini not only reclaims a mythic past; he also makes it a contemporary imperative: "the portrayal of a late-medieval Italian society in ideological and economic crisis [. . .] becomes an allegory of late capitalist society" (102). Furthermore, as Oswald Stack points out, in abandoning Boccaccio's dialect of the rising Florentine middle class for that of the Neapolitan subproletariat, Pasolini underscores the point that the latter class alone retains "the mythical features" of the Italian past (48).

Guerrini's 1971 film Decameron N°. 2: Le altre novelle del Boccaccio is part of what Bondanella (291) and Mario Quargnolo (165) note and Giovanni Grazzini (323–26) laments as a "mania of sequels" (my phrase) released in Italy after Pasolini's film. In a review of the film, David McGillivray sums up Guerrini's approach to his putative source: "Unfortunately, there is little consistency (apart from a consistently anachronistic score) and one can marvel at the illogicality of a film which continually requires its cast to strip naked and then goes to inordinate lengths to camouflage the results" (26).

Missing in Guerrini's film is any attempt to situate the film's plot in some greater context. The six tales—all more or less based on Boccaccio and most involving adultery—are told by and to an unidentified group who sit around a large fire in the center of some great hall. Their costumes and those of the characters in the tales suggest the medieval, but the film is little more than a codpiece bawdy comedy—Boccaccio reduced (badly) to what passes in the director's mind for the titillating. In the first tale (5.10), Pietro di Vinciolo, we are told, marries a younger woman to gratify his ego. Unfortunately, no one in the film version of the tale is that much older or younger than anyone else. Whereas Boccaccio suggests that the wife's deception of her husband and her subsequent infidelity resolve themselves in a menage à trois, Guerrini's version of the tale has the husband really in love with the man who has just cuckolded him with his wife. The other five tales retold by Guerrini depart less radically from Boccaccio.

In the tale of Ferondo (3.8), an abbot tricks Ferondo into believing he is in purgatory, so that the abbot can sleep with the gullible man's neglected wife. In the tale of Alibech (3.10), the title character yearns to be a Christian and travels to the desert to find a hermit who will show her the way to God. Instead, she leads the hermit and several other holy men astray. The famed beauty of Madonna Beatrice (7.7) compels the student Anichino to disguise himself as a servant in her husband Egano's house. The student sleeps with the wife, who directs the deception of her husband in such a way that she gains his unwitting blessing for her continued liaisons with Anichino. A husband's supposed sanctity proves his undoing in the tale of Frate Puccio (3.4), whose desire to be a saint provides a famed preacher with an opportunity to offer Puccio's long-suffering wife a bit of heaven on earth. And finally, marital discord and jealousy are easily resolved when neighbors Zeppa di Mino and Spinelloccio Tavena (8.8) decide to share their wives with each other.

As the final credits for Guerrini's film roll down the screen, a voice-over announces "all words are good [. . .] but may become harmful when wrongly used." The irony here is, of course, unintended. Guerrini reduces Boccaccio to cheap titillation, as do most of the films based on the *Decameron* made immediately after Pasolini's. Pasolini, then, unwittingly set a standard from which films based—at least nominally—on the *Decameron* have since generally digressed. He went on to reject his own film of the *Decameron* for a combination of political and aesthetic reasons.[6] But that rejection must be seen, as Lawton points out, within the greater context of Pasolini's life work ("Rejection" 167–73).

For students and for all those who attempt to make distant texts come alive for them, the three most readily available film versions of Boccaccio's *Decameron* offer interesting lessons. Great literature can be translated into film, but such translations require great filmmakers. Clearly, neither Fregonese nor Guerrini—though for different reasons—was capable of, or even interested in, accomplishing a commendable transition from page to screen. Pasolini, in contrast, largely succeeded in the task by offering a personal reading of his source in which he incorporated himself both as translator and as character: "No Italian artist since Dante has sat so sternly and lovingly in judgment of his country, and no artist has experienced so thoroughly the pain of exile within the peninsula" (Lawton, "Rejection" 172).

NOTES

[1]The dialogue in Pasolini's *Decameron* and Guerrini's Decameron *N°. 2* is in Italian; the videotape versions of each film provide English subtitles.

[2]Students may also find puzzling the copy on the box for the videotape version of Decameron *Nights* issued by Hollywood Movie Greats (a division of California Video Distributors). Joan Collins, who only gained superstardom decades later, receives top billing on the front of the box as the film's star; her name appears above the title in typeface larger than that used for the title: "Joan Collins / in / Decameron Nights / *with* Louis Jourdan and Joan Fontaine" (italics mine). The synopsis of the film's plot on the back of the box identifies Collins as the beautiful "earthly siren" who comes between "the sensuous story-spinner" Boccaccio and "his lady love" Fianetta [sic] in an "all-star spectacular" that is "brought to life in grand entertaining style." In good medieval fashion, Dame Fortuna's wheel continues to turn.

[3]The other two films in the trilogy—*Il racconti di Canterbury* (1972) and *Il fiore delle mille a una notte* (1974)—also deconstruct literary texts. Unfortunately the screenplays for all three films are available only in Italian. See Pasolini's *Trilogia della vita*.

[4]Lawton's important essay has been reprinted under various titles. I cite the version that appears in the Norton Critical Edition of the *Decameron*, which also includes all the tales that Pasolini translated into film.

[5]With the exception of three other actors and himself, Pasolini used ordinary people who had never acted before and who were cast from the streets of Naples to play the fifty-four roles in his film.

[6]The text of the rejection, "Abiura dalla 'Trilogia della vita,'" is printed along with the screenplays for the trilogy (Pasolini 7–11).

The epigraph on p. 164 is taken from Pasolini's *Trilogia* (68).

APPENDIX
FILMOGRAPHY

The following filmography lists films based at least nominally on the *Decameron*. Silent films based on the *Decameron*, like silent films in general, often survive without directorial or other credits.

The Adventures of Boccaccio. Dir. unknown. Great Britain, 1910.

La Bambole. Dir. Dino Risi, Luigi Comencini, Franco Rossi, and Mauro Bolognini. Italy, 1964.

Boccaccesca. Dir. Alfredo De Antoni. Italy, 1927.

Boccaccio. Dir. Michael Curtiz. Austria, 1920.

Boccaccio. Dir. Marcello Albani. Italy, 1940.

Boccaccio / Nights of Boccaccio. Dir. Bruno Corbucci. Italy, 1972.

Boccaccio '70. Dir. Federico Fellini, Luchino Visconti, and Vittorio De Sica. Italy, 1962.

Boccaccios Liebesabenteuer. Dir. Bruck Reinhard. Germany, 1920.

Bosco d'amore / Wood of Love. Dir. Alberto Bevilacqua. Italy, 1981.

Le calde notti del Decamerone */ The Hot Nights of the* Decameron. Dir. Gian Paolo Callegari. Italy, 1971.

Una cavalla tutta nuda. Dir. Franco Rosetti. Italy, 1972.

The Decameron. Dir. Pier Paolo Pasolini. Italy, 1971.

Decameron. Dir. Koji Makamatsu. Japan, 1975.

Decameron *francese*. Dir. Jacques Scandelari. Italy, 1973.

Decameron *Nights*. Dir. Herbert Wilcox. Great Britain, 1924.

Decameron *Nights*. Dir. Hugo Fregonese. Great Britain, 1953.

Decameron *N.° 2: Le altre novelle del Boccaccio*. Dir. Mino Guerrini. Italy, 1972.

Decameron *N.° 3: Le più belle donee del Boccaccio / Decameron's Jolly Kittens*. Dir. Italo Alfaro. Italy, 1972.

Decameron *N.° 4: Le più belle novelle del Boccaccio*. Dir. Paolo Bianchini. Italy, 1972.

Decameron *'69*. Dir. Bernard Clarens, Jean Herman, Louis Grosspierre, Jean Desaillers, and Serge Korber. France, 1969.

Decameron *'300*. Dir. Mauro Stefani. Italy, 1972.

Decamerone. Dir. Gennaro Righelli. Italy, 1911.

Il Decamerone *nero / The Black* Decameron. Dir. Piero Vivarelli. Italy, 1972.

Il Decamerone *proibitissimo / The Forbidden* Decameron */ Sexy Sinners*. Dir. Franco Martinelli. Italy, 1972.

Il Decamerone *proibito / The Prohibited* Decameron. Dir. Carlo Infascelli. Italy, 1972.

Decameroticus. Dir. Pier Giorgio Ferretti. Italy, 1972.

Fratello homo, sorella bona—nel Boccaccio superproibito / Get Thee to a Nunnery / Roman Scandals '73. Dir. Mario Sequi. Italy, 1973.

I fuorilegge del matrimonio. Dir. Valentino Orsini, Vittorio Taviani, and Paolo Taviani. Italy, 1963.

Giovanni Boccaccio. Dir. unknown. Italy, 1910.

The Golden Supper. Dir. D. W. Griffith. United States, 1910.

Gua Fu Shi Ri Tan / Decameron *of a Widow*. Dir. Xiao Feng. China, 1996.

Die Liebesgeschichten von Boccaccio / *Boccaccio* / *Love Tales of Boccaccio*. Dir. Herbert Malsch. Germany, 1936.

Love Boccaccio Style. Dir. Sam Phillips. United States, 1977.

Novelle galeotte d'amore dal Decameron / *Decameron 3*. Dir. Antonio Margheriti. Italy, 1972.

Novelle licenziose di vergini vogliose / *Licentious Tales of Lusty Virgins*. Dir. Michael Wotruba. Italy, 1972.

Quando le donne si chiamavano madonne. Dir. Aldo Grimaldi. Italy, 1972.

Racconti proibiti di nulla vestiti / *Master of Love*. Dir. Brunello Rondi. Italy, 1973.

A zsarnok szíve avagy Boccaccio magyarországon / *Boccaccio in Hungary* / *Heart of a Tyrant*. Dir. Miklós Jancsó. Hungary, 1981.

The *Decameron* Web: Teaching a Classic as Hypertext at Brown University

Massimo Riva

In 1995 the *Decameron* Web first made its appearance on the Internet. By April 2000, it had received over two hundred thousand visits and about fifteen hundred Guestbook entries. The *Decameron* Web is an archive of information pertinent to the reading and studying of Giovanni Boccaccio's *Decameron*. Assembled by graduate and undergraduate students under the direction of their instructors at Brown University, it is accessible to the general public on the World Wide Web at http://www.brown.edu/Research/Decameron. It currently comprises the original Italian text in a searchable format (the Branca edition published by Einaudi and the seventeenth-century English translation, attributed to John Florio).[1] In addition, it features numerous documents and images meant to elucidate the cultural and literary context of the *Decameron*, including a variety of student projects exploring literary topics, cultural relations, and the visualization of the text in various media; an on-site news group and Chat Chamber, a feature meant to provide free real-time discussion among its users; and a system of electronic subscription to an e-mail newsletter that will periodically disseminate information related to Boccaccio and medieval Italian culture in general.

Is There a Hypertext in This Class?

One can plausibly say that printing technology has shaped our notion of text: by binding and reproducing it in the physical form of a book, it has given the text both a status and a stable configuration (much more stable and accessible, for example, than that of old manuscripts). The act of reading and, perhaps to a lesser extent, the act of writing have been profoundly conditioned by this long-standing configuration. Now, in this "late age of print," as Jay Bolter calls it (150), that status and stability have started to crumble. We live at the dawn of an age whose primary notion of text is virtual rather than actual. A text is more and more the appendix of a technological process, and the acts of reading and writing are directly dependent on a complex instrumental apparatus: contemporary didactic approaches to literary texts cannot ignore the new learning environment that virtually links the circumscribed space of the classroom to a world wide web of information.

Traditional teaching methodology is largely based on and geared to the production of written documents (papers, exams, etc.). The use of electronic technology greatly expands the scope and nature of these documents to include a variety of multimedia materials. Contemporary technology can thus facilitate and enhance in unprecedented ways the complex cognitive and learning activities involved in reading a late medieval text such as the *Decameron*: in fact, hypertext expands the medieval notion of the gloss or commentary and conflates it with the visual form of manuscript illumination and text illustration, resulting in a new, cognitively enriched, interactive process of reading, writing, and learning.

Let me start, then, by condensing a rather complex set of theoretical questions into one (to paraphrase the title of Stanley Fish's well-known work that marked, in 1980, an original point of departure in the debate on literary postmodernism): Is there a hypertext in this class? The class in question studies Boccaccio's *Decameron* in English translation, taught every year in the spring semester at Brown University. And the answer to the question, I would suggest, is yes: a hypertext exists even in the traditional setting of an old-fashioned classroom, long before we sit in front of a computer. Then in what sense may we speak of the *Decameron* not just as a great book, or simply as a text, but rather as a hypertext? The answer to this question is complex, yet we can begin with this simple proposition: we can speak of the *Decameron* as a hypertext in a virtual sense. As such, the textual structure of the *Decameron*, with its combination of macro- and microcomponents—the so-called frame and the hundred novellas—virtually suggests what we might call a hypertextual, multilinear type of reading. In addition, as a milestone of the Western canon,[2] the *Decameron* invites its readers to follow its multifarious threads within a variety of narrative traditions. But instead of venturing into a discussion of the *Decameron* as a model work for hypertextual reading,[3] I explain my original proposition by illustrating the concrete organization of the course.

Since Boccaccio drew equally from the high humanistic and popular culture of his times, the *Decameron* can be considered both a summa of late medieval culture and an encyclopedia of early modern life. The work thus provides a particularly effective entry into late medieval and early modern culture as a whole. One crucial aspect of the course design is the attempt to meld two major streams of *Decameron* criticism, the cultural-historical and the narratological, and, at the same time, to have students interact with two textual practices based on two different interfaces: the book and its electronic or hypertextual version. In this course, I approach the *Decameron* as a cultural encyclopedia and a narrative grammar, insisting that these two fundamental perspectives critically interact with each other: on the one hand, a close reading of the text within its historical context raises general anthropological, ethical, and cultural issues; on the other hand, the text is explored as a self-contained narrative universe, generating its own rules and governed by a complex set of linguistic, semiotic, and rhetorical codes. In practice, this translates as follows: students enrolled in this course are given the opportunity to read the *Decameron* as a book and also to read and search it in electronic form, in both the Italian original and in English translation. (Project participants are currently working to put online a more recent translation—J. M. Rigg translation, London, 1921—than the seventeenth-century version we originally adopted for copyright reasons.) In addition, students are offered the opportunity to conduct their research and write their papers about the *Decameron* both in a traditional and in a nontraditional way while getting acquainted with critical scholarship.

The most obvious of the new functions activated by the digitalization of a text is that of electronic concordances.[4] Yet the very notion of concordances acquires in an electronic environment an unprecedented extension, because it can include a potential hypermedia repertoire of images, sounds, and so forth, which, as stated above, virtually expands the medieval notion of the gloss or commentary and conflates it with the visual form of text (manuscript) illumination. One can thus imagine a (hyper)text that, created mostly by young monks (our students) under the supervision of their elders (instructors), pushes both these notions, dependent as they are on the configuration of the book, to evolve beyond the boundaries of the book universe. In a sense, when we experiment with a new technology, we are transferring and adapting ancient or medieval notions of humanist scholarship and literacy to the new environment of the late-twentieth-century "e-literate" (Kaplan) classroom. And the *Decameron* can be the intermediary in this operation.

Is There a Class in This Hypertext? The Decameron Web

When we began work on the Web project at Brown, we had to decide on the design of the interface between the conventional and the experimental components of the course: the book and the hypertext in relation to the text and also in relation to the various literary and didactic practices they involve. The challenge was how to use the hypertext system as a creative tool for multiple alternative textual practices within a virtual community of active readers already engaged in reading the *Decameron* as a book. The most important decision taken by the instructor (as the primary designer of the course) was that of mirroring the inner formal architecture and the dialogical structure of the text within the community of its readers. The fundamental idea behind the *Decameron* Web is the projection of the virtual inner structure of the book into the new visual and cognitive form of a hypertextual environment ("Hypertext"—as Michael Joyce underlines—"is, before anything else, a visual form" [206].) Since the collective creators of this environment are the students and their instructors, the first step was that of re-creating the virtual community of readers already contained by or in the text.

The course organization follows: each of the ten to fifteen students usually enrolled in the course is assigned the virtual identity of one of the ten narrators of the *gentile brigata*, while the instructor takes responsibility for the virtual identity of the author-narrator. The composition of this community of readers thus somewhat reflects the subtle hierarchical structure embodied in the text (and the classroom). Moreover, it also reflects another peculiar characteristic of the *Decameron*'s supporting framework: the ten narrators are at the same time the (oral) storytellers, the (ideal) audience, and the primary commentators of the *novelle*, while the author-narrator is the great codifier of the written text as a whole. The basic numerological structure that governs the text is also adopted as the organizational principle of the course work and of the hypertext design. Thus class discussions are organized following the ten-day structure of the text: in a typical twelve-week term, roughly one week and two class meetings for each *giornata*, plus one week for the introduction and one for the conclusion. Each student, or member of the learning *brigata*, is in charge of the week's discussion, according to the order of queens and kings also established by the text. Each student is responsible for the introduction and interpretation or discussion in class of the novella recounted each day by the narrator he or she represents (of course, all students have to read all the *novelle* in order to actively participate in the discussion). The discussion is conducted in class as well as in a virtual environment, an electronic news group where the students and instructor exchange ideas and information and post articles or news of common interest. (Thanks to the *Decameron* Web news group and Chat Chamber, this discussion can be effectively extended to the virtual community of Boccaccio readers and scholars, across the Internet.)

These activities directly translate into the hypertextual design. Each student has to write a short, interpretive commentary for each of the *novelle* recounted by the narrator he or she represents; at the same time, he or she has to develop ideas for additional contextual documents that will enrich the encyclopedic side of the *Decameron* Web. The contributions to this encyclopedic exegesis of Boccaccio's work range from standard sequences of one- to two-page documents linked to each other and representing original student work or review and discussion of critical sources to more ambitious hypermedia projects according to the student's specific interdisciplinary interests and abilities. The documents can thus take the form of images, graphs, maps, visual, or audio recordings.

Each week, for an additional period of two hours, the course meets in a multimedia laboratory, where students sit in front of computers and either discuss their projects with instructors or simply work on their projects, further exploring the Web and looking for possible links and additional resources. (A number of sample links to the ever-growing resources for medievalists on the Web are accessible directly from the *Decameron* Web.) This lab time is also used for initial training of those students (very few, nowadays, at Brown) who are not yet familiar with hypertext, the Internet, or HTML (Hypertext Markup Language); these students find help directly on the *Decameron* Web and can also attend additional training classes offered on campus.

Another task the students undertake is adding links from one set of documents to the other and from their documents to the *Decameron* text, thus creating a crossed path of nonlinear reading possibilities. What scholars have called concordances and glosses evolve into a glossary or index of key words, themes, and motifs and a variety of possible reading paths that link one story to the other and their commentaries, as well as to a number of contextual documents. Thus the students enrolled in the class effectively become *Decameron* virtual "Wreaders," the term coined by George Landow in 1992 (*Hypertext*) to describe the active reader of hypertext (see also Landow, *Hypertext 2.0*, 220). It is a concept reminiscent of the operations performed by the reader-character-narrator in Italo Calvino's *Castle of Crossed Destinies*: the designing of a series of interpretive paths, all strictly related to and emanating from the book's original structure yet also part of a combinatory process of reading that suggests its own alternative itineraries. This active role played by the students also implies a new role for the instructors in their capacity as editors of the *Decameron* Web.[5] Instead of being (as in Calvino's fictional example) the masterminds behind this hermeneutic game or simply the virtual custodians of the letter of the text and of its correct or authentic interpretation, the instructor and teaching assistants become the supervisors of a series of collective and interactive reading, writing, and linking activities, which result in both a learning experience and an interpretive process whose true protagonists are the students as "empirical readers" in the never-ending process of becoming model readers (to use Umberto Eco's terminology in *The Role of the Reader* [7–11]). A few words need to be said about the nature of these activities.

As stated above, a fundamental task of hypertextual design is that of envisioning a new visual form, or interface, for the *Decameron*. Following are a few examples of the variety of student projects. One team of students studied the creation of an interactive geographical map of the whole *Decameron*, which will allow, when perfected, an easy nonlinear navigation of its fictional worlds. All the countries, lands, cities, villages, and even certain streets or piazzas mentioned in the text will eventually be identified, documented, and linked to all the spots in the text where they appear (an encyclopedic enterprise not so distant from Boccaccio's own interest in topography and geography, which will also be discussed in the commentaries to the project).[6] For each (or the most important) of these topographical sites, a critical note will explain their strategic position in the narrative geography of the *Decameron* (whose center will obviously be a fictional topography of Florence, radiating from the ideal center of Santa Maria Novella, the meeting place of the *brigata*, and the palace gardens near the city where the ten storytellers retreat). When existing technology is perfected, the reader might even be able to walk the virtual map of Andreuccio's night in Malpertugio or navigate the Mediterranean seas with Landolfo or Alatiel. Part of this encyclopedic geography of the *Decameron* will inevitably be the fictional worlds, the fantastic realms of medieval folklore evoked by some of the most brilliant of its narrative performances (e.g., Frate Cipolla's sermon) in the form of a series of links to illustrated documents on medieval popular culture and traditions. This example clearly refers to what I have characterized above as the potential evolution of hypermedia illumination.

For students more interested in theoretical issues raised by contemporary technology, another task is that of studying the various possible representations and simulations of the *Decameron* as a virtual narrative world or the representational models used to explain the complex architecture of the text, starting with a review of all the cognitive models produced by scholars to date: from Chinese boxes to a labyrinth to an architectural edifice to Todorovian and Proppian grammars of narrative functions, and so forth. The students involved in this project could also produce their own interactive map of the *Decameron*, based not on a geographical approach but on one of the following alternative models: a bidimensional, iconographical model, in which the members of the *brigata* (and the author-narrator) appear sitting in a circle in an enclosed garden, exchanging places according to their rotation in the order of each day, their individual figures clickable as a link to the novelle they tell, or a tridimensional one, in which a series of pictures (old illustrations of various editions of the book), aligned in Albertian perspective, are the doorways or gateways to the corresponding loci of the text and its mapping, as in a memory gallery or palace. Other students are involved in exploring the *Decameron*'s visualization in different media (ranging from prints to paintings to theater and film).

As already stated, this complex interaction between the text and its visual form or interface with the reader (which will be further pursued by other students in the future) clearly evokes the fundamental role that images played in medieval illuminated manuscripts and in the making and reading of those texts, with an added dimension made possible only by today's hypertextual or hypermedia technology. The complete digitalization of all the illustrations of the *Decameron* ("Decamerone *visualizzato*"), starting with Boccaccio's own hand-drawn images, for example, would allow a new perspective on how to explore, read, and imagine the text, providing a link between the cultural-historical perspective suggested by a review of all its illustrations to date and a new, ongoing creative exploration of the deep visual grammar of the *Decameron*.

Other hypermedia projects involve voice recordings, such as readings in Italian of linguistically or narratologically relevant passages of the text, and emphasize both the oral substrata of storytelling and its performance in relation to the rhetorical codification of a written text. Additional documents will illustrate the pivotal position of the *Decameron* in the historical codification of the Italian language. Projects may also involve the musical recordings of ballate or canzoni, inspired by the ballads or songs or dances that close each day of the *Decameron*, or musical passages that evoke the work's musical atmosphere, the cultural aura emanating from the so-called frame story within the context of fourteenth-century music. And, of course, there will be more and more contextual exploration of medieval culture, including exercises in the identification of sources and in comparative intertextuality, and so forth. All this is, in perspective, very exciting—and clearly still evolving. The *Decameron* Web is still at an early stage, although it is rapidly growing, at the rate of about 100 to 150 documents every semester. So far, the most important result of the experiment is that students as members of the virtual community of *Decameron* Web "Wreaders" are the codesigners of the whole project. The idea, however, is to eventually open the *Decameron* Web to contributions from the greater virtual community of *Decameron's* readers, all those who are interested in participating in an ongoing discussion of this classic great book.

Hyperbook, Hyperlibrary (and Beyond)?

I can now briefly return to my initial set of theoretical issues. To illustrate how the new hypertextual environment is in many aspects suggestive and evocative of the textual world of medieval or early modern culture, and yet represents a radical departure from that world, I could quote Dante's *Comedy* (as have both Eco and Bolter). At the apex of Dante's journey, which is also the climax of his book, Dante has a vision of his textual universe: he witnesses the explosion of a metaphorical ideal book into what sounds from his description like a visualized hypertext:

> Nel suo profondo vidi che s'interna,
> legato con amore in un volume,
> ciò che per l'universo si squaderna:
>   sustanze e accidenti e lor costume
> quasi conflati insieme, per tal modo
> che ciò ch'i' dico è un semplice lume. [. . .]   (*Paradiso* 300; 33.85–90)

> In its profundity I saw—ingathered
> and bound by love into one single volume—
> what, in the universe, seems separate, scattered:
>   substances, accidents, and dispositions
> as if conjoined—in such a way that what
> I tell is only rudimentary. [. . .]   (*Paradiso* 301)

The "semplice lume" 'simple glimmer of that light' could be viewed as a glimpse at the universal interface: thus reread, Dante's volume, which from its original conflation spreads open or scrolls down into the universe, is a metaphor adaptable to the age of electronic writing. A volume of volumes, in which the gravitational laws of reading and writing are created and modified in the process along with the grammar that holds them together, may be an apt metaphorical (although perhaps a touch metaphysical) description of a hypertextual universe. One might even find the theological image of angelic intelligences evocative of the new virtual community made possible by the ensuing age of global (instant) communication.[6] The *Divine Comedy*, the greatest book if not the great code of our literary tradition, can thus be envisioned as a long, linear, and ascending stroll on the way to the instantaneous and simultaneous vision or insight of the universe as a book (*volumen* and codex), a true apotheosis of reading. It is curious, though, that Eco—who quotes Dante's passage in one of his "walks in the fictional woods"—does so in the essay dedicated to the narrative virtue of lingering (*indugio*). I think this should be taken as a sensible warning. Is Eco telling us, perhaps, that through our infatuation with hypertextual velocity, simultaneity, and so forth, we risk losing, on our textual journey, the patient way to the revelation or salvation that linear reading entails? The truth is that, on the threshold of this vision (that is, a vision of the future of textuality), scholars are faced with less metaphysical but no less intriguing dilemmas about the nature of textuality and its dynamic role within our complex cognitive and learning activities.

Speaking of great books, such as the Bible, the *Divine Comedy*, and the *Decameron*, Eco introduces the category of *sgangherabilità* ("disjointed nature," as the English translation reads [Eco, *Walks* 128]). I actually prefer the (equally untranslatable) category of *squinternabilità*. To unhinge, to unstich, to pull to pieces or chunks is a fairly accurate description of what a hypertextual system seems to do to a book or to a text. And yet, isn't that what our readings (any reading) do to some extent, in the silence of our minds, where words float and fall into place and in sequence without being bound to pages or paragraphs? (Even our so-called photographic memory is bound to change nature in a hypermedia environment.) Now, comparing three virtual hyperbooks like the Bible, the *Divine Comedy*, and the *Decameron* (also an interesting allusion to the progressive "secularization" of the Book), Eco writes that, while the structures of the Bible and the *Divine Comedy* seem to imply or allow the paradoxical property he calls *sgangherabilità* the *Decameron* does not:

> The immense and age-old popularity of the *Bible* is due to its disjointed nature, stemming from the fact that it was written by several different authors. The *Divine Comedy* is not disjointed at all, but because of its complexity, the number of characters it deals with, and the events it recounts (everything concerning heaven and earth, as Dante said), every line of it can be put out of joint and used as a magic spell or as a mnemonic device [. . .]. But although the *Divine Comedy* can be put out of joint, the *Decameron* cannot, since each tale is to be taken in its entirety [. . .].   (*Walks* 159)

The idea that it is impossible to unbind the *Decameron* or take it apart at the seams would seem an obstacle to its transformation or transcodification into a hypertext (at least a certain type of hypertext). Yet one could reply that it is precisely the architecture of the *Decameron* that hints at a virtual hypertextual structure, a profane or thoroughly secularized alternative (the human comedy) to the theological model represented by Dante's divine *Comedy*. It is no coincidence that, judging from the variety of projects dedicated to the *Decameron* and the *Divine Comedy* in these early stages of the new technological paradigm, both works stimulate our technological imagination more than any other great book.

The inherent textual integrity of the *Decameron* lies as much in its unity as a book as in its fragmentation into individual narrative and textual subunits (the one hundred novelle, with their multiple readings and interpretations); these are narrative microuniverses that contain and suggest multiple possible navigations, multiple textual journeys (as opposed to the one, master journey through the three realms of the under- or otherworld on which the *Comedy*, for example, is centered) across the boundaries of fictional time and space (the earthly geography of the *Decameron*). The very framework devised by the author-narrator thus becomes the mechanism that makes possible a multiplicity of readings, without necessarily compromising its unity. The crucial point is this: if from the compositional point of view of the author-narrator this architectural organization can be envisioned as the infrastructure of a complex, unifying plan, from the point of view of the reader (or wreader) the same textual architecture represents the flexible infrastructure of interpretive freedom. As I have said, electronic linking is a crucial aspect of this interpretive freedom and therefore of our experiment with hypertext; it is also the most problematic aspect presented so far. Electronic linking is the most important result of the recodification of a typescript into a compuscript, of a printed book into an electronic (hyper)book. In actuality, electronic links are the traces of prior readings, highlighted as possible paths that the current reading can take, leaving the active reader (the reader-writer) the choice to follow or not to follow virtually infinite (or indefinite) paths of internal correspondences (be they linguistic, semantic, thematic, symbolic, etc.). This choice path is further complicated by the fact that hypertextual, online systems at any moment allow the active reader to jump altogether out of the textual boundaries of a self-contained book universe, into the multiverse of a virtually unlimited hyperlibrary growing out of the hyperbook as its own ideal encyclopedia (or exegetical apparatus, or glossary) but also independent from it. This hyperlibrary has the virtual boundaries of the whole Internet or World Wide Web, currently growing at an exponential rate in every direction.

The risk of losing oneself in this maze of simultaneous correspondences is one our active readers (let us say, our students) are increasingly exposed to, particularly if they do not have at their disposal the anchors that can tether them to a point of departure; to focus their interest. The very accessibility of texts within the new universal framework of their electronic interface can jeopardize any attempt at maintaining a sound historical perspective. And yet the new environment can also stimulate students to reach a new and heightened awareness of how the combinatorial process of learning (and reading) works. Providing the anchors that are counterbalancing the centrifugal and centripetal forces of the hypertextual environment is a crucial task for those who design an instructional hypertext. Nevertheless, here lies a fundamental theoretical and practical question: who is (or should ultimately be) the designer-controller of this new hypertextual environment? It is an open question that involves the very definition of the future virtual community of readers and learners.

It is my conviction that hyperreading and learning are inherently (virtually) nonhierarchical communicative practices, although undoubtedly still practices limited to new e-literates (the new elites, somewhat ironically envisioned by Kaplan, to which our Brown students belong). Of course, new hierarchies of teaching and learning might be implemented even by or in the new environment; it seems fairly clear, though, that in this new technological context instructors are forced to abandon their essential prejudices on textuality and instead adopt a more open pragmatic or dialogical approach. The ultimate question, therefore, is not what the *Decameron* as a hypertext virtually *is* but what it can virtually *become*, while remaining itself a hyperbook in a new learning and reading environment. Because a text (any text, as the new technological environment allows one to better understand) is inseparable from the interactive process of reading and writing that has both produced it and itself continues to produce.

What started out as the limited historical memory of a course taught at Brown University, a course archive so to speak, has branched out to the World Wide Web, thus turning a didactic experiment into an ongoing dialogue of "Wreaders," which, if not yet comparable to the angelic intelligences of an ideal community of scholars, represents a step forward toward a communicative and pedagogical practice of a new type, in a radically transformed global learning environment. It might well be that in the course of this experiment, the *Decameron*, like a talisman in the hands of apprentice sorcerers, will appear to lose its architectural compactness, as its foundations as a book seem to crumble. At the same time, its inner dialogical structure as a text will expand, becoming a textual universe of a new kind, both actual and virtual, by opening new possibilities to the reading process. The virtual game of the *Decameron* (storytelling), could be replayed, time and again, as a communicative and dialogical learning game in a truly polyphonic fashion within the new epistemological paradigm. Literary and technological imagination could converge in a realization of the implicit utopia of reader-response criticism, where reading and textual analysis flow together in a truly open academic community.

NOTES

In 1999 the *Decameron* Web project was awarded a two-year grant by the National Endowment for the Humanities. This essay benefited from contributions by Giorgio Melloni, Michael Papio, Sergio Parussa, Giuliana Picco, and Giuseppe Strazzeri.

[1]The Italian text was digitized by Nanda Cremascoli and her students and is available from various sites, including *Liber-liber*, or Project Manuzio. The English translation is accessible out of copyright through Oxford Text Archives and other sources. We are currently working on obtaining the rights to a contemporary English translation.

[2]As Harold Bloom, in his *Western Canon*, put it, "Ironic storytelling whose subject is storytelling is pretty much Boccaccio's invention, and the purpose of this breakthrough was to free stories from didacticism and moralism, so that the listener or reader, not the storyteller, became responsible for their use, for good or for ill" (102–03).

[3]We have argued this in Papio and Riva's "La novella tra testo e ipertesto: Il *Decameron* come modello."

[4]With the help of the Brown University Scholarly Technology Group and thanks to

the grant from the NEH, we have completed and are now in the process of testing an SGML (Standard General Markup Language) encoding of the text according to the guidelines called TEI (Text Encoding Initiative) Lite. In 2001 it will be available at our site, allowing students, teachers, and scholars more advanced explorations of the *Decameron's* textual universe. Both graduate and undergraduate students are actively involved in this project.

[5]In addition to the editorial board, the project participants have now created an advisory board composed of prominent *Decameron* and Boccaccio scholars. Their periodic supervision will be fundamental to guaranteeing the quality of the materials included in the *Decameron* Web.

[6]One of the main search functions activated by the SGML encoding (Geographical Places) allows users to perform these operations quickly.

[7]The implicit (critical) reference is to Pierre Levy's "atheology" of *Collective Intelligence* (*L'intelligence collective*), ch. 5.

NOTES ON CONTRIBUTORS

Robert E. Bayliss is a PhD student in comparative literature and Spanish literature at Indiana University. His work focuses on Cervantes, the tradition of courtly love, and its influence on Spanish Golden Age literature.

Marga Cottino-Jones is professor of Italian at the University of California, Los Angeles. She is the author of many articles on Italian literature. Her books include *Order from Chaos*, *Introduzione a Pietro Aretino*, and *An Anatomy of Boccaccio's Style*.

Raymond-Jean Frontain is professor of English at the University of Central Arkansas. His specialties include the Bible as literature, the English Renaissance, gay and lesbian studies, and comedy. He is the editor or coeditor of several volumes, including *The David Myth in Western Literature*, *Poetic Prophecy in Western Literature*, *Old Testament Women in Western Literature*, and *Reclaiming the Sacred: The Bible in Gay and Lesbian Culture*.

Steven M. Grossvogel is associate professor of Italian at the University of Georgia. He is the author of *Allusion and Ambiguity in Boccaccio's* Filocolo. His articles on Boccaccio have appeared in *Studi sul Boccaccio*, *Italiana*, and *Il Veltro*.

Robert W. Hanning is professor of English and comparative literature at Columbia University. He is a fellow of the Medieval Academy of America and the holder of fellowships from the ACLS, Guggenheim, and NEH. He is the author of many articles, the coeditor of an anthology and two essay collections, and the cotranslator of the *Lais* of Marie de France. He is the author of *The Individual in Twelfth-Century Romance* and *The Vision of History in Early Britain*.

Kevin J. Harty is professor of English at La Salle University. He has published extensively on cinematic depictions of the Middle Ages. He is author of *The Reel Middle Ages: American, Western and Eastern European, Middle Eastern, and Asian Films about Medieval Europe* and editor of *King Arthur on Film: New Essays on Arthurian Cinema* and *Cinema Arthuriana: Essays on Arthurian Film*.

Robert Hollander is professor in European literature in the Department of Romance Languages and Literatures at Princeton University. He is the author of some twenty books and more than seventy articles, including *Allegory in Dante's* Commedia, *Boccaccio's Two Venuses*, *Dante's Epistle to Cangrande*, and *Boccaccio's Dante*. He has twice been a member of the National Council on the Humanities and has served as president of the Dante Society of America. His honors include the Gold Medal of the City of Florence in recognition of his work on Dante and honorary citizenship in Certaldo.

Bonnie D. Irwin, associate professor of English at Eastern Illinois University, has focused her work on the frame tale. Her articles have appeared in *Oral Tradition*, the *Encyclopedia of Folklore and Literature*, and the *Encyclopedia of Medieval Folklore*. She is currently writing a book on the *Seven Sages of Rome* and the *Book of Sindibad*.

Victoria Kirkham is professor of Romance languages at the University of Pennsylvania. She is the author of *The Sign of Reason in Boccaccio's Fiction* and *Fabulous Vernacular:*

184   NOTES ON CONTRIBUTORS

Boccaccio's Filocolo *and the Art of Medieval Fiction*; and is coauthor, with Anthony K. Cassell, of Diana's Hunt / Caccia di Diana: *Boccaccio's First Fiction*. She has a long-standing interest in relations between literature and the visual arts, which she has explored in a number of articles on Dante, Boccaccio, the sixteenth-century poet Laura Battiferra, and Italian cinema.

Julia Reinhard Lupton received her PhD in Renaissance studies from Yale University, where she studied Boccaccio with Giuseppe Mazzotta. She is associate professor of English and comparative literature at the University of California, Irvine. She is co-author, with Kenneth Reinhard, of *After Oedipus: Shakespeare in Psychoanalysis* and *Afterlives of the Saints: Hagiography, Typology, and Renaissance Literature*. She is founding director of Humanities Out There, an outreach program between UCI's School of Humanities and local schools.

Angelo Mazzocco is professor of Spanish and Italian at Mount Holyoke College. He is the author of *Linguistic Theories in Dante and the Humanists*. His articles have appeared in numerous journals and in such publications as *Poesia e Poetica delle Rovine di Roma*; *Rome in the Renaissance: The City and the Myth*; *Umanesimo a Roma nel Quattrocento*; and *ACTAS del Congreso Internacional de Historiografía Lingüística: Nebrija V Centenario*.

Elizabeth H. D. Mazzocco is associate professor of French and Italian at the University of Massachusetts, Amherst. She has written articles on epic, chivalry, Boiardo and language pedagogy, and she is the author of *Parliamoci a quattr'occhi*, a laser disc for elementary Italian. She is currently writing a book on the topic "Humanism and Chivalry at the Court of Ercole I D'Este: The Case of Matteo Maria Boiardo."

Giuseppe Mazzotta is Charles C. and Dorathea S. Dilley Professor of Italian at Yale University. He is the author of many articles on Italian literature. His books include *Dante, Poet of the Desert*; *The World at Play in Boccaccio's* Decameron; *The Worlds of Petrarch*; and the forthcoming *Cosmopoiesis: A Renaissance Experience*.

James H. McGregor is associate professor of comparative literature at the University of Georgia. He was a fellow of the American Academy in Rome in 1981–82. His publications include several articles and two books on Boccaccio's minor works: *The Image of Antiquity* and *The Shades of Aeneas*. He has translated Luigi Guicciardini's *The Sack of Rome* and representative literary texts for *Renaissance Naples*.

Michael Papio is assistant professor of Italian at the College of the Holy Cross and is coeditor of the *Decameron* Web. He has published articles on Dante, Boccaccio, the novella tradition and cinema and is the author of *Keen and Violent Remedies: Social Satire and the Grotesque in Masuccio Salernitano's* Novellino. He is currently working on a study of horror in the early Italian short story.

F. Regina Psaki is associate professor of Romance languages at the University of Oregon. Her publications include "The Play of Genre and Voicing in Boccaccio's *Corbaccio*," "Arthurian Women in the Italian Tradition," and "Lïenor and the Poetics of Ellipsis." She has served as vice president and president of the Society for Medieval Feminist Scholarship.

Massimo Riva is associate professor of Italian studies and modern culture and media at Brown University. He is the author of *Saturno e le Grazie: Malinconici e ipocondriaci* *nella letteratura italiana del Settecento.* He is creator and coeditor of the hypertext project the *Decameron* Web, coeditor of the Pico Project, and editor of the forthcoming *Site/ Seeing: Mapping Contemporary Italian Fiction.* He is currently at work on a book entitled "The Virtual Garden: The Hyper-Novel from Boccaccio to Eco."

Aldo Scaglione is E. M. Remarque Professor of Literature at New York University. His publications include *Nature and Love in the Late Middle Ages, Ars Grammatica, The Classical Theory of Composition, The Theory of German Word Order, The Liberal Arts and the Jesuit College System, Knights at Court,* and *Essays in the Arts of Discourse.* He has edited the works of Boiardo, miscellanies on Ariosto and Petrarch, *The Emergence of National Languages,* and *The Image of the Baroque.* He is editor of the Peter Lang series Studies in Italian Culture.

Janet Levarie Smarr is professor of comparative literature at the University of Illinois, Urbana. Her books include *Italian Renaissance Tales, Boccaccio and Fiammetta: The Narrator as Lover, Boccaccio's Eclogues,* and the edited volume *Historical Criticism and the Challenge of Theory.* She is currently writing a series of essays and a book on women writers of the sixteenth century and coediting a collection of essays on the subject "Italian Women and the City."

SURVEY PARTICIPANTS

The scholars and teachers listed below participated in the survey on approaches to teaching the *Decameron*. Without their generous efforts the volume would be greatly diminished.

Gloria Allaire, *Ohio University*
Robert E. Bayliss, *Indiana University*
JoAnn Cavallo, *Columbia University*
Marga Cottino-Jones, *University of California, Los Angeles*
Giuseppe Faustini, *Skidmore College*
Pier Massimo Forni, *Johns Hopkins University*
Raymond-Jean Frontain, *University of Central Arkansas*
Tommasina Gabriele, *Wheaton College*
Steven M. Grossvogel, *University of Georgia*
Robert W. Hanning, *Columbia University*
Kevin J. Harty, *LaSalle University*
Frank G. Hoffman, *Susquehanna University*
Robert Hollander, *Princeton University*
Bonnie D. Irwin, *Eastern Illinois University*
Victoria Kirkham, *University of Pennsylvania*
Dennis Looney, *University of Pittsburgh*
Julia Reinhard Lupton, *University of California, Irvine*
Angelo Mazzocco, *Mount Holyoke College*
Elizabeth H. D. Mazzocco, *University of Massachusetts, Amherst*
Giuseppe Mazzotta, *Yale University*
Marilyn Migiel, *Cornell University*
Michael Papio, *College of the Holy Cross*
Tom Peterson, *University of Georgia*
F. Regina Psaki, *University of Oregon*
Nancy Reale, *New York University*
Massimo Riva, *Brown University*
Aldo Scaglione, *New York University*
Karl-Ludwig Selig, *Columbia University*
Michael Sherberg, *Washington University in St. Louis*
Janet Levarie Smarr, *University of Illinois, Urbana*
Paul Spillinger, *University of Central Arkansas*
Kay Stanton, *California State University, Fullerton*
David J. Wallace, *University of Minnesota*
Elizabeth Walsh, *University of San Diego*

WORKS CITED

Aarne, Antti. *The Types of the Folktale: A Classification and Bibliography*. Ed. and trans. Stith Thompson. 2nd rev. ed. FF Communications 184. Helsinki: Suomalainen Tiedeakatemia, 1961.

Accademici Intronati di Siena. *Gl'ingannati*. Bari: LaTerza, 1979.

Almansi, Guido. *The Writer as Liar: Narrative Technique in the* Decameron. London: Routledge, 1975.

Alpern, Hyman, ed. and trans. *Three Classic Spanish Plays*. New York: Washington Square, 1963.

Alpert, Michael, trans. *Two Spanish Picaresque Novels*. New York: Penguin, 1969.

Antal, Frederick. *Florentine Painting and Its Social Background: The Bourgeois Republic before Cosimo de' Medici's Advent to Power*. Cambridge: Harvard UP, 1986.

Aretino, Pietro. *La cortigiana*. Turin: Einaudi, 1980.

Ariosto, Ludovico. *La cassaria*. Turin: Einaudi, 1976.

———. *La Lena*. Turin: Einaudi, 1976.

———. *Il negromante*. Turin: Einaudi, 1976.

———. *I suppositi*. Turin: Einaudi, 1976.

Auerbach, Erich. "Frate Alberto." *Mimesis: The Representation of Reality in Western Literature*. Trans. Willard R. Trask. Princeton: Princeton UP, 1953. 203–31.

Axton, Richard. "Gower—Chaucer's Heir?" *Chaucer Traditions: Studies in Honor of Derek Brewer*. Ed. Ruth Morse and Barry Windeatt. Cambridge: Cambridge UP, 1990. 21–38.

Balduino, Armando. "Fortune e sfortune della novella italiana fra tardo Trecento e primo Cinquecento." Picone, Di Stefano, and Stewart 155–73.

Ballerini, Carlo, ed. *Atti del Convegno di Nimega sul Boccaccio*. Pubblicazione dell'Istituto di Lingua e di Letteratura Italiana dell'Università Cattolica di Nimega. Bologna: Patron, 1976.

Baratto, Mario. *Realtà e stile nel* Decameron. Vicenza: Pozza, 1970.

Barberi Squarotti, Giorgio. *Il potere della parola: Studi sul* Decameron. Naples: Federico, 1983.

———. *Prospettive sul* Decameron. Turin: Einaudi, 1989.

Barbina, Alfredo. *Concordanze del* Decameron. Florence: Barbera, 1969.

Barolini, Teodolinda. "Giovanni Boccaccio (1313–1375)." *European Writers: The Middle Ages and Renaissance*. Ed. W. T. H. Jackson. Vol. 2. New York: Scribner's, 1983. 509–34.

———. " 'Le parole sono femmine e i fatti sono maschi': Toward a Sexual Poetics of the *Decameron* (*Dec*. II.10)." *Studi sul Boccaccio* 21 (1993): 175–97.

———. "The Wheel of the *Decameron*." *Romance Philology* 36 (1983): 521–39.

Battaglia, Salvatore. *Contributi alla storia della novellistica*. Naples: Pironti, 1947.

Battaglia Ricci, Lucia, ed. *Novelle italiane: Il Trecento*. Milan: Garzanti, 1982.

Beardwood, Alice. *Alien Merchants in England, 1350–1377: Their Legal and Economic Position.* Cambridge: Medieval Acad., 1931.

Bec, Christian. *Les marchands écrivains: Affaires et humanisme à Florence 1375–1434.* Civilisations et Sociétés 9. Paris: Mouton, 1967.

Becker, Marvin B. *Florence in Transition.* 2 vols. Baltimore: Johns Hopkins UP, 1967.

———. *Medieval Italy: Constraints and Creativity.* Bloomington: Indiana UP, 1981.

Bergin, Thomas. *Boccaccio.* New York: Viking, 1981.

Bernardo, Aldo S., and Anthony L. Pellegrini, eds. *Dante, Petrarch, Boccaccio: Studies in the Italian Trecento in Honor of Charles S. Singleton.* Binghamton: Center for Medieval and Early Renaissance Studies, 1983.

Bettinzoli, Attilio. "Per una definizione delle presenze dantesche nel *Decameron.* I: I registri ideologici, lirici, drammatici." *Studi sul Boccaccio* 13 (1981–82): 267–326.

———. "Per una definizione delle presenze dantesche nel *Decameron.* II: Ironizazzione ed espressivismo antifrastico-deformatorio." *Studi sul Boccaccio* 14 (1983–84): 209–40.

Bibbiena. *See* Dovizi, Bernardo.

Billanovich, Giuseppe. *Restauri boccacceschi.* Rome: Storia e Letteratura, 1947.

Bloch, R. Howard. *Medieval Misogyny and the Invention of Western Romantic Love.* Chicago: U of Chicago P, 1991.

———. *The Scandal of the Fabliaux.* Berkeley: U of California P, 1986.

Bloom, Harold. *Western Canon.* New York: Harcourt, 1994.

Boccaccio e dintorni: Miscellanea di studi in onore di Vittore Branca 2. Biblioteca dell' "Archivum Romanicum." Serie 1. Storia, letteratura, paleografia 179. Florence: Olschki, 1983.

Boccaccio, Giovanni. *Amorosa visione.* Trans. Robert Hollander, Timothy Hampton, and Margherita Frankel. Bilingual ed. Hanover: UP of New England, 1986.

———. *Decameron.* Ed. Vittore Branca. Milan: Mondadori, 1976. Florence: Einaudi, 1980. Milan: Mondadori, 1985. Boccaccio, *Tutte le opere,* vol 4.

———. *Decameron.* Ed. Vittore Branca. 2 vols. Florence: Le Monnier, 1960.

———. *Decameron.* Ed. Vittore Branca. 3 vols. Florence: Sadea, 1966.

———. *Decameron: Edizione critica secondo l'autografo Hamiltoniano, Scrittori Italiani e testi antichi pubblicati dall'Accademia della Crusca.* Ed. Vittore Branca. Florence: Olschki, 1976.

———. *Decameron.* 1981. Trans. G. H. McWilliam. 2nd ed. Harmondsworth: Penguin, 1995.

———. *Decameron.* Trans. Mark Musa and Peter Bondanella. New York: NAL, 1982.

———. *The Decameron.* Ed. Mark Musa and Peter Bondanella. Norton Critical Edition. New York: Norton, 1977.

———. *Decameron.* Trans. John Payne. Ed. Charles S. Singleton. 3 vols. Berkeley: U of California P, 1982.

———. *Decameron.* Ed. Cesare Segre. Milan: Mursia, 1967.

———. Decameron: *Edizione diplomatico-interpretiva dell'autografo Hamilton 90.* Ed. Charles S. Singleton. Baltimore: Johns Hopkins UP, 1974.

———. *Decameron.* Trans. Guido Waldman. Oxford: Oxford UP, 1993.

————. Il Decameron *di Messer Giovanni Boccacci, Cittadino Fiorentino.* Florence: Giunti, 1573.

————. *Filocolo.* Boccaccio, *Tutte le opere,* vol. 1, 61–675.

————. *Tutte le opere di Giovanni Boccaccio.* Vittore Branca, gen. ed. 10 vols. Milan: Mondadori, 1967–1998.

Bolter, Jay. *Writing Space: The Computer, Hypertext, and the History of Writing.* Hillsdale: Erlbaum, 1991.

Bondanella, Julia Conaway, and Mark Musa, eds. *The Italian Renaissance Reader.* New York: Dutton, 1987.

Bondanella, Peter E. *Italian Cinema from Neorealism to the Present.* Rev. ed. New York: Continuum, 1991.

Borges, Jorge Luis. "Blindness." *Seven Nights.* Trans. Eliot Weinberger. London: Faber, 1984. 107–21.

Borlenghi, Aldo. *La struttura e il carattere della novella italiana dei primi secoli.* Milan: Goliardica, 1958.

Bosco, Umberto. Il 'Decameron': *Saggio.* Rieti: Biblioteca Editrice, 1929.

Bourland, Cathy. "Boccaccio and the *Decameron* in Castilian and Catalan Literature." *Revue Hispanique* 12 (1905): 1–232.

Bowron, E. P. "Giorgio Vasari's *Portrait of Six Tuscan Poets." Minneapolis Institute of Arts Bulletin* 60 (1971–73): 43–54.

Bragantini, Renzo, and Pier Massimo Forni, eds. *Lessico critico decameroniano.* Turin: Bollati Boringhieri, 1995.

Branca, Vittore. *Boccaccio medievale e nuovi studi sul* Decameron. 1956. 5th ed. Florence: Sansoni, 1981.

————. *Boccaccio: The Man and His Works.* Trans. Richard Monges. Cotrans. and ed. Dennis J. McAuliffe. New York: Harvester, 1976.

————, ed. *Boccaccio visualizzato.* 3 vols. Turin: Einaudi, 1999.

————. "Boccaccio visualizzato I: 1. Interpretazioni visuali del *Decameron*; 2. Un primo elenco di codici illustrati di opere di Boccaccio." *Studi sul Boccaccio* 15 (1985–86): 85–148.

————. "Boccaccio 'visualizzato' dal Boccaccio II: Possibile identificazione nel Parigino It. 482 di una redazione del *Decameron* anteriore all'autografo degli anni Settanta." *Studi sul Boccaccio* 22 (1994): 225–34.

————. *Giovanni Boccaccio: Profilo biografico.* 2nd ed. Florence: Sansoni, 1992.

————. *Linee di una storia della critica al* Decameron *con bibliografia boccaccesca completamente aggiornata.* Biblioteca della 'Rassegna' 23. Milan: Alighieri, 1939.

————. "Un *lusus* del Bruni cancelliere: Il rifacimento di una novella del *Decameron* (IV, 1) e la sua irradiazione europea." *Leonardo Bruni cancelliere della Repubblica di Firenze: Convegno di studi (Firenze 27–29 ottobre 1987).* Ed. P. Viti. Florence: Olschki, 1990. 207–26.

————. "Ostensione del cuore e «Amore e Morte.»" *Forma e parola: Studi in onore di Fredi Chiappelli.* Ed. Dennis J. Dutschke et al. Rome: Bulzoni, 1992. 155–73.

Branca, Vittore, and Giorgio Padoan, eds. *Boccaccio, Venezia e il Veneto: Civiltà veneziana.* Saggi 25. Florence: Olschki, 1979.

———. "Bolletino bibliografico. I: Integrazioni alle bibliografie di studi boccacciani pubblicati dal Traversari e dal Branca. II: Indicazioni di studi boccacciani pubblicati dal 1938 al 1950." *Studi sul Boccaccio* 1 (1963): 445–516.

Brucker, Gene A. "Florence and the Black Death." Cottino-Jones and Tuttle 21–30.

———. *Florentine Politics and Society, 1343–1378.* Princeton: Princeton UP, 1962.

———. *Renaissance Florence.* New York: Wiley, 1969.

Bruni, Francesco. *Boccaccio: L'invenzione della letteratura mezzana.* Bologna: Mulino, 1990.

Bruni, Leonardo. *Le vite di Dante e del Petrarca.* Ed. Antonio Lanza. Rome: Izza, 1987.

Bryan, William F., and Germaine Dempster, eds. *Sources and Analogues of Chaucer's Canterbury Tales.* 1941. New York: Humanities, 1959.

Burton, Richard F., trans. *The Book of the Thousand Nights and a Night.* Ed. Leonard C. Smithers. 12 vols. London: Nichols, 1898.

Callmann, Ellen. "Subjects from Boccaccio in Italian Painting, 1375–1525." *Studi sul Boccaccio* 23 (1995): 19–78.

Calvino, Italo. *The Castle of Crossed Destinies.* Trans. William Weaver. New York: Harcourt, 1979.

Cambridge Italian Dictionary. Barbara Reynolds, gen. ed. 2 vols. Cambridge: Cambridge UP, 1981.

Camille, Michael. *The Gothic Idol: Idology and Image-Making in Medieval Art.* Cambridge: Cambridge UP, 1991.

Carmichael, Ann G. *Plague and the Poor in Renaissance Florence.* Cambridge: Cambridge UP, 1986.

Castiglione, Baldassare. *Il cortegiano con una scelta delle opere minori* [*The Courtier*]. Vol. 31 of *Classici Italiani.* Turin: Unione Tipografico-Editrice Torinese, 1955.

Cazalé-Bérard, Claude. "Filognia/Misoginia." Bragantini and Forni 116–41.

Cazalé-Bérard, Claude, and Michelangelo Picone, eds. *Atti del Convegno "Gli Zibaldoni di Boccaccio: Memoria, scrittura, riscrittura."* Firenze, 26–28 aprile 1996. Florence: Cesati, 1998.

Cervantes Saavedra, Miguel de. Novelas ejemplares: *Estudio preliminar, edición y notas de Julio Rodríguez-Luis.* Madrid: Taurus, 1983.

Chaucer, Geoffrey. *The Canterbury Tales. The Riverside Chaucer.* Larry Benson, gen. ed. 3rd ed. Boston: Houghton, 1987. 3–328.

Chiarini, Gioachino, ed. *Novelle italiane: Il Quattrocento.* Milan: Garzanti, 1982.

Cholakian, Patricia Francis. *Rape and Writing in the* Heptaméron *of Marguerite de Navarre.* Carbondale: Southern Illinois UP, 1991.

Cholakian, Patricia Francis, and Rouben Charles Cholakian, eds. and trans. *The Early French Novella.* Albany: State U of New York P, 1972.

Ciardi DuPré dal Poggetto, Maria Grazia. "Boccaccio 'visualizzato' dal Boccaccio I: 'Corpus' dei disegni e cod. Parigino It. 482." *Studi sul Boccaccio* 22 (1994): 197–224.

———. "L'iconografia nei codici miniati boccacciani dell'Italia centrale e meridionale." Branca, *Boccaccio visualizzato* 2: 3–152.

Ciccuto, Marcello, ed. *Novelle italiane: Il Cinquecento.* 2nd ed. Milan: Garzanti, 1989.

Cicero. *De Inventione*. Trans. H. M. Hubbell. Loeb Classical Lib. Cambridge: Harvard UP; London: Heinemann, 1976.

Clements, Robert J., and Joseph Gibaldi. *The Anatomy of the Novella: The European Tale Collection from Boccaccio and Chaucer to Cervantes*. New York: New York UP, 1977.

Cohn, Samuel Kline. *The Cult of Remembrance and the Black Death: Six Renaissance Cities in Central Italy*. Baltimore: Johns Hopkins UP, 1992.

Consoli, Joseph P. *Giovanni Boccaccio: An Annotated Bibliography*. Garland Medieval Bibliographies 9. New York: Garland, 1992.

Cottino-Jones, Marga. "Observations on the Structure of the *Decameron* Novella." *Romance Notes* 15 (1973): 378–87.

———. *Order from Chaos: Social and Aesthetic Harmonies in Boccaccio's* Decameron. Washington: UP of America, 1982.

Cottino-Jones, Marga, and Edward F. Tuttle, eds. *Boccaccio: Secoli di vita: Atti del Congresso Internazionale Boccaccio 1975*. L'Interprete 4. Ravenna: Longo, 1977.

Crane, T. F. "The Sources of Boccaccio's Novella of Mitridanes and Natan (*Dec*. X, 3)." *Romanic Review* 12 (1921): 193–215.

Curtius, Ernst Robert. *European Literature and the Latin Middle Ages*. Trans. Willard R. Trask. New York: Harper, 1963. Princeton: Princeton UP, 1990.

Daniel, Norman. *The Arabs and Medieval Europe*. London: Longman, 1975.

———. *Islam and the West: The Making of an Image*. Edinburgh: Edinburgh UP, 1966.

Dante Alighieri. *La commedia secondo l'antica vulgata*. 2. *Inferno*. Ed. Giorgio Petrocchi. Florence: Le Lettere, 1994.

———. *The Divine Comedy: Inferno*. Ed. and trans. Charles S. Singleton. 2 vols. Princeton: Princeton UP, 1970.

———. *The Divine Comedy of Dante Alighieri: Paradiso*. Dual-language ed. Trans. Allen Mandelbaum. New York: Bantam, 1984.

———. *Inferno*. Trans. Allen Mandelbaum. Berkeley: U of California P, 1980.

D'Antuono, Nancy L. *Boccaccio's 'Novelle' in the Theater of Lope de Vega*. Madrid: Porrua Turanzas, 1983.

David, Michel. "Boccaccio pornoscopo?" *Medioevo e rinascimento veneto con altri studi in onore di Lino Lazzarini. I: Dal Duecento al Quattrocento*. Padua: Antenore, 1979. 215–43.

Degenhart, Bernhard, and Annegrit Schmitt. *Corpus der italienischen Zeichnungen 1300–1450*. Vol. 1., pt. 1. Berlin: Mann, 1968.

Delcorno, Carlo. "Metamorfosi boccacciane dell'exemplum." *Exemplum e letteratura: Tra Medioevo e Rinascimento*. Ed. Delcorno. Bologna: Mulino, 1989. 265–94.

———. "Note sui dantismi nell' *Elegia di madonna Fiammetta*." *Studi sul Boccaccio* 11 (1979): 251–94.

Delcorno Branca, Daniela. " 'Cognominato Prencipe Galeotto.' Il sottotitolo illustrato del Parigino It. 482." *Studi sul Boccaccio* 23 (1995): 79–88.

de' Negri, Enrico. "The Legendary Style of the *Decameron*." *Romanic Review* 43 (1952): 166–89.

De Sanctis, Francesco. *Storia della letteratura italiana*. Florence: Sansoni, 1965.

Dinshaw, Carolyn. *Chaucer's Sexual Politics*. Madison: U of Wisconsin P, 1989.

Dizionario della lingua italiana. Ed. Giocomo Devoto and Gian Carlo Oli. Florence: Le Monnier, 1995.

Dombroski, Robert S., ed. *Critical Perspectives on the* Decameron. London: Hodder, 1976.

Donato, Maria Monica. "Per la fortuna monumentale di Giovanni Boccaccio fra i grandi Fiorenti: Notizie e problemi." *Studi sul Boccaccio* 17 (1988): 287–342.

Dovizi, Bernardo. *La Calandria*. Turin: Einaudi, 1978.

Durling, Robert M. "Boccaccio on Interpretation: Guido's Escape (*Decameron* VI.9)." Bernardo and Pellegrini 273–304.

———. "A Long Day in the Sun: *Dec*. 8.7." *Shakespeare's 'Rough Magic': Renaissance Essays in Honor of C. L. Barber*. Ed. Peter Erickson and Coppelia Kahn. Newark: U Delaware P, 1985. 269–75.

Eagleton, Terry. *Literary Theory: An Introduction*. Minneapolis: U of Minnesota P, 1983.

Eco, Umberto. *The Role of the Reader: Explorations in the Semiotics of Texts*. Bloomington: Indiana UP, 1984.

———. *Six Walks in the Fictional Woods*. Trans. William Weaver. Cambridge: Harvard UP, 1994.

El Saffar, Ruth. *From Novel to Romance: A Study of Cervantes' Novelas ejemplares*. Baltimore: Johns Hopkins UP, 1974.

Enciclopedia dantesca. Ed. Umberto Bosco. 6 vols. Rome: Istituto della Enciclopedia italiana, 1970–78.

Esposito, Enzo. *Boccacciana: Bibliografia delle edizioni e degli scritti critici (1939–1974)*. Ravenna: Longo, 1976.

Fajardo, Salvador J. "The Frame as Formal Contrast: Boccaccio and Cervantes." *Comparative Literature* 36 (1984): 1–19.

Fassò, Luigi. "La prima novella del *Decamerone* e la sua fortuna." *Saggi e ricerche di storia letteraria (Da Dante al Manzoni)*. Milan: Marzorati, 1947. 84–90.

Ferrante, Joan. "The Frame Characters of the *Decameron*: A Progression of Virtues." *Romance Philology* 19 (1965): 212–26.

———. "Narrative Patterns in the *Decameron*." *Romance Philology* 31 (1978): 585–604.

Fido, Franco. "Architettura." Bragantini and Forni 13–33.

———. "Dante personaggio mancato del *Decameron*." Cottino-Jones and Tuttle 177–89.

———. *Il regime delle simmetrie imperfette: Studi sul* Decameron. Milan: Angeli, 1988.

———. "Rhetoric and Semantics in the *Decameron*: Tropes and Signs in a Narrative Function." *Yale Italian Studies* 2 (1978): 1–12.

Fish, Stanley. *Is There a Text in This Class? The Authority of Interpretive Communities*. Cambridge: Harvard UP, 1980.

Foley, John. *The Singer of Tales in Performance: Voices in Performance and Text*. Bloomington: Indiana UP, 1995.

Foscolo, Ugo. "Boccaccio." Dombroski 15–25.

Foucault, Michel. "What Is an Author?" *Textual Strategies: Perspectives in Post-Structuralist Criticism.* Ed. Josue Harari. Ithaca: Cornell UP, 1979.

Franklin, Margaret. "A Note on Boccaccio in Hiding." *Source* 14.1 (1994): 1–5.

Galigani, Giuseppe, ed. *Il Boccaccio nella cultura inglese e anglo-americana.* Ente nazionale Giovanni Boccaccio Pubblicazioni 2. Florence: Olschki, 1974.

Gehl, Paul F. *A Moral Art: Grammar, Society, and Culture in Trecento Florence.* Cornell: Cornell UP, 1993.

Gelernt, Jules. *World of Many Loves: The* Heptaméron *of Marguerite de Navarre.* Chapel Hill: U of North Carolina P, 1966.

Getto, Giovanni. *Vita di forme e forme di vita nel* Decameron. Turin: Petrini, 1986.

Gibaldi, Joseph. "The *Decameron* Cornice and the Responses to the Disintegration of Civilization." *Kentucky Romance Quarterly* 24 (1977): 349–57.

Gower, John. "Tale of Constance." *Confessio Amantis.* Ed. G. C. Macaulay. 1901. London: Oxford UP, 1969. 146–73. Vol. 1 of *The English Works of John Gower.* 2 vols. Early English Text Society, ES 81.

Graedel, Leonie. *La cornice nelle raccolte novellistiche del Rinascimento e i rapporti con la cornice del* Decameron. Florence: Cenacolo, 1959.

Grande dizionario della lingua italiana. Ed. Salvatore Battaglia and Giorgio Barberi Squarotti. 19 vols. to date. Turin: Unione tipografico-editore torinese, 1961– .

Grazzini, Giovanni. "Al cinema col Boccaccio." *Boccaccio e dintorni* 323–26.

Green, Louis. *Chronicle into History.* Cambridge: Cambridge UP, 1972.

Green, Thomas. "Forms of Accommodation in the *Decameron*." *Italica* 45 (1968): 297–313.

Griseri, Andreina. "Di fronte al «*Decameron*» : L'età moderna." Branca, *Boccaccio visualizzato* 1: 155–211.

Grossvogel, Steven. "What Do We Really Know of Ser Ciappelletto?" *Il Veltro* 40 (1996): 133–37.

Haddawy, Husain, trans. *The Arabian Nights.* New York: Norton, 1990.

Hankey, Teresa. "Salutati's Epigrams for the Palazzo Vecchio at Florence." *Journal of the Warburg and Courtauld Institutes* 22 (1959): 363–65.

Hastings, Robert. *Nature and Reason in the* Decameron. Manchester: Manchester UP, 1975.

Henri d'Andeli. Le Lai d'Aristote *d'Henri d'Andeli.* Ed. Maurice Delbouille. Paris: Belles Lettres, 1951.

Hind, A. M. *Early Italian Engraving: A Critical Catalogue with Complete Reproduction of All the Prints Described.* 1938. Lichtenstein: Nendeln, 1970.

Hirth, Georg, ed. *Kulturgeschichtliches Bilderbuch aus drei Jahrhunderten: Picture Book of the Graphic Arts, 1500–1800.* 1882–90. New York: Blom, 1972.

Hitti, Philip K. *Islam and the West: A Historical Cultural Survey.* New York: Van Nostrand, 1962.

Hollander, Robert. "Boccaccio's Dante." *Italica* 63 (1986): 278–89.

———. "Boccaccio's Dante: Imitative Distance." *Studi sul Boccaccio* 13 (1981–82): 169–98.

———. *Boccaccio's Dante: The Shaping Force of Satire*. Ann Arbor: Michigan UP, 1997.

———. *Boccaccio's Last Fiction: Il Corbaccio*. Philadelphia: U of Pennsylvania P, 1988.

———. "The Proem of the *Decameron*: Boccaccio between Ovid and Dante." *Miscellanea di studi danteschi in memoria di Silvio Pasquazi*. Ed. Alfonso Paolella, Vincenzo Placella, and Giovanni Turco. Vol. 1. Naples: Federico, 1993. 423–40.

———. "The Sun Rises in Dante." *Studi sul Boccaccio* 14 (1983–84): 241–55.

Hollander, Robert, and Courtney Cahill. "Day Ten of the *Decameron*: The Myth of Order." *Studi sul Boccaccio* 23 (1995): 1–58.

Holleran, Andrew. *Ground Zero*. New York: NAL, 1989.

Holmes, G. A. "Florentine Merchants in England, 1346–1436." *Economic History Review* 2nd ser. 13.2 (1960): 193–208.

Horster, Marita. *Andrea del Castagno: Complete Edition with a Critical Catalogue*. Ithaca: Cornell UP, 1980.

Jacobus de Voragine. *The Golden Legend*. Trans. and adapt. Branger Ryan and Helmut Ripperger. Salem: Ayer, 1969.

Jaunzems, John. "Structure and Meaning in the *Seven Sages of Rome*." *Studies on the Seven Sages of Rome and Other Essays in Medieval Literature: Dedicated to the Memory of Jean Misrahi*. Ed. H. Niedzielski et al. Honolulu: Educ. Research Assoc., 1978. 43–62.

Joyce, Michael. *Of Two Minds: Hypertext Pedagogy and Poetics*. Ann Arbor: U of Michigan P, 1995.

Juvenal. *The Satires of Juvenal*. Trans. Rolfe Humphries. Bloomington: Indiana UP, 1958.

Kaplan, Nancy. "Politexts, Hypertexts, and Other Cultural Formations in the Late Age of Print." *Computer-Mediated Communication Magazine* 1 Mar. 1995 <http://metalab.unc.edu/cmc/mag/1995/mar/kaplan.html>.

Kass, Robert. "Review of *Decameron Nights*." *Catholic World* Dec. 1953: 223–24.

Kern, Edith. *The Absolute Comic*. New York: Columbia UP, 1980.

Kirkham, Victoria. "L'immagine del Boccaccio nella memoria tardo-gotica e rinascimentale." Branca, *Boccaccio visualizzato* 1: 85–144.

———. "John Badmouth: Fortunes of the Poet's Image." *Boccaccio 1990: The Poet and His Renaissance Reception*. Ed. Kevin Brownlee and Kirkham. Spec. issue of *Studi sul Boccaccio* 20 (1991–92): 355–76.

———. "Painters at Play on the Judgment Day (*Decameron* VIII 9)." *Studi sul Boccaccio* 14 (1983–84): 256–77.

———. "A Preliminary List of Boccaccio Portraits from the Fourteenth to the Mid-Sixteenth Centuries." *Studi sul Boccaccio* 15 (1985–86): 167–88.

———. "Renaissance Portraits of Boccaccio: A Look into the Kaleidoscope." *Studi sul Boccaccio* 16 (1987): 284–305.

———. *The Sign of Reason in Boccaccio's Fiction*. Florence: Olschki, 1995.

Kirkham, Victoria, Susy Marcon, Paul Watson, and Vittore Branca, eds. "Boccaccio visualizzato II." *Studi sul Boccaccio* 16 (1987): 247–305.

Kushner, Tony. *Angels in America: Part Two: Perestroika*. New York: Theatre Communications Group, 1994.

The Lady of Vergi [*La Châtelaine de Vergi*]. Ed. and trans. Leigh A. Arrathoon. Merrick: Cross-Cultural Communications, 1984.

Landow, George P. *Hypertext: The Convergence of Contemporary Critical Theory and Technology*. Baltimore: Johns Hopkins UP, 1992.

———. *Hypertext 2.0*. Baltimore: Johns Hopkins UP, 1997.

Lane, Edward William, trans. *The Arabian Night's Entertainments; or, The Thousand and One Nights*. New York: Tudor, 1927.

Langer, Susanne K. *Feeling and Form: A Theory of Art*. New York: Scribner's, 1953.

Larner, John. *Culture and Society in Italy, 1290–1420*. New York: Scribner's, 1971.

———. *Italy in the Age of Dante and Petrarch, 1216–1380*. London: Longman, 1980.

La Roncière, Charles de. "Tuscan Notables on the Eve of the Renaissance." *Revelations of the Medieval World*. Ed. Georges Duby. Trans. Arthur Goldhammer. Cambridge: Harvard UP, 1988. 157–310. Vol. 2 of *A History of Private Life*. Ed. Philippe Aries and Duby.

Lawton, Ben. "Boccaccio and Pasolini: A Contemporary Reinterpretation of *The Decameron*." Boccaccio, *Decameron* [Norton] 306–21.

———. "The Evolving Rejection of Homosexuality, the Sub-proletariat, and the Third World in the Films of Pier Paolo Pasolini." *Italian Quarterly* 21–22 (1980–81): 167–73.

Lee, Alfred C. *The* Decameron: *Its Sources and Analogues*. 1909. New York: Haskell, 1967.

Lefkowitz, Mary. *Lives of the Greek Poets*. Baltimore: Johns Hopkins UP, 1981.

Levy, Pierre. *L'intelligence collective: Pour une anthropologie du cyberspace*. Paris: La Découverte, 1994.

Lifton, Robert J. *The Life of the Self*. New York: Simon, 1976.

Lope de Vega. *See* Vega Carpio.

Lopez, Roberto S. *The Commercial Revolution of the Middle Ages, 950–1350*. Cambridge: Cambridge UP, 1976.

Lopez, Roberto S., and I. Raymond. *Medieval Trade in the Mediterranean World*. New York: Norton, 1967.

Lupton, Julia Reinhard. *Afterlives of the Saints: Hagiography, Typology, and Secular Literature*. Stanford: Stanford UP, 1996.

Luther, Martin. *Table Talk* [*Tischreden*]. Ed. and trans. Theodore G. Tappert. Vol. 54 of *Luther's Works*. Philadelphia: Fortress, 1967.

Machiavelli, Niccolò. *La Clizia*. Milan: Mursia, 1989.

———. *La mandragola*. Milan: Mursia, 1989.

Mahdi, Muhsin. *The Thousand and One Nights*. Leiden: Brill, 1995.

Mann, Jill. *Chaucer and Medieval Estates Satire*. Cambridge: Cambridge UP, 1973.

Marcus, Millicent. *An Allegory of Form: Literary Self-Consciousness in the* Decameron. Stanford French and Italian Studies 18. Stanford: Stanford UP, 1979.

———. *Filmmaking by the Book: Italian Cinema and Literary Adaptation*. Baltimore: Johns Hopkins UP, 1993.

———. "Misogyny as Misreading: A Gloss on *Decameron* 8.7." *Stanford Italian Review* 4 (1984): 23–40.

Marguerite de Navarre. *L'Heptaméron*. Ed. Nicole Cazauran. Paris: Société d'Enseignement Supérieur, 1976.

———. *The Heptaméron*. Trans. John S. Chartres. 5 vols. London: Soc. of English Bibliophilists, 1894.

———. *The Heptaméron*. Trans. and introd. Paul A. Chilton. London: Penguin, 1984.

———. *L'Heptaméron*. Ed. Michel François. 1960. Paris: Classiques Garnier, 1977.

———. *The Heptaméron*. Ed. and trans. Walter K. Kelly. 2 vols. London: Bohn, 1855.

———. *L'Heptaméron*. Ed. Yves Le Hir. Paris: PUF, 1967.

———. *L'Heptaméron*. 1853–54. Ed. A. J. V. Le Roux de Lincy and Anatole de Montaiglon. 3 vols. Paris: Slatkine, 1969.

———. *L'Heptaméron*. Ed. S. de Reyff. Paris: Flammarion, 1982.

———. *The Heptaméron*. Trans. W. M. Thompson. London: Temple, 1896.

Marie de France. *The Lais of Marie de France*. Trans. Robert Hanning and Joan Ferrante. Durham: Labyrinth, 1982.

Marino, Lucia. *The Decameron Cornice: Allusion, Allegory, and Iconology: Boccaccio's Allegorical Case of a Humanistic Theory of Literature*. L'Interprete 14. Ravenna: Longo, 1979.

Martone, Valerie, and Robert L. Martone, eds. and trans. *Renaissance Comic Tales of Love, Treachery, and Revenge*. New York: Italica, 1994.

Mathieu-Castellani, Gisèle. *La conversation conteuse: Les nouvelles de Marguerite de Navarre*. Paris: PUF, 1992.

Mazzoni, Francesco, ed. *Il Boccaccio nelle culture e letterature nazionali*. Ente nazionale Giovanni Boccaccio Pubblicazioni 3. Florence: Olschki, 1978.

Mazzotta, Giuseppe. "Games of Laughter in the *Decameron*." *Romanic Review* 69 (1978): 115–31.

———. *The World at Play in Boccaccio's* Decameron. Princeton: Princeton UP, 1986.

McGillivray, David. "Review of Decameron *No. 2*." *Monthly Film Bulletin* 40 (1973): 26.

McNeill, William. *Plagues and Peoples*. Garden City: Anchor, 1976.

Mee, Charles L., Jr. "How a Mysterious Disease Laid Low Europe's Masses." *Smithsonian* 20 (1990): 66–79.

"Le meunier et les II. clers." Bryan and Dempster 126–47.

Migiel, Marilyn. "The Untidy Business of Gender Studies; or, Why Is It Almost Useless to Ask if the *Decameron* Is Feminist?" Psaki and Stillinger, forthcoming.

Mirollo, James V. "Renaissance Short Fiction." *European Writers: The Middle Ages and Renaissance*. Ed. W. T. H. Jackson. Vol. 2. New York: Scribner's, 1983. 927–56.

Molho, Anthony, ed. *Social and Economic Foundations of the Italian Renaissance*. New York: Wiley, 1969.

Morello, Giovanni. "Disegni marginali nei manoscritti di Giovanni Boccaccio." Cazalé-Bérard and Picone 161–77.

Muscetta, Carlo. *Giovanni Boccaccio*. Rome: Laterza, 1986.

———. "Giovanni Boccaccio e i novellieri." Sapegno (1965) 316–558.

Naddaff, Sandra. *Arabesque: Narrative Structure and the Aesthetics of Repetition in the 1001 Nights*. Evanston: Northwestern UP, 1991.

Nelson, T. G. A. *Comedy: The Theory of Comedy in Literature, Drama and Cinema.* Oxford: Oxford UP, 1990.

Neri, Ferdinando. "Il disegno ideale del *Decameron.*" *Storia e poesia.* Turin: Chiantore, 1944. 73–82.

Norton Anthology of World Masterpieces. Ed. Maynard Mack et al. 6th ed. 2 vols. New York: Norton, 1992.

Il novellino. Ed. Cesare Segre. Trans. Gérard Genot and Paul Lavivaille. Paris: Union Générale, 1988.

Nurmela, Tauno. "Physionomie de Boccace." *Neuphilologische Mitteilungen* 60 (1959): 321–34.

O Cuilleanain, Cormac. *Religion and the Clergy in Boccaccio's* Decameron. Rome: Storia e Letteratura, 1984.

Olson, Glending. *Literature as Recreation in the Later Middle Ages.* Ithaca: Cornell UP, 1982.

Osgood, Charles G., trans. and ed. *Boccaccio on Poetry: Being the Preface and Fourteenth and Fifteenth Books of Boccaccio's* Genealogia Deorum Gentilium. Indianapolis: Liberal Arts, 1956.

Ovid. *Heroides.* Trans. Grant Showerman. Loeb Classical Lib. Cambridge: Harvard UP; London: Heinemann, 1971.

———. *Metamorphoses.* Trans. Frank Justus Miller. Loeb Classical Lib. Cambridge: Harvard UP; London: Heinemann, 1971.

Pabst, Walter. *Novellentheorie und Novellendichtung.* Hamburg: Cram, 1953.

Padoan, Giorgio. *Il Boccaccio, le muse, il Parnaso e l'Arno.* Biblioteca di lettere italiane: Studi e testi 21. Florence: Olschki, 1978.

Papio, Michael, and Massimo Riva. "La novella tra testo e ipertesto: Il *Decameron* come modello." *Dal primato allo scacco: I modelli narrativi italiani tra Trecento e Seicento.* Ed. Gian Mario Anselmo. Rome: Carocci, 1998. 65–85.

Parker, Deborah. "Vasari's *Portrait of Six Tuscan Poets*: A Visible Literary History." *Visibile Parlare: Dante and the Art of the Italian Renaissance.* Ed. Parker. Spec. issue of *Lectura Dantis* 22–23 (1998): 45–62.

Pasolini, Pier Paolo. *Trilogia della vita.* Bologna: Mondadori, 1975.

Passavanti, Jacopo. *Specchio di vera penitenza.* Ed. Maria Lenardon. Florence: Libreria Editrice Fiorentina, 1925.

Patterson, Lee. *Chaucer and the Subject of History.* Madison: U of Wisconsin P, 1991.

Pellegrini, Carlo, ed. *Il Boccaccio nella cultura francese.* Ente nazionale Giovanni Boccaccio Pubblicazioni 1. Florence: Olschki, 1971.

Petrarch [Francesco Petrarca]. *Letters of Old Age: Rerum Senilium Libri I–XVIII.* Trans. Aldo Bernardo, Saul Levin, and Reta A. Bernardo. 2 vols. Baltimore: Johns Hopkins UP, 1992.

Petronio, Giuseppe. *I miei* Decameron. Roma: Ruiniti, 1989.

Petrus Alfonsi. *The* Disciplina clericalis *of Petrus Alfonsi.* Ed. and trans. Eberhard Hermes into German. Trans. P. R. Quarrie into English. Berkeley: U of California P, 1977.

Picone, Michelangelo. "Dal lai alla novella: Il caso di Ghismonda (*Dec.* IV.1)." *Filologia e Critica* 16 (1991): 325–43.

Picone, Michelangelo, Giuseppe Di Stefano, and Pamela D. Stewart, eds. *Formation, codification et rayonnement d'un genre médiéval: La nouvelle.* Montreal: Plato, 1983.

Polo, Marco. *The Travels of Marco Polo.* Trans. Ronald Latham. New York: Penguin, 1982.

Potter, Joy Hambuechen. *Five Frames for the* Decameron: *Communication and Social Systems in the Cornice.* Princeton: Princeton UP, 1982.

———. "Woman in the *Decameron.*" *Studies in the Italian Renaissance: Essays in Memory of Arnolfo B. Ferruolo.* Ed. Gian Paolo Biasin et al. Naples: Soc. Ed. Napoletana, 1985. 87–103.

Psaki, Regina, and Thomas C. Stillinger, eds. *Boccaccio and Feminist Criticism.* Forthcoming.

Quargnolo, Mario. *Dove va il cinema italiano?* Milan: Pan, 1972.

Radcliff-Umstead, Douglas. "Boccaccio's Adaptation of Some Latin Sources for the *Decameron.*" *Italica* 45 (1968): 171–94.

Ramat, Raffaello. "L'introduzione alla 'quarta giornata.'" *Saggi sul Rinascimento.* Florence: La Nuova Italia, 1969. 50–69.

Ravel, Maurice. *L'heure espagnole.* Libretto by Franc-Nohain [Maurice-Etienne Legrand]. Mineola: Dover, 1996.

Raymond, Marcel. *Vérité et poésie.* Neuchâtel: La Baconnière, 1964.

Ricapito, Joseph V. "Boccaccio and the Picaresque Tradition." *The Two Hesperias: Literary Studies in Honor of Joseph G. Fucilla on the Occasion of His Eightieth Birthday.* Americo Bugliani, gen. ed. Madrid: Porrua, 1977. 309–28.

Ricci, Pier Giorgio. "Dominus Iohannes Boccaccius." *Studi sul Boccaccio* 6 (1971): 1–10.

———, ed. *Trattatello in laude di Dante.* Boccaccio, *Tutte le opere,* vol. 3, 423–538.

Rigg, A. G., ed. and trans. *Gawain on Marriage: The Textual Tradition of* De coniuge non ducenda. Toronto: Pontifical Inst. of Mediaeval Studies, 1986.

Riley, E. C. *Cervantes's Theory of the Novel.* Oxford: Clarendon, 1962.

Robinson, James Harvey. *Petrarch: The First Modern Scholar and Man of Letters.* New York: Putnam, 1898.

Rochon, André. *Formes et significations de la "beffa" dans la littérature italienne de la Renaissance.* Paris: Université de la Sorbonne Nouvelle, 1972.

Rodax, Yvonne. *The Real and the Ideal in the Novella of Italy, France, and England.* Chapel Hill: U of North Carolina P, 1968.

Ross, Harris. *Film as Literature, Literature as Film.* New York: Greenwood, 1987.

Rossi, Massimiliano. "I dipinti—Introduzione: La novella di Sandro e Nastagio." Branca, *Boccaccio visualizzato* 2: 153–231.

Rotunda, Dominic P. *Motif-Index of the Italian Novella in Prose.* Indiana University Publ. Folklore Ser. 2. 1942. New York: Haskell, 1973.

———. "A Tabulation of Early Italian Tales." *U of California Publications in Modern Philology* 14 (1930): 331–43.

Roush, Sherry. "Renaissance Modes of Italian Poetic Self-Commentary." Diss. Yale, 1999.

Rudnick, Paul. *Jeffrey.* New York: Plume, 1994.

Rumble, Patrick. *Allegories of Contamination: Pier Paolo Pasolini's* Trilogy of Life. Toronto: U of Toronto P, 1996.

Runte, Hans R., J. Keith Wikeley, and Anthony J. Farrell. The Seven Sages of Rome *and* The Book of Sindbad: *An Analytical Bibliography*. New York: Garland, 1984.

Ruzzante [Angelo Beolco]. *I due dialoghi*. Turin: Einaudi, 1974.

Saadi. The Bustan *of Sadi*. Trans. A. Hart Edwards. Lahore: Sh. Muhammad Ashraf, n.d.

Sacchetti, Franco. *Il Trecentonovelle*. Ed. Emilio Faccioli. Turin: Einaudi, 1970.

Sanguineti White, Laura. *La scena conviviale e la sua funzione nel mondo del Boccaccio*. Florence: Olschki, 1983.

Sapegno, Natalino, ed. *Il Trecento*. Vol. 2 of *Storia della letteratura italiana*. Ed. Emilio Cecchi and Sapegno. Milan: Garzanti, 1965. 2nd ed. 1987.

Scaglione, Aldo. "Giovanni Boccaccio; or, The Narrative Vocation." Cottino-Jones and Tuttle 81–104.

———. *Knights at Court: Courtliness, Chivalry, and Courtesy from Ottonian Germany to the Italian Renaissance*. Berkeley: U of California P, 1991.

———. *Nature and Love in the Late Middle Ages: An Essay on the Cultural Context of the* Decameron. Berkeley: U of California P, 1963.

———. "Storytelling, the *Novella* and the *Decameron*." *The Western Pennsylvania Symposium on World Literatures Selected Proceedings, 1974–1991: A Retrospective*. Ed. Carla E. Lucente. Greensburg: Eadmer, 1992. 1–24.

Schevill, Ferdinand. *Medieval and Renaissance Florence*. 2 vols. New York: Harper, 1961.

Schiller, Gertrud. *Iconography of Christian Art*. Trans. Janet Seligman. Vol. 1. Greenwich: New York Graphic Soc., 1971.

Segre, Cesare. *Lingua, stile e società*. Milan: Feltrinelli, 1974.

———, ed. *Strutturalismo e critica*. Milan: Saggiatore, 1985.

———. *Le strutture e il tempo*. Turin: Einaudi, 1974.

Serafini-Sauli, Judith. *Giovanni Boccaccio*. Twayne World Author 644. Boston: Twayne, 1982.

Shaffer, Peter. *Lettice and Lovage: A Comedy*. New York: Harper, 1990.

Sherberg, Michael. "The Patriarch's Pleasure and the Frametale Crisis: *Decameron* IV–V." *Romance Quarterly* 38 (1991): 227–38.

Shklovsky, Viktor B. *Theory of Prose: O teorii prozy*. Trans. Benjamin Sher. Elmwood Park: Dalkey, 1990.

Singleton, Charles. "On Meaning in the *Decameron*. " *Italica* 21 (1944): 117–24.

Smarr, Janet Levarie. *Boccaccio and Fiammetta: The Narrator as Lover*. Urbana: U of Illinois P, 1986.

———, ed. and trans. *Italian Renaissance Tales*. Rochester: Solaris, 1983.

———. "Symmetry and Balance in the *Decameron*." *Medievalia* 2 (1976): 159–87.

Sontag, Susan. *AIDS and Its Metaphors*. New York: Farrar, 1988.

———. *Illness as Metaphor*. New York: Farrar, 1978.

Southern, R. W. *Western Views of Islam*. Cambridge: Harvard UP, 1978.

Sozzi, Lionello. *La nouvelle française de la Renaissance*. Turin: Giappichelli, 1975.

Stack, Oswald. *Pasolini on Pasolini*. Bloomington: Indiana UP, 1970.

Stefani, Marchionne di Coppo. *Cronaca fiorentina*. Ed. N. Rodolico. Vol. 30 of *Rerum Italicorum Scriptores*. Città di Castello: Lapi, 1927.

Stewart, Pamela D. "Boccaccio e la tradizione retorica: La definizione della novella come genere letterario." *Stanford Italian Review* 1 (1979): 67–74.

———. "La novella di Madonna Oretta e le due parti del *Decameron*." *Yearbook of Italian Studies* (1973–75): 27–40.

Stillinger, Thomas C. "The Language of Gardens: Boccaccio's Valle delle Donne." *Traditio* 39 (1983): 301–21.

Stych, F. S. *Boccaccio in English: A Bibliography of Editions, Adaptations, and Criticism*. Westport: Greenwood, 1995.

Symonds, John Addington. "The Novellieri." *The Renaissance in Italy*. Vol 2. New York: Mod. Lib., 1935. 199–229.

Tartaro, Achille. "La prosa narrativa antica." *Letteratura italiana*. Ed. A. Asor Rosa. Turin: Einaudi, 1984. 623–713.

Tetel, Marcel. "Ambiguité chez Boccacce et Marguerite de Navarre." Pellegrini 557–65.

———. *Marguerite de Navarre's* Heptaméron: *Themes, Language, and Structure*. Durham: Duke UP, 1973.

Thompson, N. S. *Chaucer, Boccaccio, and the Debate of Love: A Comparative Study of the* Decameron *and the* Canterbury Tales. Oxford: Clarendon, 1996.

Tirso de Molina [Gabriel Téllez]. *Cigarrales de Toledo*. Madrid: Imprenta "Renacimiento," 1913.

Todorov, Tzvetan. *Grammaire du* Decameron. Hague: Mouton, 1969.

Tournoy, Gilbert, ed. *Boccaccio in Europe: Proceedings of the Boccaccio Conference, Louvain, Dec. 1975*. Louvain: Louvain UP, 1977.

Trapp, J. B. "The Iconography of Petrarch in the Age of Humanism." *Quaderni Petrarcheschi* 9–10 (1992–93): 11–73.

Traversari, Guido. *Bibliografia boccaccesca: Scritti intorno al Boccaccio e alla fortuna delle sue opere*. Città di Castello: Lapi, 1907.

Trexler, Richard C. *Public Life in Renaissance Florence*. New York: Academic, 1980.

Trevet, Nicholas. *Chronique*: "Story of Constance." Bryan and Dempster 165–81.

Vaglio, Anna. *Invito alla lettura di Boccaccio*. Milan: Mursia, 1988.

Vasari, Giorgio. *Le vite de' più eccellenti pittori, scultori e architettori; nelle redazioni del 1550 e 1568* [*Lives of the Artists*]. Ed. Rosanna Bettarini and Paola Barocchi. 7 vols. Florence: Sansoni, 1966– .

Vega Carpio, Lope de. *Lope de Vega: Five Plays*. Ed. R. D. Pring-Mill. Trans. Jill Booty. New York: Hill, 1961.

Velli, Giuseppe. *Petrarca e Boccaccio: Tradizione-memoria-scrittura*. Padua: Antenore, 1979.

Verdi, Giuseppe. *Falstaff*. Libretto by Arrigo Boito. New York: Dover, 1980.

Viano, Maurizio. *A Certain Realism: Making Use of Pasolini's Film Theory and Practice*. Berkeley: U of California P, 1993.

Villani, Filippo. "The Life of Giovanni Boccaccio." Boccaccio, *Dec.*, Musa and Bondanella (Norton Critical Ed.) 188–91.

————. *Le vite d'uomini illustri fiorentini*. Ed. Giammaria Mazzuchelli. 2nd ed. Florence: Magheri, 1826.

Villani, Giovanni. *Nuova cronica*. Ed. Giuseppe Porta. 3 vols. Parma: Guanda, 1990.

————. *Nuova cronica*. Ed. and trans. Rose E. Selfe and Philip H. Wicksteed. London: Constable, 1906.

Villani, Matteo. *Cronica*. Ed. Francesco Dragomanni. 2 vols. Florence: Sansone Coen, 1847.

Voznesenskaya, Julia. *The Women's* Decameron. Trans. W. B. Linton. Boston: Atlantic Monthly, 1986.

Wallace, David. *Chaucerian Polity: Absolutist Lineages and Associational Forms in England and Italy*. Stanford: Stanford UP, 1997.

————. *Giovanni Boccaccio*: Decameron. Landmarks of World Literature. Cambridge: Cambridge UP, 1991.

Ward, Benedicta. *Harlots of the Desert: A Study of Repentance in Early Monastic Sources*. Kalamazoo: Cistercian, 1987.

Watson, Paul F. "The Cement of Fiction: Giovanni Boccaccio and the Painters of Florence." *MLN* 99 (1984): 43–64.

————. *The Garden of Love in Tuscan Art of the Early Renaissance*. Philadelphia: Art Alliance, 1979.

————. "Gatherings of Artists: The Illustrators of a *Decameron* of 1427." *TEXT: Transactions of the Society for Textual Scholarship* 1 (1981 for 1984): 147–56.

————. "On a Window in Parnassus." *Artibus et historiae* 16 (1987): 127–48.

————. "A Preliminary List of Subjects from Boccaccio in Italian Painting, 1400–1550." *Studi sul Boccaccio* 15 (1985–86): 149–66.

————. "The Spanish Chapel: Portraits of Poets or a Portrait of Christian Order?" *Memorie domenicane* ns 11 (1980): 471–87.

Wilkins, Ernest Hatch. *A History of Italian Literature*. Rev. Thomas Bergin. Cambridge: Harvard UP, 1974.

Williams, Robert. "Boccaccio's Altarpiece." *Studi sul Boccaccio* 19 (1990): 229–40.

The World of Learning 1999. 49th ed. London: Europa, 1999.

Wright, Herbert G. *Boccaccio in England, from Chaucer to Tennyson*. Fairlawn: Essential, 1957.

Zayas y Sotomayor, María de. *The Disenchantments of Love [Desengaños amorosos]*. Ed. and trans. H. Patsy Boyer. Albany: State U of New York P, 1997.

————. *The Enchantments of Love: Amorous and Exemplary Novels*. Ed. and trans. H. Patsy Boyer. Berkeley: U of California P, 1990.

————. *Novelas ejemplares y amorosas o* Decameron *español*. Ed. Eduardo Rincón. Madrid: Alianza, 1968.

————. *Parte segunda del Sarao y entretenimiento honesto: Desengaños amorosos*. Ed. Alicia Yllera. Madrid: Catedra, 1998.

Ziegler, Philip. *The Black Death*. New York: Day, 1969.

Zinsser, Hans. *Rats, Lice, and History*. Boston: Atlantic Monthly, 1935.

INDEX OF NAMES

Modern Language Association of America

Approaches to Teaching World Literature

Joseph Gibaldi, series editor

Kingston's The Woman Warrior. Ed. Shirley Geok-lin Lim. 1991.

Lafayette's The Princess of Clèves. Ed. Faith E. Beasley and Katharine Ann Jensen. 1998.

Lessing's The Golden Notebook. Ed. Carey Kaplan and Ellen Cronan Rose. 1989.

Mann's Death in Venice *and Other Short Fiction*. Ed. Jeffrey B. Berlin. 1992.

Medieval English Drama. Ed. Richard K. Emmerson. 1990.

Melville's Moby-Dick. Ed. Martin Bickman. 1985.

Metaphysical Poets. Ed. Sidney Gottlieb. 1990.

Miller's Death of a Salesman. Ed. Matthew C. Roudané. 1995.

Milton's Paradise Lost. Ed. Galbraith M. Crump. 1986.

Molière's Tartuffe *and Other Plays*. Ed. James F. Gaines and Michael S. Koppisch. 1995.

Momaday's The Way to Rainy Mountain. Ed. Kenneth M. Roemer. 1988.

Montaigne's Essays. Ed. Patrick Henry. 1994.

Novels of Toni Morrison. Ed. Nellie Y. McKay and Kathryn Earle. 1997.

Murasaki Shikibu's The Tale of Genji. Ed. Edward Kamens. 1993.

Pope's Poetry. Ed. Wallace Jackson and R. Paul Yoder. 1993.

Shakespeare's King Lear. Ed. Robert H. Ray. 1986.

Shakespeare's Romeo and Juliet. Ed. Maurice Hunt. 2000.

Shakespeare's The Tempest *and Other Late Romances*. Ed. Maurice Hunt. 1992.

Shelley's Frankenstein. Ed. Stephen C. Behrendt. 1990.

Shelley's Poetry. Ed. Spencer Hall. 1990.

Shorter Elizabethan Poetry. Ed. Patrick Cheney and Anne Lake Prescott. 2000.

Sir Gawain and the Green Knight. Ed. Miriam Youngerman Miller and Jane Chance. 1986.

Spenser's Faerie Queene. Ed. David Lee Miller and Alexander Dunlop. 1994.

Stendhal's The Red and the Black. Ed. Dean de la Motte and Stirling Haig. 1999.

Sterne's Tristram Shandy. Ed. Melvyn New. 1989.

Stowe's Uncle Tom's Cabin. Ed. Elizabeth Ammons and Susan Belasco. 2000.

Swift's Gulliver's Travels. Ed. Edward J. Rielly. 1988.

Thoreau's Walden *and Other Works*. Ed. Richard J. Schneider. 1996.

Voltaire's Candide. Ed. Renée Waldinger. 1987.

Whitman's Leaves of Grass. Ed. Donald D. Kummings. 1990.

Wordsworth's Poetry. Ed. Spencer Hall, with Jonathan Ramsey. 1986.

Wright's Native Son. Ed. James A. Miller. 1997.